I0632250

ROLLING THUNDER

A personal exploration into
the secret healing powers
of an American Indian
medicine man

ROLLING THUNDER

by Doug Boyd

Delta

A DELTA BOOK

Published by
Dell Publishing
a division of
The Bantam Doubleday Publishing Group, Inc.
666 Fifth Avenue
New York, New York 10103

The trademark Delta® is registered in the U.S. Patent and Trademark Office.

ISBN 0-440-55052-1
Reprinted by arrangement with
Random House, Inc.

Printed in the United States of America
20   19

Introduction

Almost everyone who has ventured even slightly into the spiritual world of the American Indian can relate inexplicable happenings. Most often to the outsider these appear as tangential occurrences, no more mystifying than a clever performance by a professional magician on a stage. The non-Indian tends to reject the unexplainable; to him there is no logic in these experiences. He has been taught that everything within his levels of consciousness can be explained by the rigid laws of matter, energy, and probability—by the rules of technology.

Although modern man's industrial society has swept across the spiritual worlds of American Indians, almost destroying them as it has already shattered technological man's traditional religions, there are surviving pockets of native American culture within almost every tribe which has managed to survive. The secrets of the earth spirit are kept by older "medicine" men and women who pass them on to disciples, to younger tribal members who have rejected the values of the technological society which surrounds them.

Rolling Thunder, the subject of this book, is a keeper of tribal secrets—a modern medicine man. After witnessing one of Rolling Thunder's healing rituals at a conference sponsored by the research department of the Menninger Foundation, Doug Boyd decided to open his mind fully to the mysteries of such secret healing powers as might be revealed to him. Boyd's book is an account by a contemporary white man of the inner existence of American Indians, an exploration into what some accept as the "real" world. To the believer or to the skeptic, Boyd's experiences form a penetrating and challenging story of a world that is little known to most Americans.

Dee Brown

Author's Note

I am grateful to Richard Clemmer, Anne Habberton, and Sandra and Fred Gey for their help and support in my work with Rolling Thunder. And I am grateful to the people who were part of the events in this book—to Chief Frank Temoke, Rolling Thunder's family, Mad Bear, Semu Huaute, Oscar Johnny, Alice Floto, Mel Dayley, Dolly Gattozzi, and members of the Committee of Concern for the Traditional Indian—to name only a few.

All the Native Americans in my story are well-known public figures who have asked for help in the communication of their messages. Hoping to both acknowledge and assist their useful work, I have respectfully included their names in these pages.

My special thanks go to Ruth and Arthur Young of the Foundation for the Study of Consciousness, for their financial support of the field work. I also thank Alyce and Elmer Green, E. Dale Walters, and the entire staff of the Voluntary Controls Program at the Menninger Foundation and those others of the Menninger Foundation who encouraged and supported this work. (And I hasten to acknowledge that sponsorship of my research does not constitute endorsement of my findings.)

This project was begun as a report to the Voluntary Controls Program of the Menninger Foundation's Research Department, and if it had become just that, it would have been a very different book. But I got more from Rolling Thunder than explanations. What I got from Rolling Thunder I got by observing the man and by observing his way of life. I got a true life story.

I decided that by sharing these observations I might be able to share the insight, perspective and energy they have given me. One day in September 1972 Rolling Thunder gave me his permission to do this and said he had a good feeling about it. Beyond that he has not had to do with the book. I wanted it that way because, though I must admit I have written with the bias of an admirer, I have been able to tell more than he would have said about himself. Not that I have told his secrets, for I don't know them—I have shared only what many others have also observed—but I have been able to say, for example, that he is a healer and a spiritual leader, and Rolling Thunder would not have called himself these things.

So these are the words of the learner and not of the teacher. If there is any misinterpretation of events or meanings, the error is mine and not Rolling Thunder's. My gratitude to Rolling Thunder, therefore, is not so much for this book as for the insight, perspective and energy that his association has given me, and for that no amount of gratitude will ever be enough.

DOUG BOYD

Contents

ROLLING THUNDER

1

Rolling Thunder

Perhaps I expected a spectacular character in glorious feathers and beads. When I first saw Rolling Thunder he was wearing a red and white shirt with an Indian design, plain khaki pants and an old brown hat with a large eagle feather in it, and he looked plain.

He was talking to someone across the room from me. At times he looked aside, squinting, staring into space. I was to become familiar with that squint, that sensitive face, but at the moment my only thought was of stereotypical Indians, stoic and plain, with hats, boots and cheap suitcases going from place to place looking for work or waiting for buses.

It was April 15, 1971, and I was at White Memorial Camp at Council Grove, Kansas, waiting to hear Rolling Thunder speak. I was a member of a research team studying voluntary control of psychological and physiological states; we had just completed a lengthy study at the Menninger Foundation of the Himalayan yogi, Swami Rama, recording physiological measurements in the laboratory while he demonstrated his ability to voluntarily produce beta, alpha, theta and delta brain rhythms, to control the flow of blood in his right hand, to produce a temperature difference of about ten degrees between the right and left sides of his palm, to speed and slow his heart at will, and to stop his heart from pumping blood. We had listened to his lectures on the purpose and practice of yoga—control of the body and mind—and we had seen him perform some unusual and impressive methods of diagnosis and healing. I had come to see Rolling Thunder because of what I had experienced with the Hindu swami.

Rolling Thunder took a seat in the front row of the hall, and Dr. Stanley Krippner began to introduce him to the audience, a group of about eighty-five people from Iceland, Japan, Germany, Canada and various places in the United States who had come to Council Grove to discuss the new science of consciousness and explore dimensions for further growth through shared research and experience. Dr. Krippner is director of the William C. Menninger Dream Laboratory at the Maimonides Memorial Hospital in Brooklyn, and had invited Rolling Thunder to speak to the Menninger Foundation's third annual conference on voluntary control of internal states. He began by telling us how he had met Rolling Thunder and about a healing performed by Rolling Thunder at which he had been present. He said that no one had known for sure whether Rolling Thunder would speak, that he had spent the days since the beginning of the conference observing and conversing with the participants before deciding whether or not he would give his talk. This was the traditional three days a medicine man takes to make a decision or to accept a patient.

"Now as Rolling Thunder starts his discussion this afternoon," Dr. Krippner announced, "he has asked us to adhere to the medicine man tradition. You don't interrupt a medicine man until he's done speaking. After he finishes his talk he will be happy to answer questions, but while he is in the middle of his talk please do not interrupt. As I say, this is just part of the tradition, this is the style in which he is used to speaking. It certainly has been a priviledge for all of us to have met with Rolling Thunder here at the conference and I'm glad that he has decided that he will favor us with something to say to the whole group at this time."

Rolling Thunder reached the stand with a few deliberate steps. He took a long, slow drink from a pop bottle he had been holding and then set that down like a gentle tap of a gavel. The old brown hat with the eagle feather stayed on his head; I felt it was intended to be there. It seemed as if he was watching himself walk to the stand, take the drink, and set the bottle down. He lifted his eyes and for a moment watched us looking at him. I felt that he knew exactly what he was doing.

"Well, my friends," he began, "I'll speak to you as clearly as possible. This is my first association in spiritual matters with white people, and that's why I was hesitant to come here. Indians out where I live sit and talk all night long about spiritual things. I want to make it very clear that I will not reveal any of the rituals or sacred ceremonies that are not supposed to be revealed. Those cannot be revealed at this time. American Indians have quite a lot of things that are secret and cannot be revealed.

"As long as ten years ago I could not talk to you about any spiritual things regarding the American Indians because after the conquest of this continent, those things were hidden. We go by signs in the times, and they change as we go along. The pattern of life changes, and we were shown about six years ago that the time had come when we could travel and mix with white people and we would find people in different places with good hearts and we could talk with them. Like I say, this is one of my first experiences on the outside regarding spiritual matters. So things are getting a little better.

"Some of the young white generation out there are different

from the old generation, and they like Indians, they like people, and they like for us to come and talk with them. I'm one of the very few that seem to speak that high English—as they say— and in my home country I often have to speak for my people. They have to talk with Indian agents, judges and district attorneys when they have troubles and I'm the one who has to do that.

"But I was born to be a medicine man. Many people ask me how you become a medicine man. You don't just hire out; you don't just read a book or go to school; it doesn't come that way. I've had some people tell me they'd like to be a healer. Well, maybe so. I've had some people tell me they'd like to be a medicine man, but I want to point out this is something I've never talked about before—the pathway they follow and some of the things involved—and it's not easy. In the first place you have to be born for it and some people have asked me how you know. How do the bees in the hive know the queen bee? The Indians know; they said we know our own, and you know your own.

"We don't do anything that shows, and we don't do anything for show. No amount of money in the world can buy the medicine of the traditional Indian. I had one white fellow fly to my country a while back. He was the son of the president of a big company up in New York. He came in a private plane and offered me $10,000 to cure some red bumps he had all over his back. He asked if I could cure him and I said, 'Yes, I can cure you.' He said, 'Well, will you?' I said, 'No, not now. You come back one year from today and maybe I'll doctor you if you'll talk to my helpers first and bring tobacco when you come.' And I also said, 'Withdraw your offer of the $10,000.'

"There are some things in this life that you cannot buy, and the American Indians live according to that standard. We can't go to the drugstore and buy our medicine. You cannot come and buy a medicine man. He can either take a case or he cannot take it. He's the most independent person in the world, and I'm not overstating this. He's the only person who can walk off a field during a battle or walk out of a meeting any time he chooses. It is not to be obnoxious, because that's just the way it is. We answer to one sovereign and one sovereign only, and that's the Great Spirit himself over all. We walk in his path and that's the only way we can preserve ourselves and the only way that we can help others. So I couldn't doctor that man who offered me the $10,000 cash if I had wanted to. If I had, I would have paid for it myself, because I know it would have been wrong and I would have suffered greatly if I had done a thing like that. But immediately the next day I doctored an old man who was paralyzed—had been for years—and doctors and hospitals had not cured him. He gave me this medallion which I appreciated more than the $10,000, and it has my name in the beadwork. 'Rolling Thunder.' "

There in Council Grove Rolling Thunder spoke for the first time to psychiatrists, psychologists and physicians about the long and difficult path of spiritual pursuit and training from birth through apprenticeship to becoming a healer. He told of the process of self-realization, of seeking and knowing one's own identity. He talked about self-purification and cleansing and related some of his personal experiences as a medicine man. He talked about nature—about plants, animals and all the inhabitants of the earth—and how mankind's strength and ultimate survival depend not upon an ability to manipulate and control, but upon an ability to harmonize with nature as an integral part of the system of life.

I listened to Rolling Thunder with intermittent thoughts of Swami Rama. I felt in Rolling Thunder the same sense of total, unwavering focus on the moment, the same focus I had often felt from Swami Rama. Rolling Thunder had the same orderly system of awareness and discipline that was often manifest in the remarkable power and beauty of the swami. Moreover, Rolling Thunder expressed ideas and concepts that I had heard from spokesmen from India, Japan and Tibet. He said there was a law of nature that causes all things to be balanced, a law that says that nothing comes free, that all things must be paid for, that all wrongs must be righted. Teachers from all over the world have spoken of this law of karma. Rolling Thunder told how medicine men and others of similar practices communicate without words. Practitioners of all times and places, from witch doctors to shamans to yogis, swamis and sages, have had this ability.

He talked about the history of the Indian nation and its origins in "the beginning of time as we know it . . . when the earth would shake as we walked upon it," and "it was so hot you couldn't get away from the heat. There were people here, but they were a little different. There are remnants of those first people, like this Big Foot over in northern California and the Yeti in Tibet." Some of the ancient peoples came here in ships to escape from a land that was sinking into the South Pacific. "Some of them," he said, "are still here, and we know who they are. So all Indians are not even the same complexion and they don't all look alike any more than European peoples or any other people. We have meetings once a year in Hopi country, under the ground in *kivas,* where representatives of all tribes—medicine men and chiefs—come together. Then our sacred writings are brought out, read and interpreted.

"There are many different tribes and languages," he continued, "yet we communicate very well amongst ourselves. We have ways of communication too that I think you might understand. For instance, I met another medicine man from Quebec, Canada, named Peter Mitten. I met him in New York at a meeting of the Iroquois, but when we met we didn't talk. We didn't need to. There are others the same way and I've also met traditional peoples from the Far East and from Africa and the West Indies. If they are on the same spiritual level and they reach a certain stage of development, they don't have to talk. In the old days when two Indian chiefs would meet on the trail, many times they never talked. I remember when I was growing up a lot of the old men sat out in the sun and never talked, but they could communicate very well—better than we do today, sometimes, because they understood each other."

He talked about herbs, which he called "helpers," and told how, when he goes to gather herbs, he can feel them before he sees them. Often herbs just appear where they are needed. Weeds, he said, don't exist. We call plants we don't want "weeds," but to Rolling Thunder all plants have a purpose that should be respected. He said that plants live in families and have tribes and chiefs. When someone goes to gather herbs, he pays his respects to the chief by making an offering. Then he actually speaks to the plant, saying that he is about to take a number of the group, but no more than is needed, and for good purpose. The need and the purpose are primary. Peyote is another agent-helper whose purpose is good, but it can be misused through misunderstanding.

He talked about receiving the power of certain animals and certain reptiles by taking their lives with his bare hands and taking their power within himself—even the poison of the rattlesnake—and then never taking the lives of those creatures again. And when it is necessary to kill an animal for food or clothing, apologies are made to that animal for having to take its life, and every part of the animal is put to good use. There is no wanton slaughter among the Indians.

Then he talked about making water into medicine. This, he said, was something he could give to us, something those of us who were listening might someday find useful in the right time and place.

"I'll tell you a few things that you can take with you. You can start with this. You can take a glass of water and pray over it and make medicine out of it. A lot of times the Indians will be caught with no medicine and they want to cure a fever or something like that. They'll take a glass of water, pray over it in the morning when the sun's coming up. When the sun's rising in the morning, vibrations—what you would call vibrations in the earth, we call it the Great Spirit's power—are strongest then and they're bringing forth new life. When the sun starts to rise we make our prayer, and when you see the bottom of the sun, that's when it ends. Let the rays of the sun hit that water and you can make the medicine out of it if you want to do that and you need that medicine."

Rolling Thunder offered us the idea that experiments do not cause things to happen. Events are caused by their natural causes. There is no experiment other than a real situation. The example of the water illustrates the predicament of contemporary "science" in dealing with Indian medicine. How can "science" make any valid test of American Indian medicine if it is too "scientific" to include all the conditions of the real situation? In this case the real situation includes the need for an unordinary result and the belief that the need will bring that result. It includes a certain attitude toward the sun and the earth and all of nature. It includes a certain viewpoint about the relationship between the sun, the earth, the healer and the glass of water, and it includes a feeling about the conscious presence of the Great Spirit. Absent from the real situation are skepticism and judgment. I can think of scientists I know who would be embarrassed to investigate American Indian medicine if they should be required to work within these conditions. Yet they are simply the conditions that exist when things happen.

Another lesson has to do with the concept of agents. The glass of water was an agent. I did not learn all about agents at Council Grove that day and I have not learned it all at this writing, but Rolling Thunder's remarks about the glass of water began that learning: "Now you can start with this. You can make the medicine if you want to do that and if you need that medicine."

When Rolling Thunder spoke of herbs he called them "helpers." I was thinking about plants producing pharmacological results by virtue of their biochemical make-up. What Rolling Thunder was talking about, however, was the way a person thinks about and speaks to these plants—perhaps the chemistry is beside the point in certain cases. The water that becomes a powerful medicine would likely remain water in a laboratory. No doubt most doctors would conclude that whatever medicinal effects might be attributed to a glass of water must be "all in the mind." This, I think, is part of the truth about agents. I am beginning to think that all of one's condition, including one's body and one's environment, is in the mind and that the changes that take place in the external world occur first in the mind. If this is so, it is possible to think of agents as media through which mental changes are focused onto the external world. In the months that followed the conference at Council Grove, I saw Rolling Thunder accomplish many extraordinary "external changes" in which a variety of things, including the pure tobacco smoke from his pipe and even a small black bug, played important roles. I will be able to sense what these things are and how they work when I can see how that glass of water relates to the sun, the earth, the mind, the right ritual and the need for the medicine.

Much of what Rolling Thunder said would seem incredible to the Western intellect. Yet this native American gave voice to thoughts and ideas that have been common knowledge for centuries among his people. However strange and unusual his words might be to contemporary Western researchers, they were not at odds with ideas that have come out of many other cultures. It occurred to me then as I first listened to Rolling Thunder that there might be valuable information in the areas of self-mastery and man/nature relationships that contemporary American culture has failed to find in its rigorous institutional pursuits.

Rolling Thunder concluded: "So this spiritual power is supposed to be used in a good way and to help people, and I don't mean just sick people either. You can use it to help keep people from getting sick; you can use it for friendship and for good feeling among your family and among people wherever you go.

And I think that if there are enough of you, there will even come a time when you can use it to bring about better government—and maybe you could even use it to influence the Bureau of Indian Affairs."

For a moment he stood motionless and looked at us. "Thank you," he said. "And now you can ask some questions if you'd like."

Immediately many people raised their hands enthusiastically. There were several questions that Rolling Thunder did not wish to answer, and several others that he disposed of with only a very brief comment. But there were some that he willingly answered at length.

Someone asked if he would tell how a person could find his own purpose in life, his identity.

"Yes," he said, "when our young people are twelve or thirteen years old, they go out and pray on the high mountain at certain sacred places while an older person waits at the foot of the mountain. They go up there with no clothes, just a blanket, no food or water, for as long as three days. If they drop off to sleep, they wake up praying. Then there comes a time when they have a vision showing them what they're supposed to do. They won't know the meaning of it, most likely, so they come on down to the base of the mountain and tell the older person; then they go together to the medicine man and tell of the vision again, and the medicine man looks into it. Next they have the name ceremonies and decide what the meaning of this dream is and how it's interpreted. That person then gets a feeling and a name, and they know their purpose in life."

Someone else asked if Rolling Thunder was training someone to take his place, if he had an apprentice.

"That's a very good question as to who will take my place. You know, years ago, see, they tried to kill off all the chiefs and the medicine men. That's no overstatement, though it may not be in the histories. My grandfather went that way. The next one, if he's got a son or a grandson, and for seven generations that seed is still alive and the Indians learned long ago to hide some of them away when those things were going on. Even today they hide out some of the kids so they don't get kidnapped and sent off to these schools. So it may not happen the next generation or the next generation and then the third or fourth generation there might be one crop up that's going to be a medicine man. So they'd have to kill all the people for seven generations to wipe out all the medicine men, and it's not even decided by the people. I have a son who's going to be a medicine man and I also have sons of others that you might say attach themselves to me, who become my sons and work with me. All these young people will be medicine men. It's kind of like a school, only we take just so many. We don't take just any and everybody. In the first place, it's meant to be for the one we take.

"Not too long ago a man came to my country to be doctored —from the outside, you know. If they don't know the customs they get in trouble and they get us in trouble. We have to watch that kind very closely. He didn't bring me any tobacco either, and that's very important. But anyway I felt sorry for him because he's a young man who needed a lot of help. So I went ahead anyway and he was all right. His mind was quite confused, but he became all right.

"Then he wanted to be a medicine man. Well, a lot of them do, I guess. So I told him that I'd have to take three days to look into that. We're allowed three days to look into something to see if we want to take it. We can, as I say, take it or we can not take it; it's our choice. Anyway, I did have the desire to help this man, so I told him I would take three days and I'd let him know. About a day and a half or so went by until he called me and wanted to know whether I was going to teach him any medicine. Very impatient. I guess everybody's in a hurry in this world today. So I don't remember saying it—it just came out some way—but I told him, 'No, I'm not going to teach you Indian medicine. If I do you'll be a witch and a bad one and you'll hurt yourself; you'll hurt a lot of people around you.' The young man got very angry He had it in his head that he was going to be a medicine man and that's all there was to it. He was using a lot of things that we don't use. Even his temper and everything else was against him. He didn't talk about preparing himself first, either. So anyway, he left my home and he went to live with another family and he took the man out to doctor him the way he had seen me doctor—tried to copy my methods; nobody could steal my medicine. So that young man who was doing the doctoring, his hair and his eyebrows caught fire and that should have been a warning to him. Well, they finally put him on a plane out of the country before he could get into any more trouble. He lost his job and his band that he was working with broke up and a lot of things started to happen right away. I'm sure he won't make that mistake again."

People began to ask about diseases and rituals; Rolling Thunder said, "I can't tell you that at this time. Wait until after the medicine ceremony tonight and I might talk a little more."

Rolling Thunder had offered to perform a healing ritual for a young man who was a participant in the conference and had been injured in a soccer game just before coming to Kansas. He had been kicked with a spiked shoe and the hole in his leg had healed over and become infected underneath. There were many doctors at the conference, but there was no medical equipment and some of the doctors thought the injured man should be taken to a hospital. Rolling Thunder had looked at the wound, and during the three days since the beginning of the conference, while he was deciding about his talk, he had also decided to treat the young man's leg. He had decided that the Indian medicine ritual should take place that evening at seven o'clock in the hall where the talk had been given.

When the lecture and the questions ended, there were less than two hours before the ritual. Supper was soon to be served in the dining room.

"I wonder if someone could get some raw meat from the kitchen," Rolling Thunder said as people began to leave the room. "I'll need to have about a pound of raw meat in a dish and a large basin with about an inch or two of water in it. Could someone have these things here by seven o'clock?"

2

Healing Ritual
at Council Grove

At seven o'clock almost everyone who had heard Rolling Thunder speak that afternoon was in the lecture hall. In the front of the room sat the injured man, a young man with long hair and a beard. His right pants leg was rolled up to the knee and I could see the painful-looking bruise. Earlier that day, while Rolling Thunder was answering questions, I had glanced around the lecture hall looking for the injured man. I learned that he had been in bed during the lecture. It had become too painful for him to walk or even stand on his injured leg.

The room was silent. The cameras and recorders that had been in the room earlier were absent. Beside the chair where the injured man sat were a large basin with some water in it and a bowl containing the bright red meat. Rolling Thunder entered at the back of the room and walked down the center aisle

carrying the old suitcase that was his medicine bag. He wore
the old brown hat with the feather in it.

No introduction was needed. We all knew that the man in the
front of the room had a painful, infected leg injury and that
Rolling Thunder was about to perform an Indian medicine
healing ritual. Rolling Thunder had explained in his lecture
that there had once been a large number of medicine men
throughout the land, but now the nearest Indians were miles
away. Most of the leaders were gone. "There is no longer a chief
or a medicine man in this territory," Rolling Thunder said. "I
had to look into that when I first came here. This was once a
place where Indians gathered to hold council. That's how it got
its name, Council Grove. But now I find that there are no chiefs
or medicine men in this area."

Had it been otherwise, Rolling Thunder would have made
contact: tradition requires permission to perform a healing
ritual in another man's domain.

Rolling Thunder approached the chair where the injured
man sat and placed his suitcase on the floor. He looked quietly
at his patient and then he whispered something. The young man
began taking off his shoes. Rolling Thunder knelt on the floor
and opened his suitcase. He took out a number of things. I
could identify only a large feather with a handle and a rather
ordinary pipe. He took off his hat and I noticed he had soft,
graying hair. He filled the pipe and put it to his mouth. Then
he turned to face us. Holding the pipe between his teeth, he
stood and looked at us. I became awkwardly aware of the group
of spectators; but then Rolling Thunder spoke and the awkward
feeling left.

"Among my own people at home I have assistants to make
these preparations," Rolling Thunder said. "They even light
my pipe for me." He struck a match and for a moment he
continued to watch us as he held the flaming stick between two
fingers. "But here I guess I have to do these things myself." He
sucked at the flame, and puffs of smoke billowed. As I watched

I pictured myself standing beside him holding the match to his pipe. I almost wished I could have been standing there. At that moment we ceased being an audience. We were patient, and healer, and concerned observers. There was a feeling of harmony in the room.

My mind jumped back to an afternoon in October 1970 when Swami Rama performed a psychokinetic demonstration in our laboratory in Topeka. A pair of long aluminum knitting needles were crossed to form an X and mounted on a spindle so that with a slight push they would rotate on a horizontal plane. The needles on their spindle were placed on a coffee table about four feet in front of the Swami, who was seated lotus-position on a couch. A protractor was placed around the spindle so that any movement of the needles could be accurately observed. Swami Rama was to cause the needles to turn on the spindle by using a certain chant and the force of his gaze. Seven researchers were in the room to watch the demonstration. I was seated on the couch beside the Swami. I had the responsibility of steadying the Swami with a wooden rod in case the intense concentration or force should cause him to tip to the side. The needles moved twice on the spindle; both times it happened at precisely a moment when the Swami was making a high-pitched nasal *eee* sound, the sound of his command. But even more memorable to me than the apparently extraordinary manner in which an object was caused to move was my awareness of my sense of responsibility as a participant. I remembered my thoughts as I stood outside the room where Swami Rama had sat in meditation to prepare himself for the experiment. I wondered if I should be in meditation, for if Swami Rama did things with thoughts, feelings, confidence or state of consciousness playing an important role, what about the seven investigators who were to observe? Would not our feelings and our state of mind influence the result?

*   *   *

As the healing ritual was about to begin I watched Rolling Thunder inhale long, deep puffs on the pipe and let the smoke rise from his mouth. I felt a sense of responsibility. I knew at once that those of us who were watching could affect the outcome of the ritual, and I realized that Rolling Thunder had used his pipe and his match and his words about assistants to bring us into the role of participants. I thought of the familiar situations in which attitudes create atmospheres. A practiced instructor can create a tangible atmosphere of confidence in a classroom through direct outward projection from his own mind of a conscious state of clarity and a feeling of calm. Or one student can negate the elucidative effect of a lecture by projecting his own state of confusion. Now in the light of much closer acquaintance with Rolling Thunder, I can recall his words as he lit his own pipe for the ritual that April evening. Out of his perception, his unusual sense of communication, and his straight and simple manner came words and gestures superbly suited to creating a strong feeling of confidence and an attitude of cooperation.

Rolling Thunder drew upon the pipe four times, once facing east, once facing north, once south, and once west.

> "To the East where the Sun rises.
> To the North where the cold comes from.
> To the South where the light comes from.
> To the West where the Sun sets.
> To the Father Sun.
> To the Mother Earth."

Rolling Thunder handed his pipe to his patient. The injured man also drew four times on the pipe and deeply inhaled the smoke. Rolling Thunder spoke to him in a matter-of-fact tone. "Why do you want to be relieved of this condition? Do you just want to feel better, or what are you going to do? Is there anything else that you would like to improve or change? Is there anything else you would like to say? Because whatever you say now, that's the way it's going to be."

The young man spoke without hesitation. He was not embarrassed. His voice was clear and serious. He explained his injury and said he wished to have it healed. Then he stopped talking. Rolling Thunder apparently wanted to establish more reason, so he questioned his patient about his plans and why he felt it important to have the painful infection removed. The man said that there was much work to be done and he needed to be free from his injury to better involve himself in important social projects.

Rolling Thunder turned to face the man and began a very high, wailing chant. I could not see his face. For a moment I imagined that his mouth and eyes were closed and that the sound was coming out of the top of his head. It was not an ordinary sound, but a high-pitched wailing. The sound must have come from Rolling Thunder, yet it seemed to come from a point above where he stood. When the sound stopped, Rolling Thunder placed the man on his back. There was no definable change in Rolling Thunder's physical form, but there was something about the attitude of his stance that made him look very different. Suddenly he thrust his head on the wound and sucked at it with his mouth. The sucking lasted for several minutes. It was a strange scene—the patient lying on his back, the medicine man bent over him, his beaded medallion hanging from his neck and his mouth upon the patient's leg. But it was even stranger to hear. From Rolling Thunder came sniffing, howling and wailing sounds unlike any of the ordinary sounds made by a man.

Rolling Thunder lifted his mouth from his patient's leg. He held his lips tightly together. Still bending over, he turned and took a few steps. With his back to the observers he leaned over the basin and vomited violently. The sniffing, sucking, wailing and vomiting was repeated again and again. Then Rolling Thunder began placing his hands upon the wound. Twice during this procedure he spit upon one palm, rubbed his hands together vigorously and placed both palms at once upon the injured area.

The patient was returned to his chair and Rolling Thunder knelt to pick up the large feather with the handle. With the feather he made brisk sweeping motions over the patient's entire body—about his head, along his arms, over his chest and his back, and down his legs to his feet. The feather never quite touched the man or his clothing. Rolling Thunder watched through squinted eyes as he swept. It seemed he was seeing something that was invisible to me. Several times he stopped sweeping and turned aside, and with a strong snap of his arm shook the feather at the raw meat.

He put his things back into his case and closed it. In the afternoon he had suggested that he might answer more questions after the ritual was over, but now he picked up his bag and said, "I don't feel like answering questions at this time. I don't feel too good just now." He pointed to the patient sitting in the chair. "You can talk to him." He started through the aisle with his suitcase in one hand and his hat in the other. Then he turned and looked back. "Now that meat should be burned to ashes. And make sure that no one touches it."

When Rolling Thunder left the room several doctors moved forward and examined the patient's leg. The consensus was that the color had returned to normal, the swelling had decreased, and the flesh around the wound was flexible instead of hard. The young man reported that the pain was gone.

People began milling around. Two large tables were pulled out from the back wall, and the patient, who had been in bed with pain, began an active game of ping-pong.

I watched the game, but as I watched I thought about the ritual. I knew I had not seen enough of what had really happened. I felt something good had been accomplished and that I would like to understand it better. I thought of countless Indians who for centuries held healing rituals—neither hypothesizing nor validating results, but simply experiencing them. No doubt there are a variety of unknown ways in which this nature-force or power can work, but Rolling Thunder had explained that the power belongs to the Great Spirit. This seemed to me an appropriate expression when I considered that the Great Spirit is a name, when there must be one, for the collective conscious will-energy of the universe and that one who is sufficiently prepared and purified becomes a clear channel for this power.

I left while the ping-pong game was still in process. I wanted to see Rolling Thunder, so I decided to go looking for him. I found him standing in the dining room talking to Dr. Elmer Green of the Menninger Clinic. I walked right to him and listened for a moment, but then began to fear I had acted hastily.

Rolling Thunder looked at me and smiled. "Hello," he said. I stood beside him until someone told me that my ride back to Topeka was waiting.

During the long ride home I went over the scene of the medicine ritual many times. All the mysterious sounds and motions could not have been more impressive to me if they had been designed solely to intrigue my sense of wonder; but I believed that everything Rolling Thunder had done had purpose and meaning. I could not fully understand that meaning, and I wanted to.

For weeks after seeing Rolling Thunder at Council Grove I thought about him. Often I saw his face in my mind or recalled words from the lecture or the strange sounds and gestures of the ritual. The Swami Rama project, or at least my part of it, was finished; there was a tentative possibility that our research program would send me to Korea. Recent news from Korea had indicated that I might find there practicing Buddhist monks with training and capabilities similar to the Swami's. I had lived in Korea for over eight years and I was looking forward to going back. So for weeks, while I retained memories of Rolling Thunder, I suppressed any desire to become involved with him at greater length. I began preparing a prospectus for a field trip to Korea to investigate Korean Buddhist training techniques and practices of self-regulation of psychophysiological states. Then one day in a conversation with Dr. Green, I heard myself say: "What I really want to do now is to meet Rolling Thunder."

Rolling Thunder."

Buffalo Horse
and Spotted Fawn

The last part of the trip to Carlin, Nevada, was a bus ride from
Salt Lake City. I didn't know where to find Rolling Thunder
or what I would say to him if I did find him. Originally I had
wanted it that way. I did not want to plan or prearrange the
meeting. Rolling Thunder had given his mailing address to
Elmer and Alyce Green as a post office box in Carlin, Nevada.
How near Carlin did he actually live?

After the conference at Council Grove, I had proposed to the
Menninger Foundation that I undertake a field trip to learn
from Rolling Thunder. Dr. Green, head of the psychophysiology laboratory and principal director of the voluntary controls research program, received my proposal with interest. I
was given a three-week provisional field assignment to meet
Rolling Thunder and look for something that might lead to

some common denominator with what we had learned from
Swami Rama, some key points regarding self-regulation and
control of internal states, the mind-body secrets we were seeking.

I started out on July 9, 1971, riding with the Greens through
Kansas and the Oklahoma Panhandle. From Flagstaff I took a
plane to Salt Lake City and on the afternoon of July 12 caught
the first westbound bus. By the time the bus was speeding across
Nevada I was beginning to feel some apprehension. This meeting with Rolling Thunder was important to me. I wanted to
carry back reports that would be useful to our research project,
but I wanted to do it in a way that would be of service to Rolling
Thunder's purpose. It seemed important to decide how to approach him and what to say. It reassured me to consider that
I was following a natural course of circumstances; the time
seemed right.

The bus pulled onto the shoulder and stopped, interrupting
my thoughts. The door opened and I saw the driver's eyes in
the mirror.

"Carlin!" he shouted.

I couldn't believe it. There was nothing here. I saw only a
Standard gas station near where we pulled off the road and two
other stations, a Texaco and a Shell, just across the highway.

"This is Carlin!" repeated the driver.

I made my way through the narrow aisle with my two suitcases and got off. The evening air was calm and fresh. I stood
on the shoulder and looked down the highway after the bus
until even the sound was gone. I was in the middle of nowhere.
Rolling Thunder might be somewhere in those distant hills that
were now disappearing in the sudden night of summer while I
was standing on an empty highway with two suitcases.

I walked to the Standard station to buy a cold drink from the
machine. "Is this Carlin?" I asked the attendant. It was Carlin.
I just wanted to be sure. From where I stood now I could see
that there was a motel just behind the Texaco station across the

highway. If I had known I could have seen its sign from the bus stop. It said STATE INN, and a sign on the other side of the same station said CAFE.

I walked across the highway and rang the bell on the office door. I waited. Nothing happened. I saw I had done the right thing because there was a note thumbtacked on the door that said, "Ring the bell." I had my finger on the button again, and a voice said, "I heard it and I'm comin' already." An elderly lady appeared, wearing a white starched dress that looked like a uniform. She was coming toward me, but very slowly, shuffling along in an old pair of slippers.

"Do you have a room?" I asked when she was reasonably close. She looked at me like she thought I was stupid. She shuffled up to the office door and fumbled slowly through a bunch of keys on a chain.

"Single is six dollars and thirty cents a day."

Inside my room I began to think again about planning. There was no real urgency now. In the morning I could find out where Rolling Thunder lived and how to get there. Perhaps the old lady might know. I would likely find her in the restaurant next door when I went in for supper, and if so I would ask her.

That restaurant was closed and when I looked in the window it looked like it had been closed for years. The old lady came out and pointed up the highway toward the Shell station. "Go eat over there." "There" was a little place with a couple of tables, about six stools at a counter, and a number of slot machines.

After a hot meal and several cups of coffee I returned to my room. I contemplated rehearsing my first encounter with Rolling Thunder. I tried talking to myself as if I were speaking to him, but it felt ridiculous. Since I had no books or magazines, I decided to just shower and sleep.

It occurred to me then how alone I was, and what an opportunity this could be. Here there were no telephones, no schedules, no waiting, no special times to be anywhere. No one in the world could possibly know where I was. No one could ring Room 3 at the State Inn. During months of training sessions with Swami Rama I had longed for a situation like this. The Swami always recommended a quiet corner somewhere in the house for daily meditation. With practice, one is supposed to become detached from all of life's distractions. But there are always the telephone, the doorbells and the appointments to remember. I thought about all my sessions with Swami Rama and of the sessions I had spent alone in my own quiet corner in Topeka. I recalled the many hours I spent in the psychophysiology laboratory, electrodes attached to my scalp, working to consciously sustain those states of deep relaxation and reverie that are associated with theta brain-wave patterns on an electroencephalogram, and I decided to take advantage of my ideal situation in this motel room. I decided to spend two days and two nights working on myself, hoping that this would be a meaningful preparation for my meeting with Rolling Thunder.

I never repeated that situation, but I've never lost the memory of it. I used those forty-eight hours of solitude for total-relaxation practice, breathing exercises, concentration and meditation. I left my room only a few times, either to eat or to stroll for a few minutes in the fresh air. I slept only a few hours. Most of the time I spent in what I thought of as a "silent alert." I wanted to establish a clear sense of direction; to align myself with my own identity and with the will and energy of my present task within a larger picture; and to become aware of those with whom I was associated and of those who were a part of my life and work. I did not experience a great degree of success in becoming directly aware of all that I had hoped to, but I did achieve a change in my thoughts and feelings. I became totally free. All apprehension and anxiety were gone. I lost my sense of importance. I no longer really cared what happened between Rolling Thunder and me. I had nothing to care about, nothing to succeed in, nothing to do.

Now that I have associated with Rolling Thunder for over two years I am convinced that those forty-eight hours of preparation allowed me to tune myself to a relevant key. I believe it was because of that preparation that I have been able to learn from Rolling Thunder, from then until now, without feeling obliged to know or to interject my own needs or questions. Had I tried to actively pursue Rolling Thunder I would have failed. As it was, I neither succeeded nor failed at anything.

I discovered that Carlin was a real town. From my window I could finally see the streets and houses that were not visible from the highway. On one of my walks during those two days I passed the Carlin post office, and I decided to go in and ask about Rolling Thunder. I had learned from the Greens that Rolling Thunder was known locally by the Anglo-Saxon name John Pope and that he worked as a brakeman for the Southern Pacific railroad.

"Ya, he lives in town here," said the lady in the post office.

"Do you know where?"

"Well, it ain't hard to find." She pointed through the wall. "Just head down that way across the tracks and ask anybody."

I went back to my room to get the tobacco that I had brought to give Rolling Thunder. Before I started out to find his house I rang the bell on the motel-office door and waited for the lady to shuffle over in her old slippers. I wanted to pay her now for this third night, since I might be returning late.

"Now, this here's my name where I've signed," she said, handing me a receipt. "I'm a widow lady. My husband died years back and left me alone here with this whole place." She made a sweep of her arm that took in at least the motel and bar, the old Texaco station, and the closed café.

"Do you know the Popes?" I asked.

"Sure I do. Helen and John Pope." She looked at me over the top of her glasses. "Do you know 'em?"

"Well, I know Ro—John Pope. I'm going to see him now.

I thought maybe you could tell me how to get there."

"Well, all you do is walk over town straight away down there. You're walkin', right?"

"Right."

"Well, you get to that overpass first. That's for people crossin' the tracks. When you cross over that, you'll see where them bars are at, and you don't go that way, you go the other way. Then you turn down the next street and go on down to where the pavement ends. It's a little old house with bushes and weeds all growin' up around it so you can't hardly see it from the road."

I walked through the little town and across the tracks with my tobacco offering in my shoulder bag. I knew the place when I saw it because there were all sorts of things growing wild around the house. I recalled Rolling Thunder talking at Council Grove about plant life and herbs, saying there were no weeds in this world. It was a grayish wooden house with a slanted roof, and it had a door right in the center and a window on each side. It looked like a cottage in a children's story. The weeds and plants grew in a sort of yard bordered at the front with a few bushes and shrubs, and a path led through the middle to the door. Some boards and wooden slats made the front door-step, and on this doorstep lay a huge Saint Bernard with its dripping tongue hanging out. I noticed a young man at the side of the house. He had long hair and looked to be Indian. He had his back turned, so he didn't see me. Because of the Saint Bernard on the doorstep I stopped well outside of the bushes that bordered the yard and waited. I had retained much of my silent state and I could have stood there for a very long time just looking at the house. But the young Indian turned around.

"Is this where Rolling Thunder lives?" I asked.

"This is where he lives, but he's not here right now. He's out on a trip. Did you want to talk to him or something?"

"I wanted to meet him if I could. Do you know when he'll be back?"

"Just a minute, I'll get my mom. You can talk to her."

When he went in he left the door open but I could not see inside from where I stood. I had apparently just met Rolling Thunder's son. I learned later that his name was Buffalo Horse and that he had a younger brother, Spotted Eagle. Though I did not yet know his name, I felt as though I knew the man. I had collected some impressions of him in my long silence that had just ended. When we spoke, the impressions came to the surface of my attention and made him seem familiar.

Rolling Thunder's wife was a large woman with a very beautiful face. She wore long black braids and a necklace. When she came out of the door she had to step around the Saint Bernard. She walked down the path and studied me for a moment. Then she sat down on an old sofa that was beside the door. A pure-white cat climbed on her lap, looking at me, and then jumped in through the open window. I tried to tell her who I was and why I was here. She watched me and listened. I kept glancing at the dog on the front step and the window where the cat had disappeared. I noticed there was another dog, a German shepherd, a few yards behind me, and that he was on a chain. It seemed that it was taking me too long to speak. Perhaps I should be quiet. I would rather have been listening. Helen Pope seemed enchanting. I had the feeling that she was terribly important, that she had come a long way, from some faraway place that could be reached through that front door, to sit on that sofa and listen to me. I imagined her coming through a series of doors, making her way first into the house and then out to the front where I was waiting. I believed that she was enchanted and that she could go anywhere she wished, but that she was here because she had a family and a lot of animals, and cared about meeting people.

"He works on the railroad and he's out on a trip right now," she said. "But if you met Rolling Thunder at Council Grove I'm sure he will be happy to talk to you. He'll return home some time tonight but he'll probably want to rest in the morning. Maybe you could come back about this time tomorrow afternoon. He should be able to talk to you then."

Her son was sitting near her in the yard balancing himself on a wooden produce box. "Where are you staying?" he asked me.

"At the motel up on the highway."

"The State Inn, right?"

"Yes."

"Because if I had your name and room number I could drive up there and pick you up whenever my dad was ready. See, you can't tell about him and I'd hate to have you walk down here again for nothing."

I repeated my name and said I didn't mind walking back.

I wanted to stay and talk with Rolling Thunder's family, but the conversation seemed to have come to a conclusion. I started back the way I had come, still carrying in my shoulder bag the tobacco I had brought. Rolling Thunder's wife and son had impressed me. They reminded me of people I had known in Korean countryside villages. They were poised and easy, informal and unpretentious. There was a natural warmth about them. They seemed as exotic to me as the Koreans. I had felt something poised and powerful in Buffalo Horse, like a coiled snake that was not threatening, a kind of terrible force completely at rest, indefinitely waiting. Perhaps my impressions should be modulated. Was I to have such ideas about every Indian I met?

Suddenly I felt like going back and talking to Buffalo Horse again. I thought it might be a mistake to appear there again before the arranged time, yet would it be unreasonable? Rolling Thunder's wife and son had been friendly and they had fit perfectly with the mood and expectations that I had established in the past two days. I could explain that I had nothing to do. So I went back.

My conversation with Buffalo Horse was much too brief.

"I don't really have time right now because I've got to go to Elko, but I can introduce you to the dude who stays in that trailer there and you can rap with him."

Since I had walked all the way back, there was nothing I could do but talk to "the dude who stays in that trailer." I was glad I did. Lynn Carlson was the son of the proprietors of a local market. His family were friends of Rolling Thunder's family—about the only local non-Indian friends they had, I learned. I told Lynn how I had met Rolling Thunder and why I had come.

"Do you think he'll remember you from Council Grove?" Lynn asked.

"I don't know. He'd remember the others from the conference before he'd remember me. I was there for only one day."

"I think you'd be right to talk to Buffalo Horse first," he said, "or someone in the family. Rolling Thunder is, well, he's—you could pick up some understanding of him from his family and they're really easy to talk to."

It was suppertime when I left the trailer and went back through town. I stopped in one of the bars near the railroad tracks because the sign said MAGAZINES. The rack was full of true confession, bold romance and movie magazines. I found an issue of *Playboy*. This would be a change from all the hours of meditation. I stopped for supper and it was dark when I got back to my room. Later there was a knock at my door. It was the lady in the slippers.

"I got a call for you over to the bar. It was Helen Pope and you're s'posed to call her back. You'll have to call from the bar. That's where the phone's at." I followed her shuffle, dragging my feet to match her pace.

"Go on ahead if you want. Have a drink while you're waitin' on me 'cause I've got the number wrote down in my notebook."

"That's all right."

"Ya got a nickel? It's a pay phone, you know."

"Won't I need a dime?"

"No, it takes nickels," she cackled, "and you can't win none back from it."

She gave me the number.

"Oh yes, hello. This is Spotted Fawn. You talked to me today and I told you to come tomorrow?"

Spotted Fawn, I thought to myself, Helen Pope is Spotted Fawn.

"Rolling Thunder got back just a while ago. There are some other visitors here and he'll probably stay up quite late. I told him about you and he said you might as well come down tonight."

The Crucial Conversation

Once again I took my shoulder bag and returned through the little town in the dark. I decided I would ask Rolling Thunder if we could talk alone. I wanted this first contact to be personal and direct, and I wanted Rolling Thunder to feel free to say whatever he wished.

I have come to know Rolling Thunder as a gentle and compassionate healer, a crafty social strategist, a skillful debater, a thoughtful and loving father, a practical outdoorsman, a carefree socialite. He can be the stern and stoic Indian or a delightful comic. He is a spiritual teacher, an enchanting storyteller, a tough, hard-working railroad brakeman, and, to the casual observer, a very plain, regular guy. I have seen him under many conditions, but I can think of no attribute, or its opposite, that would describe him on the first night we met and talked. De-

spite my initial feelings about going to a strange place, alone
and uninvited, to meet an Indian medicine man in his native
milieu, the meeting was the easiest and most natural first encounter I have ever had with anyone. No effort was needed on
my part. Rolling Thunder opened the door himself. He was
completely neutral.

"How are you? What is your name?"

"Maybe you remember me. I met you at Council Grove." I
looked inside. The atmosphere was strange yet cheerful and
friendly. On the walls there were deer horns and woven tapes-
tries. Against one wall there was a glass case filled with small
relics, some of which looked like amulets and charms. Over this
was a grand stuffed eagle with outstretched wings. The room
smelled of cedar smoke and incense. I thought of the Korean
mudangs, the Shinto mediums. They would have respect for a
place like this.

"Come on in."

Rolling Thunder introduced me to his two visitors. They
were Anne Habberton and Richard Clemmer. Anne was an
artist and Richard an anthropologist from the University of
Illinois, and they had met Rolling Thunder the previous summer. I liked them immediately. We were to spend the following
year together and much of the understanding I have gained
from Rolling Thunder is due partly to them.

The chance to talk alone with Rolling Thunder was arranged. I suggested it almost right away, but he postponed it
for some small talk and relaxation. Several times during the
conversation Rolling Thunder made a gesture that made it
appear he was about to fall asleep. He would drop his head to
one side and then let it fall backward. Each time he did he
would squint in my direction as if he were peering at someone
just beside me. Several times I nearly turned to look, but I knew
no one was there. Then he would lift his head and join the
conversation as though he had done nothing unusual. It was
uncommon behavior, yet it appeared to be such a satisfying

habit that I did not feel ill at ease. In fact I was beginning to feel very comfortable when Rolling Thunder stood up.

"Well, let's go outside, you and me, and we can get some fresh air and chat." When we were out of the house he said, "Let's sit in the car over there."

It was July 14. It must have been close to midnight. The night was cool and quiet, and I felt good. We climbed into the front seat of one of the old cars and talked for over an hour. Rolling Thunder fingered the steering wheel as if he might be driving me on some symbolic first trip. Somehow we covered most of the territory we were to explore more carefully in months to come. I remember everything about that night, except which car we sat in. Rolling Thunder had a half-dozen old vehicles in his yard, some running, some needing major repairs. Among them were a station wagon, a jeep and even an old Army half-track with a winch in the front. Many times I have looked over all his old cars, trying to remember which one was that special one; either I have forgotten or it has changed or disappeared.

I knew I must tell Rolling Thunder why I had come. He may have sensed my mission but I felt it was my business to be explicit. I was tempted to give him the tobacco first while I decided what to say. But he would want to know who was bringing it and why.

I told him that I was part of a team researching states of consciousness, volition, self-regulation and creativity, and that since the Council Grove Conference the Greens and I had felt there was much of value he could contribute in these matters, if he wished to, in the form of teaching, demonstration or explanation. I had come for such a contribution, in case there was to be any, because I believed he had information that would be helpful not only to us in our research but also to others. I believed he knew things he would like others to know. Then I said, "I feel that all this is entirely up to you and that I am only an instrument."

I waited and Rolling Thunder was silent. In fact, he was

motionless. He inhaled loudly. But he spoke gently and with neither finality nor uncertainty.

"I think I get the picture of what you're saying. You're talking pretty heavy stuff. I guess you might be disappointed. The teachings don't come like some people think. You can't just sit down and talk about the truth. It doesn't work that way. You have to live it and be part of it and you might get to know it. I say you *might*. And it's slow and gradual and it don't come easy. I guess we could just see what happens."

His words stayed with me and I later repeated them into my tape recorder. Now I appreciate their simplicity and honesty. They would have been true and fitting whatever happened. Though I claimed to be "only an instrument," I have realized considerable emotional involvement; my feelings in my work with Rolling Thunder have ranged from disappointment to excitement to ecstasy.

I said nothing and Rolling Thunder asked, "What is the Menninger Foundation?" That brought more silence. How could I describe the Menninger Foundation in a sentence or two? I wanted to avoid a nutshell definition. I also wanted him to know that though I represented the Menninger Foundation I did not necessarily represent the aims and aspirations of all departments and staff.

I explained that the Menninger Foundation was an organization with hospitals and clinics, the world's largest training center for psychiatrists, and a research department, all concerned with problems and solutions in the area of mental health. I told him few of the people there would know about him or me or what I was doing.

"I work for the research department, but even that has many parts. Our project is called the voluntary controls project. My work here would be just a part of that project."

"Well, I know a little something about that project, I guess, from Council Grove. What's the main idea behind this research?"

"The idea of self-regulation, that every person is his or her own master."

I talked about the things that Swami Rama and other subjects had done in the laboratory. I briefly explained how certain processes—biofeedback and autogenic training—were combined in this research to investigate the possibility that people can learn to voluntarily influence or regulate "automatic" functions such as heart rate, blood pressure and body temperature. Learning to gain some measure of control over these normally "automatic" processes seemed to lead to some success in the regulation of other internal states and functions such as concentration, relaxation, attention and creativity.

"You spoke at Council Grove about a sense of identity and purpose," I said, "how a person should come to know himself and become aware of his needs and motives and natural capacities. It seems to me that one's chances of acquiring awareness of self and purpose and of maintaining good health and achieving that purpose would be greatly enhanced by an understanding of how much of one's condition is voluntary, or could be voluntary."

Rolling Thunder said, "I like that voluntary part. And that gets into government and laws and the whole of what you call the system. Every man has his own identity and he has his own purpose in this world, and he has ways of finding out that identity and carrying out that purpose. No man should interfere with that."

He talked about governments, social systems, natural laws, ecology, healing, races, wars, self-regulation and karma; and he talked about all these things as they related to that word "voluntary." What he had to say in this sense was like the words of Thomas Jefferson: the best government is the least government. Rolling Thunder feels that each man has his destiny or purpose and his own karma to handle. The natural tendency of every government—to regulate people—results in government expansion of power and control to the point of mass manipulation and conformity, and is counter to the purpose for which man lives.

He explained that the Indians in all the tribes throughout America are now of two important types: traditional Indians and BIA Indians. BIA Indians have succumbed to the Bureau of Indian Affairs' contempt for Indians and its belief in their incompetency. Many have become incompetent, for without self-determination and self-direction anyone is lost. Many are alcoholics, and their suicide rate is the highest in the United States. These conditions aid the exploitation of Indians. Traditional Indians, however, still live by codes of conduct that they have carried with them during all their history. These codes are essentially codes of mutual respect and are therefore guarantees of freedom. Strict guarantees for self-direction and individual pursuit of purpose are a major part of the codes. Traditional Indians recognize no government. They participate in no political system.

"When the white man invaded our land it was an act of oppression. Now this oppression extends more and more to non-Indians as well, to minority groups, to people in under-developed lands, to people of new generations with new ideas, to all the people outside the government establishment.

"But we traditional Indians don't participate in that system. We're oppressed by it, but we don't try to be a part of it. You can't go to another people's land and try to kick everyone there off the land when they have nowhere to go, and kill most of them in the process, and then say that the ones who are left are supposed to join your club. That's wrong. We don't like their club and we won't join it. If it were a good club they wouldn't expect us to, and they'd leave our club alone. And they would leave other peoples in other countries alone. Every one has his own club. If it's a bad club, it's no one else's business. The people will learn in their own way. No good system tries to spread itself. It's good to help people, but it's wrong to spread systems. It's wrong to spread beliefs. It doesn't matter whether it's Christianity or what it is, or whether it's supposed to be the best belief in the world—and there is no such thing—it should be told only to those who ask. It's wrong to spread any ideology by intimidation, and that means Christianity, communism, capitalism, democracy or anything else.

"And by the way," said Rolling Thunder, "we are not a conquered people. We are not subjects. We have made mutual treaties with the white man, most of which the white man has broken, but there has never been a case of surrender."

The state of ecology or of modern man's environment was to Rolling Thunder another example of oppression: "Modern man talks of harnessing nature, conquering nature and making nature a servant of man. This shows that modern man doesn't know the first thing about nature and nature's ways. And the condition of the environment today proves that. Now everyone's afraid—afraid of air pollution, radioactivity and poisoned water. The land is becoming contaminated and the resources are disappearing or becoming unusable, and now people wonder whether it's too late. You can't make any kind of laws or system to control nature or to control man's inner nature, his consciousness or his natural behavior—the way he thinks and feels. That cannot be controlled. No individual or group can block another individual's path or change it against what fits his nature and his purpose. It might be done for a time, but in the end it won't work out. It will only lead to danger and fear for everyone. Even in healing we take that into account. A true healer considers a man's karma and his destiny. He has a way of looking into and understanding what is meant to be according to each individual's own progress and unfoldment. That way things are more realistic and it saves everyone a lot of trouble. Nature is sovereign and man's inner nature is sovereign. Nature is to be respected. All life and every single living being is to be respected. That's the only answer."

Listening to Rolling Thunder made me wish to get beyond the academic subject-category orientation in which I had been trained to think of politics, health and ecology, and be able to think of all these things as being related, to each other and to the whole earth. The significance of all that Rolling Thunder said rests in his unitary vision: the laws of karma, of action-reaction, man-nature relationships and all natural laws, principles of health and healing, self-regulation and social interaction can be understood only when they are seen collectively. In Rolling Thunder's view, for example, the ever-increasing accumulation of complicated and oppressive laws which have the effect of obscuring individuality and obstructing self-determination and self-regulation results from growing inattentiveness to the laws of mind and nature. In a vicious circle, these man-made laws obscure the laws of nature and promote further ignorance resulting in further chaos resulting in the apparent need for further oppression.

Somewhere in the midst of that long talk there was a pause, and I offered Rolling Thunder the tobacco pouch and the can of Sir Walter Raleigh that I had three times carried along with me.

"Oh, I left my pipe inside," he said. "Just a minute." He went inside. When he returned to the steering wheel he was carrying a long-stemmed pipe with some strings or cords attached to the stem where it joined a tall cylindrical bowl. I could not see very clearly in the dark. Right away he filled the pipe, lit it and began to puff in earnest. Then he handed the pipe to me.

"Would you like to try it?"

I did.

Setting up Camp

More than an hour had passed while Rolling Thunder talked about government and health, war and health, ecology and health, evolution and health.

"And another thing you should understand," he said. "I mentioned it at Council Grove, I believe, and I'll tell you now —that every Shoshone Indian knows something about Indian medicine. I have to know more, because it's my work, but there isn't a traditional Shoshone in this land who doesn't know something about Indian medicine. And that's the first thing you should remember from right now."

For a moment he was silent. Then turning to me suddenly he asked, "Have you got any camping equipment?" I had none. I had my recorder, tapes, camera, film, pencils and paper, and clothes for anywhere, and that was it.

"Well, I can loan you my own sleeping bag and we'll be scraping together what we've got around here tomorrow. Some of the Committee of Concern for the Traditional Indian are coming up from San Francisco. A lot of people will be here looking for evidence of the pinyon trees being knocked down. We figured camping would be the best way. I was planning to go out there with Anne and Richard tomorrow and set up camp in the Palisades. There's a nice place to camp up there in the hills, right in the canyon. You might as well join us. That'd get you out of that motel and you could stick around awhile. You know it can break a man staying in these motels. You could go on out with us in the morning and see how you like it. We don't have to decide it all now. We'll just see what happens. Can you get down here for breakfast around eight tomorrow?"

I told him I could.

"You picked a good time to show up here," he said. "You'll probably see a lot going on. It must have been meant to be. You came at the right time."

I walked back in the dark with my empty shoulder bag, and thought about all that I had heard. Rolling Thunder had knowingly established the orientation I would need in order to learn from him. It seemed hopeful.

Apparently my first lesson would be to see the destruction of pinyon-juniper forests on Shoshone land. During the question-and-answer period after his lecture at Council Grove, Rolling Thunder had told us about the chaining of forest lands. The Bureau of Land Management, under pressure from wealthy ranchers, was knocking down thousands of acres of trees on Indian treaty territory and public domain to convert the forests into grazing land. To Rolling Thunder it was man's destruction of his own environment. "In a few years it's all going to wash and there'll be no grass or sagebrush or trees or anything. It'll be a dust bowl. For the sake of a few blades of grass for a few years, they are willing to come into a desert country and destroy the trees that are in the hills, pinyon trees that the Indians have depended on for food for thousands of years." To Rolling Thunder this was a mental health issue. Already I had a sense of his understanding. I felt my ultimate task would be to relate that understanding to a style of living.

In the morning I packed my camera, recorder and notebook. I left my room key on the dresser and again walked through town to meet Anne Habberton and Richard Clemmer and ride with them to the campsite.

By early afternoon we had set up the camp that was to be our home for the rest of the summer. I learned later that Anne and Richard had arrived unexpectedly at Rolling Thunder's only hours before I met with him. In one sense, all this was in answer to Rolling Thunder's wishes. Now the three of us, with his ideas, his devices and his camping equipment, were playing the script he was writing. Members of the Committee of Concern for the Traditional Indian would arrive tomorrow.

One key point of traditional Indian thought is that there is a right time for every event and signs to indicate every right time. Only a few years ago the time had been right for traditionals to gain the lasting sympathy and respect of new non-Indian friends. The signs had long been pointing to the time. Signs like the ancient Hopi prophecy:

The day would come when the children of the white man would begin to dress like Indians, when they would begin to wear long hair, beads and headbands. That would be the generation from which would come the first true non-Indian friends.

The spontaneous formation in San Francisco of the Committee of Concern for the Traditional Indian was a confirmation of the signs and a sign itself. To the Indian it is another step in the unfolding of a very long-term plan. In Rolling Thunder's vision, that summer was the right time to bring together a number of Indians and non-Indians on Shoshone land. The purpose was to investigate and protest the destruction of the pinyon-juniper forests. The purpose and the coming together provided the medium through which everyone involved could achieve his own understanding and carry out his own tasks.

All this was part of a growing movement which was bringing about new levels of communication between Indians and non-Indians and was responsible for many new and continuing Indian activities. The Alcatraz movement had just ended, and the occupation of the island by Indians from many tribes was over, but the meaning of that occupation and its outcome had not yet been fully realized. At the same time, a struggle was taking place at Black Mesa, arising from the horrible incidents which had occurred in the course of strip-mining operations on Navajo and Hopi lands in Arizona and the Four Corners area. In California there was the continuing legal battle of the Paiute Indians to stop the diversion of Pyramid Lake for irrigation of white-owned ranches, the reclaiming of three and a half million acres of ancestral lands by the Pit River Indians, and north of San Francisco the reclaiming of the abandoned Marine Nike missile site on Indian treaty land and the establishment on the site of Deganawidah Quetzalcoatl University.

There were at times fifteen people at our campsite in the Palisades, and in this communal setting Rolling Thunder was positively jubilant. This brief but productive time fit in with his larger dreams for free schools and communes, traditional Indian communities, places of empirical learning for people of nonchallenging cultures. And it was also a good time, he thought, for Alice Floto to be here. Alice Floto was theoretically at great odds with the rest of the group. A middle-aged white woman from Salt Lake City, she was a Mormon and inclined to right-wing political views, for which ailments Rolling Thunder gave her occasional treatments. But she was also a chemist and an experienced herbalist, so she helped Rolling Thunder, too. At first she was suspicious and critical of long-haired youths who she thought wore dirty clothes and had questionable bathing habits. But in spite of herself Alice quickly grew fond of everyone and confessed her earlier prejudices, surprised that no one had noticed them.

On our first excursion out of camp we visited the Lee Indian Reservation and found a good stream to wade in. We had lunch on the thick grass, shaded by tall trees. I was selected by a very deft mosquito who left a large red swelling in the middle of my forehead. Wading into the icy stream I lifted handfuls of water to apply to the itchy spot. Alice noticed, and came over to examine the bump. She began to walk about and soon found a small fuzzy-looking plant from which she plucked several leaves and began to chew them. Spitting the soggy pulp into her fingers, she plastered it upon my forehead where it stuck and dried. Then she repeated the process. She told me this was done with the permission of Rolling Thunder, chief medicine man in that land. "It would be pretentious of me to perform even a minor treatment in his presence. But when he doctors people in my area he always asks me first. He gets my permission every time. He has that courtesy."

I sat with Alice on a large rock in the middle of the stream and learned that she had spent many years in the study and practice of various techniques of diagnosis and healing. She told me she and Rolling Thunder had often worked together. Not a few times her chemistry had been called upon to help Rolling Thunder blend some herb into a tonic or ointment. But Alice was more than a mere technician. There was something in her that gave warmth and comfort; her matronly bearing was the personification of healing, a loving kind of healing that is given without the need to serve the cause of prestige, to which use the art of healing is so often put today.

I later learned that Alice was thought of not only as a healer but also as a long-time friend of many Indians. Most traditional Indians regard the efforts of Mormons to woo them as proselytization, for which they feel considerable distaste. Though Alice may have been politically conservative, she was liberal in her religious sense, and there was no apparent effort on her part to promote Christianity among Indians.

"She has a lot of special talents and sensitivities," Rolling Thunder said to me, "and she's done a lot of good work in spite of her right-wing ideas." Rolling Thunder often referred to right-wing politics of any kind as fascist, and he spoke of fascism with profound gravity. He did not use the word lightly but he used it often, not usually about people themselves, but about ideas and actions. He was apprehensive of fascism as a growing danger in America. In my field notes I recorded that Rolling Thunder had considered fascism "the tool of the dark forces." He was more concerned with what he had called "the signs of fascism creeping up" than any of the obnoxious mischief of Communists or capitalists. He spoke of the new no-knock law as one omen that people with political power would begin to consider themselves privileged, endowed with special rights, exempt from principles of justice and honesty.

Before Rolling Thunder went out with Anne, Richard and me to set up camp, he had called Alice in Salt Lake City, about six or seven hours from Carlin. He told her there was an opportunity for her to camp out in the canyon with a bunch of long-haired hippies and she should come right away with a tent and whatever camping gear she could bring. Alice did not want to come. She insisted she could not come, and there was no point in trying to persuade her. Rolling Thunder reminded her one doesn't acknowledge a learning opportunity until the learning takes place. He told her she must come. No. Circumstances were on her side, she said. Her husband was going fishing with the tent, her car was broken down, and there was no one to care for her youngest boy. Besides, she was not feeling well, and if she improved she had other plans anyway. Rolling Thunder insisted the car could be repaired and all the other matters fixed. She would soon see that she felt fine and everything would work out very neatly. "I don't know or care how," he said, "you just come. This is meant to be and it's going to be, so I'll see you here tomorrow." Alice arrived the following day.

6

The Earth Is a Living Being

Not long after we had finished setting up camp I had a second good conversation with Rolling Thunder. There was a pleasant light-heartedness in the air as we rode from the Palisades to Rolling Thunder's home in Carlin for lunch. After lunch we were going to nearby Elko, Nevada, for provisions. I found Rolling Thunder an excellent companion for a walk or a ride or hauling water or pitching a tent or having a simple meal. At times he was downright funny. And when others wanted to be funny their humor succeeded with Rolling Thunder. Although I have never seen in him the slightest hint of anguish or despair, and he is never given to depression, he becomes obviously tired when it seems appropriate and he might show anger when it is of some use. I am convinced that every image, every mood and every reaction he displays has a purpose. Each day it was becoming clearer to me that Rolling Thunder was a teacher who could offer me insights that I could never achieve in the laboratory or discover in the library.

Rolling Thunder's house was refreshingly cool. On the table with the meat and salad was a large pitcher of lemonade, and in the other room was a squirrel-cage evaporative cooler whirring in the window. It was getting hot up in the canyon. The sun was strong and the tents were like ovens. The only comfort was to stay in the shadows of the trees, and that was not usually convenient. A nearby place to swim would be a help. There was a stream not far from the campsite, but I had not had a chance to walk that way. In any case, I had noticed an inviting-looking stream as we rode out of the hills that day. "Are those streams up there okay to swim in?" I asked.

"I don't like my kids to swim in any of these streams around here," Rolling Thunder said. "Other kids do it, and mine have, I know. But I don't like the idea. These streams are polluted and that water is dangerous, especially if you should happen to swallow any amount of it. You know, the Indians have a saying, 'Never trust the water downstream from a white man.' This land was all pure at one time. The whole country was pure, the air, the water, everything. Now there's hardly any pure water left. From the major rivers to even the little streams in secluded areas, if the white man's gotten to it, it's no longer pure. And it hasn't taken him long, it hasn't taken the white man long at all."

His words went on like a buzzing in my ears. I just kept thinking about a nice cold swim, a place that could be reached by car. I remembered someone mentioning a small lake where water ran over a wall. I wondered if Rolling Thunder would know about that lake. Perhaps he could tell me whether it would be all right and where to find it.

He was still talking; I had not really been listening, yet I must have heard all of it, and something Rolling Thunder said caught my attention. He had called the earth an organism. I had never heard it just like that. After my return from years spent in Asia, I had begun to see the oneness of the world. I could think of the world as a single mind, in a sense, by thinking of all the nations and races and problems collectively. I knew of people from many countries and from the United Nations who spoke of world consciousness. Many were urging an awareness of the reality of the earth as one planet that should not foolishly be divided into parts and the things on the earth—water, air, even people and their cultures—could not be contained by boundaries conjured up by man. Rolling Thunder had somehow gone from streams to veins of flowing blood. Somehow the sand, soil, plants, rivers, streams and air were a body. I do not recall the words, but he managed to present a number of impressions instantaneously, giving rise to new perceptions in me: this earth a body, a gigantic body of a conscious, struggling living being. The body belongs to a being, an individual with an identity and a purpose. That being exists here now. We have to be within it —like cells.

Had I been listening with all my intellectual, analytical habits, this feeling would not have taken hold. I would have heard it too literally and gotten caught up in comparisons. But my mind was off-guard. Rolling Thunder had spoken too simply, too spontaneously. One would expect such perception to come under a stormy sky or when one was looking over the land from an airplane or lying down upon some green meadow. It had come from Rolling Thunder while we were eating at his table. At any rate, that all-too-temporary awareness has never returned, exactly, only the memory. I have since thought to ask Rolling Thunder to run through the whole thing again from the beginning, just as he did then. It is an awareness that I should like to have again.

I have since come to know some part of the Indian prophecy that is preserved chiefly by the Hopi people and maintained by traditional-Indian spokesmen everywhere. The currently significant part of those prophecies pertains to an approaching transition that is often called "the day of purification." This prophecy coincides with the claims of ecologists and scientists who believe that imbalance in nature has passed the point of no return. Yet the traditional Indian does not await some kind of ecological doomsday. Instead, he awaits the moment of climax with hopeful anticipation. During our lunch Rolling Thunder said, "When you have pollution in one place, it spreads all over. It spreads just as arthritis or cancer spreads in the body. The earth is sick now because the earth is being mistreated, and some of the problems that may occur, some of the natural disasters that might happen in the near future, are only the natural readjustments that have to take place to throw off sickness. A lot of things are on this land that don't belong here. They're foreign objects like viruses or germs. Now, we may not recognize the fact when it happens, but a lot of the things that are going to happen in the future will really be the earth's attempt to throw off some of these sicknesses. This is really going to be like fever or like vomiting, what you might call physiological adjustment.

"It's very important for people to realize this. The earth is a living organism, the body of a higher individual who has a will and wants to be well, who is at times less healthy or more healthy, physically and mentally. People should treat their own bodies with respect. It's the same thing with the earth. Too many people don't know that when they harm the earth they harm themselves, nor do they realize that when they harm themselves they harm the earth. Some of these people interested in ecology want to protect the earth, and yet they will cram anything into their mouths just for tripping or for freaking out —even using some of our sacred agents. Some of these things I call helpers, and they are very good if they are taken very, very seriously, but they have to be used in the right way; otherwise they'll be useless and harmful, and most people don't know about these things. All these things have to be understood.

"It's not very easy for you people to understand these things because understanding is not knowing the kind of facts that your books and teachers talk about. I can tell you that understanding begins with love and respect. It begins with respect for the Great Spirit, and the Great Spirit is the life that is in all things—all the creatures and the plants and even the rocks and the minerals. All things—and I mean *all* things—have their own will and their own way and their own purpose; this is what is to be respected.

"Such respect is not a feeling or an attitude only. It's a way of life. Such respect means that we never stop realizing and never neglect to carry out our obligation to ourselves and our environment."

Of all the teachings I have heard, these words are the most important and the most valuable for the contemporary aspirant upon the path of Karma Yoga, the path of action. No teaching for the path of action could be more fundamental or primary than the teachings of love and respect—for oneself, for one's world, and for the Great Spirit, which is all life in all things. The aspirant can perform no greater service for his world than to be mindful that his acts, even his thoughts and speech, become a part of the condition of that world.

The lesson from that day at Rolling Thunder's is now a part of my consciousness. His words provided me an opening through which further insights could come. Whatever I do, wherever I am, I will always be at that table with Rolling Thunder.

7

Subchief Oscar Johnny

Oscar Johnny joined us in camp one evening at sunset. He drove up in his new shiny green Ford pickup, parked just off the dirt road, and walked up to the fire. He had come just in time for our evening meal. With our new outdoor appetites we prepared food in great abundance. This night it was fried chicken, a large pot of stewed vegetables, and baked potatoes from the hot coals. Oscar Johnny ate with us and then, a cup of coffee in hand, he sat by the fire and talked until after dark.

Rolling Thunder had told me about Oscar Johnny: "He's a traditional, hereditary subchief of the Western Shoshone. Now there's a man who knows a lot. You might not recognize it right off, but he knows a lot. And if you were to ask him, he wouldn't tell you."

To me Oscar Johnny looked like a dark and husky truck-driver or bulldozer operator. I later discovered he was both. He had a home on the Ruby Valley Reservation and often traveled on tribal business to all the reservations throughout Shoshone territory, but he also had a home in Elko and maintained a full-time job with road contractors. His tribal position was hereditary. His father and fathers before him had been sub-chiefs of the Shoshone. He knew the vast Shoshone lands. Like the typical Indian scout he knew every hill and valley, every river and stream, and the location of all the trees and plants that his people once depended on for food. He knew the terrain of tradition as well, but unlike the vast desert land, there were places in this psychic terrain, the centuries-old oral traditions, that were not so easily accessible. Oscar Johnny was cautious of what might be unsafe or misleading if it were told out of context to people outside of his tradition. Like Rolling Thunder, he was not inclined toward trite, opinion-serving explanations, yet he was willing to participate in the growing communication between traditional peoples and their friends in the new society, hoping to satisfy and stimulate their interest.

Oscar Johnny spoke of Shoshone customs about food and clothing, marriages and wedding costumes. He talked of parents and grandparents and the stories the elders told. Many questions were asked. I had questions too, but I remembered Rolling Thunder's saying, "If you were to ask him, he wouldn't tell you," so I did not ask.

"A boy's grandparents usually find the wife for him. They make a buckskin outfit for him to wear at the wedding. They make it when he's a kid, and put it away for the wedding day. They make it the right size to fit on the wedding day, and they put it away."

"How do they know the right size?"

"They just know. They have to know, so they know. They know the wedding day and they know the size. It has to be right, so they have to know. They know the girl too, so they make her a dress—a wedding dress. It's a buckskin dress, a

white buckskin dress, and it's the right size, too, and they put
that away until the wedding day."

"You mean the grandparents always pick out the girl their
grandson marries?"

"Well, they find her, they find the right girl."

"What about the girl's grandparents, do they agree?"

"Sure they agree. They say, 'Yes, that's the one.' "

"Do the girl's grandparents ever get to do the choosing?"

"Well, it's the same thing. If they choose the right one, it's
the same."

"How do they know which person is the right one for another
to marry?"

"Well, they just look into that and they find the one that a
person's going to marry. They find out in advance. That's the
way they pick it."

"Why don't they let the person pick his own partner?"

"Well, that's the one. That's the one he picks. That's what
I meant by the right one, it's the one he picks. They just find
her in advance. They have to find her because they have to make
that buckskin dress."

"You mean they let the people find each other and decide to
get married, but they know who they're going to be in advance?
Do they know and just not tell them?"

"Well, it don't make any difference. The young ones know
too, and then they ask. They ask their grandparents. You take
some young buck. Say he goes somewhere, say, Wyoming. He
sees the girl, the one they already found, the one they made the
dress for. He would have picked her himself. Or maybe he
doesn't know yet, maybe he feels something. So he goes to his
grandparents next day and he says, 'Have I been spoken for?
Do you know my woman? Do you know who she is? Have you
made the dress?' Of course, they know and they have made the
dress, so then he asks, 'Who is she?' But they don't say, and
then he asks more questions; he asks if she lives in Wyoming
and he asks about her looks, and he finds out that way.

"How do they do that?"

"Who knows? How about another cup of coffee? This is some pretty good coffee you've got up here."

Someone quickly reached for the coffee as though it might have some bearing on whether Oscar continued. Everyone watched him, yet he appeared unaware that he was the center of attention. I recalled Rolling Thunder's words about Oscar Johnny and I wondered whether he would have explained more if he had not been questioned. For a while no one spoke and I hoped the silence would encourage him.

"Used to be a boy's grandparents could tell him a lot," he said at last. "They just looked into the matter and then told him about it, and they helped him that way. Sometimes they told the parents and not the boy. They looked at the problems, how they'd come and go and what he'd go through. And sometimes it could be changed too. They would tell about it and then it would be changed. And sometimes they wouldn't tell, if there wasn't any use. They would know the boy's taste, what he liked and how that would change. And they could tell the things the boy would like next year and the things he would stop liking, but he didn't need to know. He would like whatever he liked, and he could like it better if he didn't know it would stop. Maybe they would just tell the parents and they would say, 'Don't get so much leather for the boy. He won't care about it next year, so just let it be. Next year he'll like beads, so you just wait and see.' "

"What do they do, predict the future?" someone asked.

"Hmmm. Well, now just what they do, that's a good question."

Oscar Johnny is allowed another long silence, and since no one spoke, he did.

"That's more in the past than now. Some things, they don't do now. And some people, they don't know. Now you take these old arrowheads, you know these arrowheads like you find out in the desert? You can find them in lots of places, California too, and old ones. Those old ones have been doctored, and you can still tell it."

"How can you tell?"

"Well, they might make an infection or something. There's something still there, still in it. You can't analyze it, you can't find it by a chemist, but you can still tell it. Now, you take any old sharp stone, even the same kind, it won't do that. If it's not a doctored arrowhead, it won't do that. If you want, you try it, you cut yourself under the skin by an arrowhead and then you'll know. Used to be the young bucks, before they went out hunting, they'd get their arrowheads, ones that had been made and were ready, and the medicine man would take these arrowheads because the bucks, too, they'd do what the medicine man told them, and they would be prepared for the next day that way."

"What did the medicine man do to the arrowheads?"

"He doctored them."

"How?"

"He had a way. He had his own things he used, I guess, but it wasn't a physical thing. He would do it in the night while the young bucks were asleep. The next morning the arrowheads would be ready. The others would know what had been done but they wouldn't watch it or discuss it. And the medicine man could treat a person in the same way if he got wounded. Somebody might get a wound or an infection or a poison, the medicine man could cure that. He could convert those chemicals. Chemicals can be converted."

"How?"

"Well, they do it in their mind first. They know how. They do it in an Indian way, but they need that knowledge and they need control to do it. You take these cigarettes. These are all chemicals in here, tar and chemicals. Maybe you don't know how many chemicals are in here. This is not natural, and the old Indians, they don't like it. They don't want these chemicals, and they don't want the smoking habit. The Indians were first to smoke tobacco and it's good, good for you. But these chemicals make you sick. Now you give one of these cigarettes to an Indian medicine man, or even an old chief, he takes it because you gave it to him. He takes it, but he doesn't get those chemicals. Never. Those chemicals make him sick. He feels it and he converts them in his own body. He converts the chemicals."

"How does he do that? How do you convert chemicals in your own body?"

Oscar Johnny looked at the man who asked. Then he shrugged his shoulders in total disinterest. "You got me."

He quietly finished his coffee while I stared into the glowing coals of the fire. If such things were possible, I thought, it would be good for us all. If he had the answers why didn't he share them? I could understand Rolling Thunder's feelings against trying to spread truth where it was not wanted. As far as I knew neither swamis nor medicine men gave advice, teaching or healing unless they were requested to do so. It was as though there were some law of invocation and response: one cannot be helped until he seeks help, cannot be taught until he tries to learn, cannot be answered unless he asks. But why had Rolling Thunder said what he did about Oscar Johnny? Why, when others did ask, did they get only a shrug of the shoulders and silence? I was sure Oscar knew much more than he had volunteered, that he could have talked until daybreak and we would have listened and learned. I felt he had no interest in being one of a privileged few. He had no notions about privileged information. Neither Oscar Johnny nor his people held exclusivistic feelings.

From the time the first foreigners set foot upon this soil, the Indians shared with them. If they had chosen to do otherwise, history from that day to now might have been vastly different. They were as willing to share their psychic knowledge and their medicine as they were to share their knowledge of how to work the land, where to hunt, how to raise corn and other crops. But the newcomers turned out to be invaders who wanted nothing from the Indian but his land, and they were willing to go to any length to get it. Indian traditions were hidden only so that they could be preserved. Then came the age of technology. In the eyes of Indians, white Americans became interested only in the shadows of things and strove to ignore and even deny the realities behind them. Many researchers and historians have published accounts of American Indians that told of impressive feats and healing techniques, yet contemporary professionals seemed afraid such accounts might contradict "modern science." The dominant attitude was an insistence that modern methods and views had to be superior to the past, and Indians were prosecuted for their practices, for performing healings, religious rituals and sacred dances. Modern America had new ideas of religion—popular Sunday morning activity, convenient source of social virtue—but when religion pretended to deal with facts about the universe it became a threat to modern science.

We sat quietly and drank our coffee. I remembered something Rolling Thunder had said the day we had lunch at his house: "These days people want everything in a hurry and they want it without much effort. That's why they miss out on a lot of things. They miss a lot of understanding because they don't want to work for it. They want all the answers, right now, easy and quick."

Oscar Johnny may have thought it would take more than one night to even set the stage for a different kind of learning. He may have thought his persistent questioners would want to debate. Maybe he would have been more accommodating if they had asked less abruptly. They might have said, "How did you learn about these things, and how can I begin to learn?" In any case, I thought, the answers will be forthcoming, even from Oscar Johnny. I thought about the ancient prophecies that spoke of the day when "the children of the white man would begin to wear long hair, beads and headbands," the day "when the Indians would find new friends among new people." There will be new people who will know how to listen, who will hear. Then the traditions will be shared.

Oscar Johnny leaned forward and placed his empty cup on

the ground. "Looks like we might all be going out to Ruby Valley in the morning."

"Are you going too?"

"Well, I'm going to try to make it if I can. Rolling Thunder said you people'd come by in the morning. Guess I'll be on my way. Sun gets up early these days."

He walked out to the road where he had parked his pickup, and drove away, as straightforward and simply as he'd talked to us that night. Never was I more certain of how poorly we judge knowledge and wisdom, who possesses it and how it is transmitted.

The Ruby Valley
Expedition

We left the Palisade campsite in the early morning for the long ride south to Ruby Valley. I rode in Alice's red Ford and Rolling Thunder drove. The red 1965 Valiant known as the "committee car" and a green Citroën belonging to another committee member followed. Including the committee people, Rolling Thunder, Alice, Anne and Richard, and myself, there were fifteen of us in three cars. For some of the others this was not the first trip to Ruby Valley. Anne and Richard and a few committee members had visited this reservation last summer and had met Frank Temoke, chief of the Western Shoshone.

A short while after we had started we parked at the side of the road and looked over the hill far below where trees had been cleared by the Bureau of Land Management. The chaining had been done long before and even the dead trees were gone. It was impossible to imagine how the area had looked in its original state. Rolling Thunder thought it would be more impressive to see some of the areas that had been chained recently. There were several areas near the route to Ruby Valley, but without Oscar Johnny it would be very difficult to find them.

Oscar Johnny had sent word that he had to remain in Elko on urgent business, so we had left without him. Rolling Thunder decided we would drive straight to Ruby Valley and back. It would be late by the time we returned to camp. As usual, Rolling Thunder drove fast. He was in good humor and laughed easily. He had to stop at every fork and intersection to wait for the others. The roads were so winding that the two cars behind could not see us. As we approached a curve at the top of a hill, he alerted us. "Now watch for this deer when we get around this curve! It's a baby fawn, still got its spots."

As we climbed the hill he continued, "Lots of beautiful deer up in here. White hunters come up here—right on the reservation sometimes—greedy, inconsiderate, destructive. Headhunters is what they are, trophy hunters after a prize, and they don't care what they kill. Sometimes they leave the carcasses along the path as they go or sometimes we find the bodies in the dump. That's not the Indian way, I can tell you that. We take what we need and no more, and nothing is wasted. And it's done in the proper way and with respect. When I hunt I take one deer and no more, and that one is chosen beforehand. I never go runnin' around searching and chasing after a deer. I'll go right to him; like I'll walk over some hill and he'll be standing there waiting for me, because that's been arranged that way and he knows it and I know—" Suddenly he pointed. "Look! See, there he is!"

I missed it. I was apparently the only one who failed to see the spotted fawn lying in the bushes near the road. It stood as we went by, according to the others, but it did not run. I had looked too far from the road. I decided that if such a thing should happen again I would not be so eager. It did happen again, many times. During the following months it wasn't un-common to hear Rolling Thunder say, "A lot of coyotes getting together up there. We'll hear them tonight," or, "There's a bird sittin' in the road right around this bend. I forget what you call him in English. I call him a . . ."

Shortly after we saw the deer, it began to rain, and it rained all the way to Ruby Valley. The light rain was accompanied by dramatic claps of thunder that seemed to roll along after the cars. We were on dirt roads made slippery by the rain, and driving became difficult. Rolling Thunder obviously enjoyed the rain. It was a hot, dry season in these parts, and this was unexpected relief.

"Listen to the rolling thunder," he said. "The thunder is really rollin' in the sky!"

Either the rain stopped by the time we got to Ruby Valley or there had been no rain there. It was hot and dry. As we drove through the reservation Rolling Thunder stopped several times, got out of the car and walked alone to some of the small, simple houses of his Shoshone friends. At one place he stood and talked for several minutes, but at others no one came to the door. "They all work at the ranches around here," he explained. "I guess this isn't the best time for meeting people. They all seem to be out in the fields taking in the hay." Later we turned onto a road that went up into the foothills. When we came to the end we got out to stretch our legs. This was a clear and quiet place; if the hills hadn't been there, you might have been able to see forever. It was one o'clock and everyone was hungry. We took out the bags of food we had prepared: carrots, celery, sandwiches, boiled eggs and potatoes. Rolling Thunder walked down a wide path and disappeared in the distance. We ate lunch strolling around the cars and lounging in the hot sun.

I began to get a feeling for the vastness of the Shoshone territory, the discontinuity of the reservations and the isolation of the people. From our campsite in the Palisades it's about fifty miles to the Lee reservation, and ninety miles south to Ruby

Valley, home of the traditional chief. The Duck Valley reservation is over one hundred miles north of Carlin and extends into Idaho. There are a few small towns or villages that are mostly Indian, but these are controlled communities where the lives and the land of the people are manipulated by the Bureau of Indian Affairs. Traditional Indian families are scattered over the immense territory. Most of them are isolated with little means of ordinary communication.

"I've been talking to a couple friends down there," Rolling Thunder said as he walked back up the path. "Now I thought you might all like to talk to them for a few minutes. They're traditional people and they don't speak English too well, but you'll be able to communicate with them. I guess you know you'll have to leave your cameras behind this time."

Two old men were sitting on a bench in front of an old wooden shack that I supposed to be their home. Their faces were dark and leathery, deeply lined. They kept their eyes toward the ground most of the time, but when they looked up their eyes were sharp and piercing. They sat very quietly. It was an awkward meeting. There seemed little to say and no way to say it. This was not true, I knew, but it seemed so at the time. One of these men was the younger brother of Frank Temoke, hereditary chief of the Western Shoshone. The other, older man carried on what little conversation there was. The visit was brief. We tried to talk about the pinyon trees and the hunters, but the only response we got was a few nods and near smiles. We shook hands and left.

"I guess that was all we could expect at this time," Rolling Thunder said as we walked back toward the cars. "Remember, most reservation Indians have never met a white man with a good heart and good intentions. But I didn't just bring you here to meet these people. I brought you here so they could meet you. Well, it's only a beginning."

Near the old Indians' cabin was a cleared area. We were told this was used for traditional festivals and important gatherings.

At one edge of the clearing we saw the cabin of subchief Oscar Johnny. Looking out in a great circle over trees and gulleys toward the distant hills, I stretched my mind to take in the many memories of this land. It wasn't hard. I had heard from Rolling Thunder the legend of Ruby Valley, the story of the signing of the treaty with the blood of an Indian. I recalled that legend now.

Our treaty, which outlines the lands which comprise the Western Shoshone Indian Nation, was made in Ruby Valley, Nevada, in 1863. Our treaty was signed by our principal chiefs and headsmen and ratified by the Congress of the United States. Our treaty was paid for in blood.

At that time, the white people were weak and few in number and it was the white man and his government who came to us asking for a peace treaty. The white people were at war among themselves and this war was called the Civil War and President Lincoln of the United States wanted to get gold from California in order to finance the war. The white man's government did not have enough soldiers to guard all of the stagecoaches that carried the gold across Nevada. It was their desire to have a treaty of peace with the people through whose lands the stagecoaches had to travel. We were those people—the Western Shoshone—and the land was ours.

So the white people and the representatives of the United States government put out the word that they were anxious to meet with the chiefs and the people of the Western Shoshone Indian Nation for the purpose of signing such a treaty. A date was set and the word was passed by runners and on horseback that there would be a feast and that all the Indians were to come. It was to be a great feast, with plenty to eat, and then the peace treaty would be signed by both parties and there would be no more fighting. The Indians were to come unarmed because they would not need their guns.

So at the appointed time the Western Shoshone and their chiefs all gathered at the designated place in Ruby Valley, and they came unarmed. The soldiers also came with the government representatives, but the soldiers had rifles which they stacked in bunches.

When the Indians had all gathered, the soldiers grabbed the rifles and killed an Indian whom they had previously captured and brought with them. They said the Indian was accused of robbing a stagecoach and that he would be an example to all Indians who might be thinking of obstructing the white man's passage through Indian lands. They they cut the Indian up and put him in a huge, black iron pot and they cooked him. And the soldiers aimed their rifles at the heads of the people and forced the people to eat some of this man they had killed. Men, women and children were all forced to eat some of this human flesh while the soldiers held their guns on the people.

It was after this terrible thing which the white man did to our people that the Treaty of 1863 was signed.

Our treaty has been paid for in blood.

We will hold to our treaty and our lands and one day the white man will have to live by the treaty and pay his debts because this is the law of balance.

One hundred years later, in October 1968, Rolling Thunder and a band of Shoshone, led by Frank Temoke, put on war paint to confront some white men who were hunting and drinking on Indian land in Ruby Valley. The white men were taken by surprise and the Shoshone warriors ran them off the reservation. The hunters never returned.

I thought about the many years of Shoshone struggle with the Bureau of Indian Affairs, the Bureau of Land Management, and the ranchers who were taking over their land. I thought of the signing of the treaty, and of the time before the white man first appeared—the hundreds of years of festivals and ceremonies. Since the coming of the white man, the harmony between the people and the land had been disturbed, and things have never been the same for the Shoshone.

On our return we made a side trip to Ely to eliminate the risk of running out of gas on the lonely reservation roads. We had supper in a restaurant in Ely, and it was well after dark when we started home.

Rolling Thunder led the way back up the mountain road

toward the pass. We could not see the cars behind us. Often I looked out the back window, but there was never even a headlight beam in the darkness. Rolling Thunder knew they were following. "They're coming along," he said every few minutes. Then, when we had nearly reached the top of the hill, he swung off onto the shoulder, making room to turn around. "I feel like they've just stopped."

I wondered how he knew. We went back down the road a few miles and came upon our two companion cars. The committee car was raised on a bumper jack and the the green Citroën was parked close behind.

As we approached the other cars Rolling Thunder shouted, "Look out!" Everyone standing around the car leaped back and the car rolled forward, off the jack! It felt as though he had made an instant prediction.

The tire was changed and we continued the trip uneventfully. That brief incident now seemed like a fleeting dream. I believe that none of us had been watching consciously—none of us had thought about what Rolling Thunder was doing. But when we were again on our way I saw those past minutes like an instant replay, and then it struck me what had happened. We had stood around half-conscious in the night, hesitating to get too close to the car that had just fallen. In what seemed an impossibly short time, Rolling Thunder had taken out the spare, gotten the car back into the air, loosened the lug bolts, removed the tire, laid it into the trunk, put on the other tire, lowered the car, and put away the tools. Rolling Thunder had done all this while everyone watched but failed to notice.

I wondered as we were riding along again whether the others were aware of what I now realized. From the time we had started out for Ruby Valley, the whole day had unfolded as if it was under the management of Rolling Thunder. Now I began to wonder whether even our being here—Alice because she was told it was meant to be, Anne and Richard because of a sudden change of plans on their way somewhere else, my own coming

from Council Grove and the others for all their varieties of
reasons—was really due to some management of events? What
Rolling Thunder had done seemed to acknowledge that. It
seemed like he had made a gesture of responsibility. He had
brought us together, picked a campsite, taken note of and provided our supplies. After the long talks, the exhibitions he
planned, arranged and guided, even the changing of a tire had
been surrendered to his hands.

Summer Flowers from Winter Snow

"I've got to start gathering my herbs," Rolling Thunder announced. "I've got a lot of herbs to gather and now is the time." It was nearly noon on a hot summer day and we were on our way to town, driving down the road that led from our canyon to the highway. Rolling Thunder had been busy and I had not seen him for several days.

"Do you have certain days for that?" I asked.

"Well, in the summertime, when they're all out real good. Some things we get earlier and some things later. It takes a long time, it's a lot of work. Some of it is around here and some pretty far away. I have to climb up into the hills sometimes. And I have to cut it and pick it and carry it back. So I have to take the chance when I get it. If I let it go, first thing you know summer'll be over and I won't have my herbs. Then, on the other hand, if the need comes up, if I need a certain herb in the wintertime and I don't have it then, I'll go out and get it. There've been times I can go right out here in the middle of winter and get a summer flower right out of the snow. That's if I need to, if the need is there. We don't do things without reason."

In the brief silence that followed, I became aware of the depth of that claim. I remembered the healing ritual at Council Grove, when Rolling Thunder had asked his patient, "Why do you want to be relieved of this condition? . . . What are you going to do?" The existence of the reason was important to the healing.

"We say there is a right time and place for everything," Rolling Thunder went on. "It's easy to say, but hard to understand. You have to live it to understand it. We live with that understanding—the fact that there's a right time—and we live in harmony with that. That way we know when to get our herbs, and where. That's how we can get them when the need is there."

The conversation ended at that point. For the rest of that day, and for some days to follow, I went over that simple conversation in my mind until I realized that I had been given a fundamental and important key. Rolling Thunder had not offered me any tangible proof that a summer flower could be taken from the snow. Perhaps there could have been a demonstration, but how meaningless it would have been! He could have done it several times to be sure that I was convinced. I could have taken pictures and shown them to others as though the whole point was whether, in fact, Rolling Thunder had actually plucked a flower from the snow. Caught up in that hopeless challenge, I would have failed to find out anything. "We don't do things without reason," Rolling Thunder had said, and giving demonstrations for evidence certainly did not occur on his list of reasons.

In any case, an example or two of this extraordinary feat

would have been of little use to me. What Rolling Thunder gave me was the secret of how it is done. The actual doing of such a thing, even for good reason, is not of great significance. The real value lies in what it indicates about the arrangement of the universe.

Rolling Thunder had explained at Council Grove that his training was experiential. In his first conversation with me he said that truth cannot be expressed verbally, that it can only be experienced: "You have to live it and be part of it and then you might get to know it." My first step was to learn what Rolling Thunder meant by understanding. Understanding is not the sort of thing my modern, establishment education had me believing it was. Understanding, to what Rolling Thunder calls the establishment mind, is simply a rather low-level dance and shuffle, a kind of churning process by which a number of ideas and concepts are juggled around with the newcomer idea until they all somehow fit together. This fitting provides a feeling of knowing which gratifies the mind. A person simply feels the satisfaction of having all his assumptions fit together, and he says, "I know."

To Rolling Thunder, knowing is being. His simple description of the arrangement of the universe is that there is a right time and place for everything. That cannot be understood by any process of speech or thought: "It's easy to say but hard to understand. You have to live it to understand it." The meaning of all this is that when Rolling Thunder talks about "a right time and place for everything—you have to live it to understand it," he is talking about becoming part of the right time and the right place. He understands right time and right place and therefore he is a part of right time and place. This means that the right time and place for the summer flower is partly his decision. To put it another way: first you identify the principle, then you practice it. Gradually you understand the principle, that is, you become one with it. When you become one with the principle it responds to your will.

It is one thing to arrive at a realization that all things have
time and place; it is quite another to put the realization into
practice. I acknowledge this truth and I speak it, I say it is so,
but I do not practice it and I am therefore not involved with
it. Rolling Thunder does practice it. Every day in every action,
in all his interrelations with the sun, the earth, clouds, mosquitoes, plants, animals and people, he practices the understanding that there is a right time and place for everything. He
does not gather herbs after sundown and he only gathers what
he needs; he does not take before he gives; he never picks plants
to throw them away; he never kills for sport; he never does
anything without reason or leaves a thing undone that has a
purpose in its doing. For him there are no weeds, no mosquito
bites, no unwanted rains. There are no dangerous plants or
animals. For him there is no fear. The wind and the rain, the
mosquitoes and the snakes are all within him. His consciousness extends to include them within its very being. What the life
of Rolling Thunder communicates is that when someone identifies himself, not with his self-image or his thinking process but
with the flowers, the snow, and all manifestations of the life
force, he can do the things of which Rolling Thunder speaks.

I acquired this explanation from Rolling Thunder through
his actions and through his very being. I have not achieved
understanding: I know that I do not know, but I also know how
to reach the point of knowing. If understanding is more difficult
than I had at first considered, and if practicing the idea of the
right time and place involves tremendous effort, then it is infi-
nitely easier than I had ever imagined to pluck a summer flower
from the snow. It is at least within the realm of possibility.

The simple remarks that Rolling Thunder made that day—
beginning with "I've got a lot of herbs to gather and now is the
time"—are an example of how an adept teacher avoids the
limitations imposed by the rational or analytical mind by delib-
erately planting a seed that in time grows in the student's mind
until he or she achieves, almost spontaneously, a full-blown

understanding. Though the unenlightened student might feel the need for evidence and reason, for immediate conclusions, the supreme teacher is above the need to prove his point or even to be understood.

Later, when Alice mentioned herb-gathering, I felt a genuine desire to help. I already knew that Rolling Thunder and Alice frequently gathered herbs together. Outsiders do not usually go along on these affairs, but I decided to ask Alice if I could accompany them. I knew, of course, that the decision would be made by Rolling Thunder. Alice said she would mention it, and she felt sure he would grant my request. A day or two later, however, Alice mentioned herb-gathering again as though she had forgotten our last conversation. Again I voiced my wishes, and again she volunteered to speak to Rolling Thunder. A few days passed and nothing more was said. I could have spoken to Rolling Thunder myself, since he had first mentioned herbs to me, but I thought I knew how it should work out. Alice would talk to Rolling Thunder, and then, if he wished, Rolling Thunder would talk to me. That was the Indian way as I understood it: you go through an assistant first. It would no doubt work out in accordance with the right time and place for everything. At least they had not yet gone off without me. I temporarily forgot the matter.

10
❦

Rain at the Abandoned Ranch

"There's an old abandoned ranch just a few minutes' ride from here," Rolling Thunder said one morning up at camp. "I like to kind of keep an eye on the place and I haven't been there for quite a while. Thought we might all go over there and have a look."

The original plan for the day had been to inspect another forest chaining site. Members of the Committee of Concern for the Traditional Indian would be returning to San Francisco in a few days. They had come to Nevada to observe the destruction that had been done to Nevada's limited forest lands by the Bureau of Land Management. The committee was concerned because these pinyon trees were being chained down on Indian treaty territory, and since the pinyon nuts were a major protein source for the Indians, their destruction was a threat to the tradition and welfare of the people. But an inspection was a discouraging prospect. It was hot and dry; the ground and the air were scorching. It was difficult to locate the areas where the trees had been chained down, and the Bureau's bulldozers were not moving at the time. It was essential to catch them in the act—dragging their anchor chain across the ground, ripping out life-giving trees at twenty acres an hour—because photographs of previously chained areas looked as though the hillsides had always been bare.

Rolling Thunder reminded us of all these problems, saying that he hoped we could somehow all be around when the chaining was resumed. He thought it would be more worthwhile this day to visit the old ranch.

"We'll take off as soon as Spotted Eagle gets here. It only takes about half an hour to drive over there." Spotted Eagle was Rolling Thunder's youngest son. He was about nineteen and, I had heard, apprentice to his father. He would be guarding our camp while we were gone, as he had done earlier when we went to Ruby Valley. When he arrived I heard Rolling Thunder instruct him: "Now people have been driving through here looking around. They've even been doing target practice up here, and you know some people couldn't care less what they shoot at—and they're not all kids either. So I don't want you going to sleep up here or wandering off somewhere." Spotted Eagle sat down in a camp chair in the shade of the large tent. The fifteen of us got into the committee's Valiant and Alice's Ford and started out for the abandoned ranch.

It was to be a good day. Rolling Thunder became the shaman that day, and at the campfire that night he was once again the teacher.

The old ranch was enchanting; at first it seemed a dead and ghostly place, but despite the broken-down house and sheds, the dead grass, and the dusty ground, the setting was peaceful. The empty ranch site lay at the foot of soft, rolling hills, dotted with large shade trees. In front of the old house was a huge log made smooth and shiny by time. Sitting on the log one could look across the road and up to a high mountain over which white-winged hawks glided in endless circles. Rolling Thunder pointed to the mountain. "Right out there where the road turns at the edge of that cliff is a sacred Indian shrine. White men blew it up. They blew the front right off of it when they built that road through there. That wasn't too long ago. Now that's why this ranch is abandoned. Years back there were Indians living all around these hills. This was their home, they weren't hurting anybody. They just wanted to be left alone. But ranchers ran them off when they came in here to take this land. Those Indians disappeared and were never seen again, and we know it's been common practice to shoot our people just to get them out of the way. Some of this ranch land has been bought and sold for millions of dollars by rich white ranchers; but it really belongs to the people they stole it from.

"Now the time has come when it is right for us to begin reclaiming some of the land that has been stolen from us, especially some of the sacred areas and the land that has been misused and mistreated, the land that our people are supposed to take care of. We don't say we own the land. When I say it belongs to us I mean we belong on this land. This land that we're standing on here today has been reclaimed for the Indian. It began when they dynamited that shrine. After that I did some work in this area. It's out of the hands of the white man now. The ranchers that were here abandoned this place because grass was dying and the hay would not grow. Even the horses and cows were getting sick and they couldn't find the reason why. I've got to come back here again pretty soon and work some more."

Rolling Thunder turned and grinned. He seemed to be elated at the thought of repossessing the land—the thought that the sacred places would be saved and the tradition would survive. As he walked around looking, smelling and touching, he appeared like someone who, coming back to inspect his garden after a too-long absence, finds everything still within the realm of easy management. His surveillance took him in widening circles, and for a few moments he was out of sight.

We began to look around inside the empty house. I walked through an old shack whose floor was almost gone and stood on the front step to watch the hawks circle the mountain. I wondered what would happen if I could sit up there alone for a few days. I became aware of holes in the side of the cliff that might be caves. I stared at the largest, highest hole and pondered how I might get a look inside. A large cloud began to form above my head, and I realized how hot and bright the sun had been. As I watched the cloud, I wondered how it got there. There was no breeze to carry it, yet there it was growing bigger and becoming blacker, like a rain cloud. This was the first such cloud I had seen; it felt refreshing and invigorating to be in its shade. I went back to join the others while the cloud grew darker.

Not more than an hour after we had arrived, we were leaving the abandoned ranch. Rolling Thunder was saying something about how a little rain would be a good idea. There was the sound of thunder directly overhead. Someone down at the Carlsons' market in Carlin had insisted it never rained in the summertime, yet it had rained on our trip to Ruby Valley and Rolling Thunder had cheered, "Listen to the rolling thunder!" Rolling Thunder got far ahead of us on the path. When we had nearly reached the road I saw him kneel beside a small sagebush. Even though he was obviously concentrating intensely, I walked right up, and knelt down beside him. Rolling Thunder was holding a tiny stick and he was poking at an ordinary stink bug. He looked at me and his face loosened for a moment.

"This will bring the rain."

He herded the big black bug about, tapping on its back to make it run and on its head to make it turn.

"Now watch!"

He quickly flipped the stick. The bug landed on its back,

righted itself and nearly stood on its head with its back end in the air. There was a loud, sharp crack: a bolt of lightning, a bright, clearly defined zigzag line.

"You see? This brings the lightning!"

Again and again the act was repeated and again and again the lightning came. It was unbelievable. I had never seen such lightning. Loud and clear, right overhead, always in the same place, the bolts came in rapid succession. It seemed to be synchronized precisely with the agitations of the bug. I might have been watching someone scratching a screwdriver on a battery pole or touching two live wires together. It became apparent as it continued that this was an uncommon but natural phenomenon produced by a real cause-and-effect relationship.

"This brings the lightning. You tease him and it brings the lightning. His irritation stimulates the lightning and that's what brings the rain."

The lightning bolts continued to come one after the other. Rising up on his haunches, Rolling Thunder jumped in a low, crouching stoop, his arm extended to reach the bug with the stick. He continued the pushing and flipping, accompanied now by a throaty cry: "Heagh, heaghhh . . ."

The others had gathered around the little bush and everyone watched as Rolling Thunder, still stooping, kicked out first one foot and then the other in a sort of dance. He looked pleased, almost mischievous.

"Now we better get out of here—fast!"

"I'll bet it's really going to come down after all that," I said. Rolling Thunder laughed.

It was a wild downpour. We were within sight of the cars when it started and we all broke into a run. The rain came in heavy sheets and beat furiously on the cars. Driving was nearly impossible. The windshield wipers provided only brief glances at the muddy road. A few minutes later, however, it was all over; the sun shone again, almost as though nothing had happened.

"Oh no, what about the things in camp!" someone remembered. We had left our clothes, towels, sleeping bags and about a half-dozen old mattresses out under the sun. I wondered if Rolling Thunder had failed to consider those things. When we reached the camp it was obvious that not a drop of rain had fallen there.

I had returned to camp in the last car behind Rolling Thunder, and when I walked back toward the tents he was already there, standing under a tree, looking at me.

"You say you like to see metaphysical things?"

I did not recall ever having said that. I am sure, in fact, that I never did. I even avoid choosing words like "metaphysical" except in some required context because I cannot be sure what such words mean—at least to others. Yet I knew exactly what Rolling Thunder meant by what he said to me. There may even have been a reason for his choice of words.

"Do you think you have seen anything of interest today?"

I agreed I had.

Later in the afternoon I found Spotted Eagle sitting at the foot of the hill behind our camp, and I questioned him about the rainmaking. If he was his father's apprentice, I thought, he should know about his father's doings.

"You know, it seems funny that it didn't rain here at all. Didn't you even notice any clouds?"

Spotted Eagle claimed not to have noticed any clouds in the sky or heard any thunder.

"But it rained hard at the abandoned ranch," I said. I looked right at him but there was no reaction.

"I think your father did it," I said. Still no reaction. "He used a bug."

Spotted Eagle's face lit up. "A stink bug!" he said. "That's what he's got me working on!"

"You can make rain with a stink bug?" I asked.

"I can't do it. Can't seem to get it down." Spotted Eagle said that in the same way he talked about a speed shift or some hot-rod maneuver. He was as restless and carefree as any nineteen-year-old, and it was difficult to picture him practicing sorcery. Yet I felt that his words were purposeful and that he would not have carelessly discussed this thing with anyone.

I had first met Spotted Eagle only a few days before. He was called Mala and at that time no one mentioned that he was Rolling Thunder's son. Spotted Eagle didn't resemble his older brother, Buffalo Horse, whom I had met when I first went to Rolling Thunder's house, but I soon realized who he was. Before I came to Carlin I had not known about Rolling Thunder's family, but when I first went to his house I began to recall specific images that had come into my mind during the two days I spent alone in the motel room—images that I had hardly been aware of at the time. One thing I remembered immediately after I first talked with Buffalo Horse was someone saying, "There are two sons, one of whom spreads inert energy that waits for good use, and the other carries about happy messages to spread good will." It is possible that I made up my "spontaneous impressions" sitting alone in that motel, but when I first saw Spotted Eagle I recognized him by those words.

"Maybe I'll get it one of these days," Spotted Eagle concluded. "It's supposed to be one of the easy ways to bring the rain once you've got your cloud together."

Later I noticed Rolling Thunder surveying the campsite, looking as he had looked at the abandoned ranch. He glanced at me and smiled. "Don't you think we could use a little rain around here too? It might be a good idea to kind of settle the dust, especially around the cooking area here."

He soon had everyone filling the largest tent with mattresses, towels, sleeping bags and food. Then he was gone again.

"Gone to see a snake, I'll bet," said Alice. "See how clear the sky is? He can make it rain, though. You watch. It'll be raining before dinner."

No rain came that night. Rolling Thunder came back to

camp just before suppertime, and standing where most of us had gathered around the pots of cooking food, announced that tonight would be the right time for him to go over some of his thoughts on the aims and methods of the committee in the coming months.

The committee had been founded in January 1969. Its first activity was to provide assistance for a traditional Navajo Indian who was tried in a federal court for refusing induction into the armed forces on treaty and religious grounds. I liked the committee's philosophy, and their policy of doing only what they were asked. "We try to help with money, with legal contacts, and where they need us for what they choose us to do," one member explained to me, "rather than sitting around thinking up ideas about 'what would be good for these Indians' and laying more white man's trips on them."

We ate our cool supper (mostly fresh vegetables) under a warm sunset; later, the night sky began to sparkle with countless stars. Then we all sat around the fire and watched the smoke rise straight up in the still air as though through a chimney. And Rolling Thunder talked. Sitting in the canvas chair, wearing the old hat with the feathers, the flickering firelight dancing upon his face, Rolling Thunder spoke as traditional teachers in all times and places have spoken, saying things that only my people seemed to have missed.

That was the central point of his message, what we had missed hearing. Man's inner nature is identical with the nature of the universe, and thus man learns about his own nature from nature herself. The technological and materialistic path of contemporary Western society is the most unnatural way of life man has ever tried. The people of this society are farthest removed from the trees, the birds, the insects, the animals, the growing plants and the weather. They are therefore the least in touch with their own inner nature. Unnatural things are so commonplace to the modern mind it is little wonder natural things seem strange and difficult to face. The important perennial truths will seem like new learning for modern Americans. This learning must come, however, before people can begin to work successfully in groups rather than as disconnected individuals, and before they can begin to deal with snowballing social problems—problems like ecological ones that challenge the potential of individuals, societies, nations and the planet to function as a single entity.

In my tent I thought I would have preferred rainmaking again that night. It occurred to me that if I were to establish the event of the rain as Rolling Thunder's doing, two such demonstrations would be much more useful than one. The first rain had been on the day of the trip to Ruby Valley, but Rolling Thunder had not said anything about that, only "Listen to the rolling thunder." I could not know whether he had done anything to bring the rain that day. Suppose it was all coincidence? Suppose that Rolling Thunder, anticipating an inevitable rain, chose to pretend that he had made it? It amused me to think, as I began to fall asleep, what a long list of coincidences would be needed to explain each recurring lightning bolt, arriving at the intended place at the intended instant. I could add that I never ran across another stink bug in Nevada before or after that day; the particular agent that was the preestablished requirement, as Spotted Eagle had confirmed the bug to be, had been in the right place at the right time.

Rolling Thunder arrived at camp early the following morning. He usually returned home late at night and drove back up about midmorning, but this day he had been awakened by a telephone call. As we all stood around, he complained at length about that call, though he seemed to think the incident was funny. He seemed in a happy mood.

"I got a phone call from that couple who were over here from Salt Lake City the other day, those people who tried to get me to become a sales representative for Shakely products. I guess their Basic-H is a pretty good washing compound and I guess they carry good, natural products. But I'm not a peddler! And they should not be peddlers around the Indians. They should not have taken their merchandise out on the Indian reservation. Imagine, they woke me up at seven-thirty in the morning to ask if I was going to sell Basic-H to the Indians for them. Well, I tried to tell them nice as I could, but I had to explain to them that you don't go out to the Indians with something to sell, not religion, not politics, not modern science or products or anything else, because that's not where it's at when you're dealing with Indians. The white man's always got to be selling something—peddle, peddle, peddle, proselytize and propagandize. Maybe that's why you people here can learn a thing or two, because you don't have anything to sell. Now let's get some of this stuff back in the tents and see if we can settle the dust around here."

Rolling Thunder walked away. He went over toward the hill behind our camp and then along the railroad tracks until he was out of sight. We carried sleeping bags and food boxes into the tents. Then we looked up at the clear, hot sky. There were no clouds, but a minute or so later we heard the distant sound of thunder, unmistakable and exciting. The sky had just begun to darken when Rolling Thunder walked back into camp, his head tilted to one side, his eyes squinting in that familiar, peering way.

"We can all go inside the big tent. It won't be too hot in there now. Then we can let it sprinkle around here for about an hour."

The air became cool and pleasant inside the tent, and everyone was cheerful. The soft, steady rain seemed to muffle the atmosphere. It was not like the downpour of the day before. From inside the tent I couldn't see if there was any lightning. There was a constant roll of thunder, though, each peal starting far in the distance, then growing louder and closer as it came rolling up through the canyon. I supposed it was raining only in our area, but surely they could hear the thunder down in

Carlin, or at least at the rock quarry at the mouth of the canyon. Someone would think it curious!

I ran to my own tent and took the cassette recorder from my suitcase, placing it on my sleeping bag, turned on. The thunder continued and back in the group I thought of the cassette, going round and round, filling up with the beautiful sound. I kept that recording for over a week and listened to it many times. The thunder was recognizable, but coming through the small speaker it was less than inspiring. It certainly could not serve as proof of anything.

I had quite carefully thought out the matter of proof, and decided that it would be both useless and impossible. I recalled Dr. Green telling me that the object of pursuing knowledge is not so much to get caught up in the matter of proof as to discover what works and then make it work. The significance or usefulness of what we know about gravity, steam power, the planets or electricity are followed, not preceded by, the theoretical explanations. Since I needed cassettes, I erased the thunder and reused the tape.

By now I had seen several demonstrations of Rolling Thunder's handling of the weather. In addition to the rain that came on the way to Ruby Valley, at the abandoned ranch and in camp, we heard thunder several evenings when he was in camp and told us to listen for it. There was never any when he was not around. Added to the list of coincidences (if they were coincidences) was the fact that whatever it was—lightning, rain or thunder—the intended phenomenon had always appeared at the intended time and place, and it was usually announced before it happened. I felt that I no longer needed to be concerned with the question of coincidence. What interested me was not whether, but *how* these things are done.

11
❧

Healing Ritual
in the Canyon

One warm summer night Rolling Thunder held a healing ritual. The day had been beautiful and peaceful; puffy cumulus clouds looking like rabbits and sheep floated slowly on a high breeze above the canyon. The hot steady sun dropped over the hill behind our camp, and dusk was long.

As darkness fell, the ceremonial fire was started. Dry field grass was pulled up and the ground scraped clean with boards and shovels to form a clear circle not far from the tents. The fire burned in a shallow pit in the center of this clearing. Three canvas chairs were placed side by side to face west across the flames. In the chairs sat the three people for whose benefit the proceedings were about to unfold. Rolling Thunder approached the fire facing east, and the ritual began.

Spotted Eagle was his father's assistant. He lit the pipe,

placed some sparkling crystals from the medicine bag in the fire and sprinkled a sandy-looking substance around it in a circle. Dipping his fingers into a can of powder, Spotted Eagle patted faces, shoulders and chests to form powdery white patterns on those of us who were participating by observing. We sat Indian-fashion on the ground in a wide half-circle about the fire. Rolling Thunder spoke, and his words were straight and simple and strong; I have rarely heard anyone speak with such clarity and precision. He began with the usual invocation:

> "To the East where the Sun rises.
> To the North where the cold comes from.
> To the South where the light comes from.
> To the West where the Sun sets.
> To the Father Sun.
> To the Mother Earth."

Then he spoke of man's spiritual predicament. He spoke of the forced adoption of Indian children into white families, the destruction of forests, the testing of chemical and biological weaponry in Nevada. He mentioned war, oppression, jealousy, hate and greed. This was not politics or protest. This was a healing ceremony, and Rolling Thunder was speaking to the Great Spirit about himself and his three patients and all of us who were listening. He was speaking about health and he began with an accounting of the situation. It appeared as if he regarded the specific conditions of his three patients a part of the total human condition.

The three patients were two members of the committee, John Welch and Ed O'Neill, and Alice Floto. They sat facing us on the opposite side of the fire, and as the darkness increased they could be seen only in silhouette.

Rolling Thunder was standing over the fire. I watched the light dance red and yellow on his face. He stooped to pick up the sacrifice that had been placed at the edge of the fire—a large portion of uncooked meat from our supplies. He placed it in the fire.

John, Ed and Alice smoked the pipe and then spoke aloud in turn about their thoughts and attitudes and personal conditions, saying what they wished to achieve through Rolling Thunder's help. Rolling Thunder left the fireside and walked over to face them. We looked at him through the flames and now he was only a shadow. Rolling Thunder stood over John for a long time. John's request at the beginning of the ceremony had been brief and clearly stated. He wanted to increase his capacity to help others, to gain deeper insight into the spiritual meanings of social problems, to learn to work more effectively in group situations, to transcend the usual personality patterns that are self-seeking and competitive. Rolling Thunder used his medicine feather and many times lay his hands upon John's head or shoulders. It was a quiet and almost motionless procedure; John sat completely still and Rolling Thunder seemed to be moving only his arms. It was dark on the other side of the fire and I couldn't see everything that was happening. At one point Rolling Thunder spit upon one hand and held it up. Then he rubbed his two hands together before placing them on his patient's body. Again he used the medicine feather to make sweeping motions in the air.

Putting the feather down, he moved behind Ed's chair, laid both hands on Ed's shoulders and began speaking to the Great Spirit. Ed O'Neill lived with a severe physical handicap that was the result of polio. I knew that Rolling Thunder had doctored him several times. He did not remove the handicap, but apparently he affected the way Ed related to his condition. I remembered Ed having once said to me, "If it were not for Rolling Thunder I could not live the life I live today." Seen through the firelight, his silhouetted form looked somehow different; an almost imperceptible change in the way he held his head or perhaps in the way he moved transformed his image. There was a moment of complete silence. No one moved and there was no sound in the whole canyon but the soft crackling of the fire. Then Rolling Thunder made a sudden emphatic exhalation, leaned forward and began to sniff, but with the sound of an animal—intense and rhythmic—not the sound of a man. The loud sniffs were interspersed with quick, sharp exhalations. Once or twice the sniffing stopped and there was an eerie howling and wailing as at the Council Grove ritual. Several times Rolling Thunder moved far off to the side to a place prepared for him outside the reach of the firelight and loudly and violently purged himself. It was an awesome proceeding but there was no sense of apprehension or anxiety, only a feeling of stupendous seriousness and wonder.

Again Rolling Thunder used his hands and the medicine feather; he apparently was following a certain pattern. Again, also, I could see that raw meat had been placed at the feet of his patients, as it had been at Council Grove. Many times the feather was shaken over this meat as though the meat was intended to absorb some sort of negative etheric substance swept from the auras of the patients.

The heavy atmosphere seemed to lift and slowly drift away, and once again a silent calm filled our canyon and the crackling of the fire became distinct. Rolling Thunder stood now and looked at Alice. When she had spoken earlier in the ceremony she had asked, among other things, that she be made able to sing again. She had said that this was extremely important to her, and then she had wept. She had been a trained professional singer but her voice had been impaired by tumorous growths in her throat that her doctor had called "little nodules that would grow much larger." She had even considered undergoing a difficult and risky surgical operation to remove them.

Rolling Thunder spoke to the Great Spirit. Taken out of context his words would sound critical of Alice's philosophy, her personal and political convictions. At the healing ceremony, however, it was apparent that he was speaking about the state of Alice's health. His words and manner were calm and straight and natural. He concluded the talk by looking into the fire and then into the sky and admonishing in a louder voice that the messengers of fear and prejudice and fascist ideas "loose their hold upon this woman." There was more silence. Then Rolling Thunder spoke very slowly: "We ask the Great Spirit that this woman be made free to do the work in the world that is meant for her to do." No one moved. I looked at Alice. She was staring into the fire and her face was stone still. Her head was slightly bowed as though she were sitting before the altar in church.

"And we ask the Great Spirit that she be given back her voice so that she can sing beautifully because that brings her happiness. We ask that she be given happiness and joy and allowed to give these things to others because happiness and joy are important to her.

"We ask that it be that way."

He picked up his medicine feather. Standing in front of Alice, his body slightly stooped and his arm outstretched, he held the feather pointed at her. Suddenly, from just behind us, came shrill hoots of an owl, one after the other. This was not simply a random owl hooting, but an owl hooting at our ceremony or at Rolling Thunder or at Alice. It was as though a small boy had been hidden in the bushes to cup his hands around his mouth and call out these hoots at just the right moment for the proper effect. If I had been a visitor there that night, that would have been my suspicion, because there was something too focused and too insistent about that call. But I knew the sound had been neither arranged nor expected. And if it were an illusion induced by all the mystery of this enchanting setting, it came to all of us at once. Everyone heard it. I could feel everyone consciously refraining from turning to look. In all the time we had been in camp no owl had been seen or heard within the canyon walls. Rolling Thunder seemed not to notice.

He moved around toward the back of Alice's chair. There were a few more hoots. It was a persistent sound. Suddenly

Rolling Thunder looked up and gazed in the direction of the sound. It was a long, steady gaze. His eyes reflected the firelight. The hooting stopped. It was never heard again. When it was apparent by Rolling Thunder's expression that the owl had been silenced, he spoke. His head was tilted slightly to one side and his gaze was steady. His voice was incredibly calm. He spoke to the owl, saying something that sounded to me like, "You over there bringing your negative message." I thought he might not have been speaking to the owl as such, but rather to what the owl represented. Then he went on, directing his words this time to the Great Spirit: "And we ask that this not come to be as the sign has been given," repeating all that he had said for Alice, and asked again "that it be that way."

His voice and his words sounded to me as if he was mindful of a certain consonance between what is desirable and what is "meant to be."

I believed I was being an objective observer, but the phenomenon of Rolling Thunder and the owl evoked some intense sensory changes. Initially I was startled and uncomfortable because I actually felt that the hooting represented some hostile challenge to Rolling Thunder or to Alice. But then, when Rolling Thunder stayed calm and simply repeated in a quiet manner what he had already said, I felt a tingling on my face and back. I was picking up a sense of well-being and control from Rolling Thunder's voice, his words and his incredible constancy.

When the ritual was finished, Rolling Thunder said simply, "That's all." His expression and posture changed and he looked around as though he had just now arrived here to do something and was about to begin it. If any sensations from that ritual lingered in our minds, a look at Rolling Thunder dispelled them. Everyone immediately got up and walked away.

I decided I wanted to be alone somewhere for a few minutes to recall all that I had seen. It seemed important to try to give it some rational form. I walked along the railroad tracks that stretched through the canyon. They glowed like streaks, providing an easy trail in the dark night.

I passed near Rolling Thunder and heard him talking to Alice. "You know," he said, in a very matter-of-fact voice, "they never give up easy." I continued walking along the tracks until I came to the old abandoned boxcars. I had often sat here to record notes on my cassettes. I stopped and looked inside. It was pitch-dark in there now and it felt unfamiliar. For a moment I thought there could be an owl or some wicked thing waiting in a dark corner, but that thought did not fit my peaceful state of mind. I hoisted myself up into the open doorway and looked out at the sky and stars.

I tried to think beyond what I had seen that night, beyond what Rolling Thunder had appeared to be doing, to what had happened in reality. I was not here to learn the procedural formula of Rolling Thunder's medicine. The powders, the feathers, the gestures and the incantations were not the most important factors. I knew that these things were agents, or perhaps the physical vehicles of agents. Like mantras, acupuncture, meditation, hypnosis, psychotherapy, even herbs and massage, they are not understandable within the limitations of the body sciences. The concepts of agents and spirit power do not fit comfortably within the confines of our accumulated knowledge. To understand these things we will need a wider grasp of the reality and the life force whence physical representations and their accompanying physical facts are made manifest.

I was not there to validate the "medical" results of the healing ceremony, but I hoped to be seeing enough of Rolling Thunder's three patients to verify the results to my own satisfaction. That's all that I could ever do with the matter of proof. As with the rainmaking, I had seen these things work, and I was interested in what was involved in making them work. Rolling Thunder's system, his method—the part I could see—was either his own device or an accumulation and synthesis of what he had learned from the teachers he had encountered in his years of apprenticeship. I suspected that what was really happening, which I apparently could not see, was an actual and constant force which existed beyond the particulars through which it could be caused to work. I knew Rolling Thunder was not breaking laws of body and mind, of chemistry and energy; rather, he was somehow making use of them. The entire ritual was an application of laws. I knew that all I had seen of Rolling Thunder, all I had heard from him, bore significantly upon the meaning of what he did at Council Grove and what he had done here this night.

At Council Grove, Rolling Thunder had said: "I want to warn you not to copy me, but work out your own method. Our people tell us to be original. If you can watch the method, though, and the way I go about it, maybe that would give you some thoughts about what to follow, what it's all about. Then you work out your own substance, your own songs, your own prayers and things to go with it. It's not good to copy."

I had a key to understanding healing as Rolling Thunder saw it. Almost everyone watching the ritual, including the patients, had been involved in the issue of the destruction of the pinyon trees. Rolling Thunder had talked with me about the tragedy of the trees when we first met. To him this issue was a health problem and a human problem, and I knew I would have to learn to see it that way if my research with him was to have any meaning. I had come from the Menninger Foundation to learn from him about self-regulation and states of consciousness. To Rolling Thunder that meant, to begin with, that I would need to be involved in the forest-chaining issue. It is involvement that is the key to understanding: without involvement I could research Indian philosophy and phenomena to my death and achieve nothing but increasing bewilderment.

All of us knew that the Bureau of Land Management was destroying thousands of acres of living, growing trees to serve the mercenary interests of a few individuals who had become politically powerful because of their wealth. In order to do this, it was necessary for the U.S. government to break a number of Indian treaties and to lie to the American public. The issue of the pinyon trees involved ignoring ecology, destroying a valuable natural food source, harming wildlife and killing millions of trees. To those of us who had become acquainted with this issue, it seemed almost impossible to believe. But Rolling Thunder had made us aware that this issue was only a shadow, a reflection of the real problem. We were led to understand that this sociopolitical issue was a manifestation of the spiritual condition of America. If the physical condition reflected the spiritual condition, then the physical solution would reflect the spiritual one. To become involved in this issue was to work on a spiritual level with spiritual matters.

Rolling Thunder's way was not to talk about the reality that he could see and understand. For those who would seek, Rolling Thunder's way was through work, through involvement with ecological, cultural, social and political matters which provides interaction with the manifestations of reality that everyone can see. Involvement provides the opportunity to think about the higher planes of reality that these things represent. Thus, one is both solving problems and elevating one's consciousness. This is the meaning of Karma Yoga.

Working with others on issues, accepting and guiding their involvement, Rolling Thunder is a spiritual teacher of the highest order. He does not bring understanding to others. He leads others to the point of understanding. Like other spiritual teachers, he has made a choice from among several paths—the path of knowledge, the path of devotion and the path of action.

Rolling Thunder's is the path of action.

I jumped down from the boxcar and started back toward camp. Tomorrow would come. I would see more rituals, I was sure, and by doing what was to be done tomorrow and in all the days to come I would come closer to seeing the real medicine.

Looking back on this evening's ritual—sitting with the others

in the wide half-circle about the ceremonial fire, looking at
Rolling Thunder's three patients across the flames, and watching his moving form in the flickering firelight—had shown me
only shadows. We who were sitting there watching the ceremony were shadows, and on the ground were shadows cast by
shadows, squirming in the firelight. All that I had seen of the
ritual had been but a reflection of reality. Rolling Thunder
might have been seeing reality; but I believed now that I had
seen neither Rolling Thunder nor what he had been doing: I
had seen only his shadow and the shadow of his actions.

12
Purification

One night, close to midnight, a dozen of our group left camp, drove out of the canyon and down the hill. There had been no supper; fasting was part of our preparation for the events to come. We stopped by a railroad crossing just outside of town and parked the cars off the road, as far out of sight as possible. We walked quietly along the highway behind Rolling Thunder. No one had spoken since we had left the campfire.

Rolling Thunder did not want us to be seen. "There are people around here who will shoot at anything if they have a reason that's good enough for them. Anyway, some of the local rednecks might get shook up at the sight of a bunch of hippies and Indians out here in the middle of the night." He did not want to have to explain to any stranger what we were about to do. We had to walk along the highway to use the bridge to get across the river. Then we could leave the road and find a path through the field to our destination. We knew that if a car should come from either direction, we must all jump off the road and lie low along the embankment and not be seen. But there were no cars, no sounds, no lights until we were on the bridge. Rolling Thunder broke the silence: "Run!"

Beams of headlights sliced through the darkness as a car rounded a distant bend. There was nowhere to hide. We had to get off the bridge before the car came. We reached the end just in time. The last man leaped over the bank just as the lights reached the spot from which he had jumped. Near the end of the bridge the land leveled off. There we all squeezed in under the bridge, taking care not to slide into the river.

"Now maybe you can get some idea of how it feels to be an Indian," Rolling Thunder said. "Always running. Always hiding. Sneaking and slinking around. Sometimes shot at, even today, and you never know when. Always hunted and chased, kicked out, sent away, herded here and there. You trust the land. You have an intimate relationship with nature, but they try to cut you off. The land gives food and shelter and medicine and cleansing, and you know these things belong to you. The land belongs to life, life belongs to the land, and the land belongs to itself. But they say, 'I take this piece, that piece is left for you, sign your name.' They take it all anyway. They signed too, but they didn't care. There was no reason or explanation because it was all wrong to begin with. They just said, 'You can walk. If you can keep walking, you might live.' Now they call it the public domain. 'Keep off, Indian, this land belongs to the public. This land is managed by the BLM, you are managed by the BIA, so keep off.' So you sneak around and if you feel guilt or fear, they prefer it that way. You have to keep your relationship with nature. Mother Earth is your friend. The land belongs to the Indian."

The car had gone right over our heads. The sound faded slowly into the distance and there was silence again. No one spoke or moved for a long, thoughtful minute.

"Let's go," Rolling Thunder said. He slid down the hill and caught the man behind him. The two of them caught the rest who followed. We were across the river now. No need to go back to the road. We found the path. Alice handed Rolling Thunder her flashlight and he led the way as we followed single file in the dark. A few minutes later we reached our destination. It was a stream, smaller and quieter than the river, a natural hot spring. Rolling Thunder called it a medicine spring. He pointed the flashlight into the rippling stream, and the beam filled with bright, white steam. When he turned off the light the stream became a silver glow—rising in the dark, its strong smell filling the air.

Crouching along the edge of the water, everyone remained silent; this was a time of purification. We stripped off our clothes and left them in neat piles on the sandy bank and then slipped slowly into the water. The bottom was soft and soothing. As our bodies worked their way deep into the hot, comfortable mud, its odors and warmth penetrated our bones. Tense muscles and minds relaxed as the hot mud began to pull on us. Ambitions, plans, hopes, worries, doubts and fears flowed out through the fingers and toes. The stars became brighter and we could begin to see stars beyond stars beyond stars. Time and motion stopped. The quiet presence of the group mind reached out to fill miles of silent space.

The earth pulled at the hands and feet, the heavy, hot water pulled at the heart, and the strong, steaming sulfur smell pulled at the breath. There was nothing but empty consciousness, and that consciousness was flowing outward, dispersing, thinning away. Rolling Thunder coughed. It was loud and sudden. I looked toward him, as the others did. We had all been gazing into the stars. As arms and legs swished in the water I began to consider the great beauty of the swishing sound. Rolling Thunder coughed again, sharp and quick. All movement stopped. Suddenly a warning passed through my mind: "Pay attention to the purification!"

Again the silence was total, but I couldn't keep the thoughts

from running through my mind. I was recalling words Rolling
Thunder had spoken back at camp, and their meaning was now
far more vivid than it had been then: "The beginning is purification, that's the first step. That's a big step and it's serious
business. There's a right way to do everything, and there's a
right way of purification. It's completely natural, I'll tell you
that much. There's nothing artificial. And purification means
purification of body and mind. You don't purify the body without cleansing the mind: that's the way it works.

"Maybe someday there will be a purification center up in
these hills. Below there might be a camp, or a meeting lodge.
There could be study and teaching and fun, too. People could
have discussions and talk and think about things. But when a
person walks up that path for purification, everything but the
person will be left behind. There will be no books or radios or
any connection with the outside world. People will leave their
clothes behind, too. The clothes will be waiting for them when
they get back, but they'll use buckskins and all the necessary
and natural means will be provided for cleansing the body and
purifying the mind. So people can leave their opinions behind
with their toothbrushes.

"In the old days when all our people lived by the tradition,
and purification was practiced by everyone, we had many
means such as sweat lodges and herbal medicines and special
rituals. Different people had different methods, but many things
were common knowledge that are mostly unknown today.
Things that are meant for a good purpose can also be used for
a bad purpose; and many of these things, if they were known
today, would be used in a wrong way. But we know that times
are changing and people will be ready to learn these things
again. Many of our new young friends have begun to seek the
way and have come to the Indian for guidance.

"There's a natural hot spring just this side of town, and we
can use it if we go there at night. It can be a sacred place of
purification. I've been there many times, and I'm willing to take

people there if they will be serious about it and use it right. I've taken people there before and at times I've had to ask them to leave because they get silly and make jokes and think wrong thoughts.

"People have to be responsible for their thoughts, so they have to learn to control them. It may not be easy, but it can be done. First of all, if we don't want to think certain things we don't say them. We don't have to eat everything we see, and we don't have to say everything we think. So we begin by watching our words and speaking with good purpose only. There are times when we must have clear and pure minds with no unwanted thoughts and we have to train and prepare steadily for those times until we are ready. We don't have to say or think what we don't wish to. We have a choice in those things, and we have to realize that and practice using that choice. There is no use condemning yourself for the thoughts and ideas and dreams that come into your mind; so there's no use arguing with yourself or fighting your thoughts. Just realize that you can think what you choose. You don't have to pay any attention to those unwanted thoughts. If they keep coming into your head, just let them alone and say, 'I don't choose to have such thoughts,' and they will soon go away. If you keep a steady determination and stick with that purpose you will know how to use that choice and control your consciousness so unwanted thoughts don't come to you any more. Then you can experience purification completely and in the right way and no impurities can exist in your mind or body at any time."

I remembered all this as if I were hearing it again. But my thoughts were again interrupted by the insistent command: "Pay attention to the purification!"

This is like meditation, I thought, or at least concentration. Purification is only a first step, and yet it apparently requires successfully controlled concentration. Here are all the problems of preparatory meditation practice. One must still the mind and hold it steady upon a certain point, neither churning, rambling,

drifting nor dreaming—but here I was again, still going on and
on . . .

"Pay attention to the purification!"

I focused my eyes on a single star and quickly found a simple
phrase, a Sanskrit mantram, to which my mind could attend.
It was a good start, but soon time began to move again as people
crawled out of the stream and up the muddy bank.

Skin tingled as the cool air touched our bodies. Breaths
quickened, the senses came alive. It was a new beginning, a
fresh awakening.

In the darkness we dressed and made our way through the
field and down the road to the cars. Those who had remained
in camp had a gigantic pot of stew waiting on the fire. It was
a marvelous fire and a tasty meal—all the more so because those
of us who had done this thing together seemed to remain of one
mind. I had no doubt that the others slept as soundly and
peacefully as I.

13

Sutras and Swamis

At last the day came when Rolling Thunder and I talked about gathering herbs. It was a quiet evening in camp. The Committee people were on their way back to San Francisco and the half-dozen of us who remained were preparing the evening meal.

"Rolling Thunder and I are planning to go herb-hunting tomorrow," Alice said to me as I watched her peel potatoes and cut them into cubes. "I've talked to him about your going with us, and he'd be glad to have you go. I told you he would. But you'll have to talk to him yourself now. He'll be staying for supper tonight and I suggest you bring it up as soon as he's eaten. That's what he wants, you know."

After supper, as we sat around the accustomed campfire, Rolling Thunder sat down beside me.

"Alice told me that you and she were planning to go out to

gather herbs tomorrow," I said. "If I may, I would really like to go along."

"Well, I think that might be okay. I don't usually take people along with me—that's not the purpose of it. Well, I have in the past, but it always happened that whoever was along would ask questions and wonder what this was for and that was for; or worse than that, they'd point their finger and shout, 'Look at that big one over there!' So I kind of gave up on it and I don't take just anybody along any more."

I said nothing.

"But you've been around now for a while and I think I know you pretty well." Rolling Thunder looked into the fire. "I would be perfectly willing to have you join us. But I will say I like it quiet, and if there are any questions, save them until afterward. At times like that I'm in a different frame of mind. You call it altered state of consciousness. That's how we communicate with plants."

For a time we watched the fire; then I remembered that he had mentioned this communication before. The night after the rainmaking he had talked to the committee people about modern man's great separation from nature and how, as a result, natural things have come to seem strange.

"I was interested to hear you talk about plant communication the other night," I said. "You mentioned that you had saved some articles about modern scientists experimenting with plants. I've heard about this before, and I've seen some of these articles. In fact I'm interested myself. I may not learn too much about herb medicine, I don't know, but I am interested in this experimentation in plant communication."

"It's not a one-way thing, you know, it's a two-way communication. I could give you something about that. Maybe someday I'll put something in writing—about how that's done —then you could carry that back with you to the Menninger Foundation."

Later I told Rolling Thunder how I had become interested

in chanting when I had worked with Swami Rama. Swami Rama had instructed me to concentrate on chanting, and I became interested in the possibility that chanting could eventually be used to produce responses in plants that could be tested under carefully controlled conditions. Through Rolling Thunder's steady questioning, we began a long discussion about the teachings of Swami Rama. I had talked about the Swami once before, because I had thought it would be useful not only for Rolling Thunder to know what I had been studying and working on, but also for me to know Rolling Thunder's ideas on some of the points that had come up in my work with the Swami. Now I found myself going over the sutras of Patanjali, which I had learned from an East Indian Swami, with an American Indian medicine man. Rolling Thunder seemed to relate to all this with total familiarity, and he had a number of comments and questions.

I became more aware then of the beauty and impact of Rolling Thunder's speech as he handled concepts I'd heard elaborated so eloquently elsewhere. This was a further learning experience for me because it gave me a chance to achieve the transcending of explanation that comes through hearing the same ideas in different words.

I told Rolling Thunder what Swami Rama had said about the principles of renunciation and nonattachment:

"Live in the world and yet above, like the lotus who has its roots in the bottom of the river but keeps its being upon the surface of the water. Enjoy the world. Do not let the world enjoy you; but you enjoy the world." Rolling Thunder liked that. He repeated the words aloud. "This is what Swami means by nonattachment," I said, "but many serious spiritual aspirants believe in renouncing the things of the world. They leave their homes and their villages and their positions and go to ashrams, caves or temples to be free from distractions and temptations, claiming that the struggle to remain nonattached is in itself a distraction. On the other hand, if the renunciate is

inconvenienced by his needs or holds in one corner of his mind
that which he has left behind, he also is distracted."

The Swami had said that there has been a "very tough and
terse" debate going on from times past on the virtues of renunciation versus nonattachment. I could guess where Rolling
Thunder would sit in such a debate. Only days before he said,
"When we're through with this earth and all these problems,
we don't have to come back. But as long as we're here we have
a job to do and a purpose to fulfill and that means dealing with
the circumstances around us."

I learned that Rolling Thunder does not believe in renunciation as a necessity or even as a possibility. He believes most
temple "renunciates" are being false with themselves and their
Mother Earth. He believes when one is done with a thing it no
longer exists for him; while it is there it is to be either followed,
honored, controlled or overcome—faced and dealt with and not
ignored. In the view of Rolling Thunder, those who have
managed to put their earthly business out of sight and mind
only postpone it, often with the result that it becomes a future
burden. That night I told him a few stories I had heard from
Swami Rama, stories I felt he might know in one form or
another. The last was the story of the Swami and the snake:

On the train to Brindavan a Swami sits beside a common man who
asks him if indeed he has attained self-mastery, as the name "Swami"
implies.

"I have," says the Swami.

"And have you mastered anger?"

"I have."

"Do you mean to say that you have mastered anger?"

"I have."

"You mean you can control your anger?"

"I can."

"And you do not feel anger?"

"I do not."

"Is this the truth, Swami?"

"It is."

After a silence the man asks again, "Do you really feel that you have controlled your anger?"

"I have, as I told you," the Swami answers.

"Then do you mean to say, you never feel anger, even—"

"You are going on and on—what do you want?" the Swami shouts. "Are you a fool? When I have told you—"

"O, Swami, this is anger. You have not mas—"

"Ah, but I have," the Swami interrupts. "Have you not heard about the abused snake? Let me tell you the story.

"On a path that went by a village in Bengal there lived a cobra who used to bite people on their way to worship at the temple there. As the incidents increased, everyone became fearful, and many refused to go to the temple. The Swami who was the master at the temple was aware of the problem and took it upon himself to put an end to it. Taking himself to where the snake dwelt, he used a mantram to call the snake to him and bring it into submission."

Rolling Thunder, who had been staring into the fire as I talked, suddenly looked at me. I began to relate what the Swami said to the snake. Immediately Rolling Thunder interrupted: "What was the mantram?"

"Oh, I don't know. I don't think the mantram itself was part of the story. At least I never heard it."

"Go ahead."

"The Swami then said to the snake that it was wrong to bite the people who walked along the path to worship and made him promise sincerely that he would never do it again. Soon it happened that the snake was seen by a passer-by upon the path and it made no move to bite. Then it became known that the snake had somehow been made passive, and people grew unafraid. It was not long before the village boys were dragging the poor snake along behind them as they ran laughing here and there. When the temple Swami passed that way again he called the snake to see if he had kept his promise—"

Again Rolling Thunder interrupted: "He didn't say anything at all about what words that Swami used to call the snake? Just thought they might probably be familiar to me. Must be something like the words I would use." Rolling Thunder did not wait for me to repeat what I had told him, but asked some question to pick the story up again.

"The snake humbly and miserably approached the Swami, who exclaimed, 'You are bleeding! Tell me how this has come to be.' The snake was near tears and blurted out that he had been abused ever since he was caused to make his promise to the Swami. 'I told you not to bite,' said the Swami, 'but I did not tell you not to hiss!'"

That was supposed to be the end of the story. Rolling Thunder quietly looked into the fire. When he saw I was finished, he considered a moment and then he looked straight up and laughed. "That's right!" he exclaimed. "That's right!" His face became serious and he stared into the fire as though he had begun to consider again. Then I felt him thinking of the pinyon forest chaining issue and the other struggles in which he was involved. His "That's right!" sounded to me like he was speaking for the snake. "Sure would be interesting to hear that mantram," he said. "You suppose Swami Rama himself would be familiar with that particular mantram?"

"If he does know, I'm sure I could find it out." But I regretted my words as soon as I'd spoken them. Would Swami tell me if he knew, and would it be permissible to ask? Even for Rolling Thunder's sake? I wondered whether Rolling Thunder would ever tell me his mantram. I would never ask him. I turned to look at him. He still stared thoughtfully into the flames. I watched the shadows from the dancing fire hammer upon him as though they were trying to deepen the lines in his face, and I could see he had nothing more to say.

Tomorrow I would go with him to gather herbs.

14

Alice Talks to Dogs and Bees

The following day I woke with the thought of gathering herbs. I waited all morning for Rolling Thunder and Alice but they did not come.

That morning Richard Clemmer's dog, Turtle, gave birth to a litter of five puppies. This was a first for her and she was hard-pressed to handle her new surprise. She was sufficiently responsive, as the day grew hot, to burrow a shady nest under a clump of bushes. But she thought to carry only one puppy with her and left the others in the sun.

At noon I discovered the dying puppies and called Anne and Richard. At that moment Rolling Thunder, Spotted Eagle and Alice arrived. Alice took the matter in hand. She laid the mother and babies in the shade of the largest tree and placed the little pups at the nipples. She talked to the mother earnestly, explaining that she had a new responsibility, that she must take care of her family. She urged the little ones to feed, but it was too late. With one motionless pup in her hands she walked over to Rolling Thunder and held it out to him. He reached out with his fingers extended, feeling not the body but the air around it.

"The life is gone, the body should be buried," he said. This happened twice again, but Alice continued to urge the remaining puppies.

Rolling Thunder called to Spotted Eagle and told him to carry an empty box or two down along the edge of the river and see if he could get a good supply of nice fat roots of yellow dock. Then he called to me. "You say you'd be interested in helping gather herbs? Why don't you go along with Spotted Eagle? He's going now, down to the river." For a moment I was disappointed. It was not herbs, it was Rolling-Thunder-gathering-herbs that I had wanted to be involved with. I realized how late it was; it was well past noon, and Indian herb-gathering always stops at sunset. Perhaps Rolling Thunder needed two teams for double efficiency? Alice left the puppies with Anne and Richard and drove off with Rolling Thunder on a separate expedition.

The river was only a short walk from camp, and I had been there before. Today the sounds and smells were very intense and things seemed more alive than ever before. I watched Spotted Eagle pull tall plants from the ground and wondered how rivers and mountains and deserts looked through his eyes. He had always lived with this life and not just observed it. Though all people once lived in direct contact with nature, there are few such people today. Those who are able to remain in touch with all nonhuman life are rare.

This was the first time I'd had any natural business in this place. It was the first time I'd truly noticed the yellow dock and all the other plants here, and surely the first time I'd ever imagined they noticed me.

I wanted to ask Spotted Eagle about the yellow dock, what

it was for and how it was used, but I remembered Rolling Thunder's warning about asking questions. I wondered whether Spotted Eagle was in an altered state of consciousness. He looked as he always did, perhaps a bit more serene. Except for a few brief sentences instructing me how to help, he was silent.

My job was to cut away the stalks as he pulled the tall plants from the ground. Only the roots were put in the boxes; the dead stems and leaves were left scattered by the river's edge. When we had finished, we took our boxes and walked back toward the camp. I broke the long silence: "Do you think we have enough roots here?"

"No, we'll get some more. We'll go get the car. I know where there's a lot more, but it's way over there." He pointed toward the railroad bridge at the end of the canyon. He said there was only one large family of yellow dock in the area where we had been. Apparently we had taken enough members of one family. We followed an old dirt road with a ridge in the middle that made loud scraping sounds on the bottom of the car. The road turned down the embankment and along the edge of the river and then ended. There was a pickup truck at the end of the road, and we pulled up right behind it. Spotted Eagle got out of the car and I followed. He said nothing. A middle-aged man appeared in the distance and walked toward us. As he came closer he began to talk. Spotted Eagle was still silent, and when the man reached us he leaned against his truck and continued talking in a loud voice about the damned weather and the damned river and about some damned thing he had seen in the river up ahead, but Spotted Eagle said nothing. Looking very polite, Spotted Eagle got back into the car, and when I did too, he backed along the road the way he had come, over the embankment, around the turn, to a place that was wide enough for the truck to get by. We waited and in a moment the man came along, backing down the road, waving as he passed. Spotted Eagle smiled at me and nodded his head. Once again we drove

down over the embankment to the end of the road, now re-
stored to a quiet peace.

We were there only a short time and had collected only a few
more roots when Spotted Eagle took his box and his axe and
put them back in the car. Again I asked whether we had collected enough roots. Spotted Eagle said nothing. As we drove
away he looked out the window, watching the river's edge.
Finally he said there were not as many separate families of
yellow dock in this canyon as he had thought, and that meant
we had collected enough.

We drove back to camp and left the yellow-dock roots in the
car to be taken to Rolling Thunder's house. Anne and Richard
were still caring for their one remaining puppy. Spotted Eagle
and I walked along the railroad tracks. He sat down on a rail
and looked up at the high cliffs on the other side of the canyon.

"I heard from Anne that Rolling Thunder is planning to go
to San Francisco," I said.

"Ya, we're thinking about leaving in the morning."

"Are you going, too?" I asked.

"Ya, I have to drive."

"How long do you think you'll be there?"

"Dad's planning on about a week, I guess."

"Ya, that's what I heard." I wanted to go with them to San
Francisco. I thought if I said this to Spotted Eagle it might be
arranged. I told Spotted Eagle that what I considered my work
right now was to be with Rolling Thunder. Ultimately, I
wanted to follow Rolling Thunder's ideas about the arrangement of my time and plans, but I did not want to spend a week
in camp just waiting.

"Just what is your work supposed to be?" Spotted Eagle
asked.

I had to consider how to answer this, because in the past few
days I had come to think that my effectiveness depended upon
my not being the arranger, upon not overanticipating my role.
When I had first talked with Rolling Thunder I felt open to any

eventuality. I had no particular questions, nothing of my own to pursue. Usually I was able to retain that openness, remaining the calm, nonattached observer, able to watch and remember. It was especially easy to be that way in Rolling Thunder's presence. But there were times when I felt impatient. Each time I had seen Rolling Thunder make rain or achieve apparent results through a healing ritual, or answer my thoughts or questions before I even mentioned them, and each time I had heard that "rolling thunder" sound follow him in and out of our canyon or down some country road, I felt elated and inspired. Yet those feelings were usually followed by impatience. I wanted to see more. I did not feel argumentative or threatened, and I did not feel a need to demand explanations. I knew that the understanding I was determined to achieve was nothing that could be accomplished by familiar mental processes.

I had already learned that the rational mind is not the source of new insights. The rational mind can be expanded to accommodate new learning, but it does not undertake learning. It is a cataloging and comparing mechanism and can see only what it contains. I knew that my techniques of perceiving and understanding could be greatly improved. I believed there were highly effective methods of learning that involved, among other things, activating and developing less familiar mental tools. I had begun to feel some changes, but I knew there was more that I could see and a better way to see it. If I felt impatience it was because of my own struggle, but when impatience occurred it felt like it was caused by all the others—by the multiplicity of people and affairs in which I had become involved. I had a sense of limited time and I felt helpless to influence the unfolding of events. I could not approach Rolling Thunder as I pleased. There were always people around and we were camped miles away from where Rolling Thunder lived. He could show up in camp whenever he wanted, but I could never go to him without having to make arrangements with others.

But somehow I always managed to work through those impatient moments. I knew that these Indian and ecological affairs had to do with humanity and nature, and that was exactly what I had come to learn about. I was not only seriously concerned, but I was also aware of my direct involvement; the situation was partly my making. Involvement was the first step toward new understanding. It was the secret of how Rolling Thunder brought the rain. I had come to see that traditional Indian philosophy regards human life as a part of the process of nature and the individual being a complete, microcosmic representation of the universe.

Rolling Thunder had told me on various occasions about the struggle between spiritual forces, the forces of light and the forces of darkness; that the Earth was a being, an individual with health problems. This reflected directly on the division of peoples, even the division of Indians. Rolling Thunder felt good about the growing number of traditional Indians. Many Indians were returning to the tradition. Many new-age young people were developing awareness of the Indian way. These people could help the Indian to reverse the present pattern of polluting, exploiting and destroying nature; in the process, the spiritual powers that the Indians have known would return to the land and to the people in it. I had to come to understand that these things were interrelated. I wanted to learn how the Indians' spiritual powers were natural powers and how these powers are acquired through caring for and communicating with nature. I wanted to learn how young people and their ecology movements and their new conscious concern for life were helping to provide the atmosphere and circumstances into which these spiritual powers could arise.

Finally I answered Spotted Eagle. "I think my work here is to do whatever your father thinks my work is."

Spotted Eagle looked thoughtful for a moment. "Yeah, I guess that's right." He was still looking toward the cliffs across the canyon, watching the large birds that never stopped circling. Realizing what his simple question had done for me, I now felt confident talking with Spotted Eagle. I began talking about the Menninger Foundation, myself, our research project on voluntary control of internal states, and about our psychophysiology laboratory. I told him about the years I had spent in Korea and my studies with Swami Rama and others. I told about what had impelled me to come to Rolling Thunder.

Spotted Eagle was stimulated by our conversation. As soon as I stopped, he spoke enthusiastically. "What I would really like to do is travel all over and meet a lot of people and learn a lot of things. I would really like to rap with a lot of different kinds of people. Like, wherever I go, I . . ." He stopped. I was not sure why. He was silent as though he was reflecting upon his own interest or maybe upon whether he should discuss it. Suddenly he said, "I just remembered something. I have to take down Alice's tent. I'd better hurry. She and Dad will probably be back in a few minutes and I was supposed to have all her stuff ready to load up. She has to drive clear back to Salt Lake as soon as they finish getting herbs."

The tent was down and nearly folded when Rolling Thunder drove into camp with Alice. Spotted Eagle ran back to the main tent to fold up Alice's camp chairs and Coleman stove.

Alice came down the path toward me, walking very fast.

"I'll have this ready in just a minute," I said.

"No, wait a minute. I want to tell you something," she puffed. "I had the most interesting experience gathering herbs up there," she said, "and I'm so anxious to tell you all about it. It couldn't have happened without Rolling Thunder. I know, but I actually communicated with the bees. I actually talked to them and they understood." She stopped short. "By the way," she said, "why didn't you go along? I thought you were going with us."

"Well, I went with Spotted Eagle."

She was thoughtful for a moment, remembering Rolling Thunder's words. "Oh," she said. "Well, let me tell you this.

I was told to tell you first." She was excited. "Rolling Thunder told me on the way back. He said, 'Now you tell Doug first and then you write it all down.' He said that you should write about the mind and the consciousness things, and that I should write about animals and wildlife. Is that what you are doing?"

"Well, maybe. I guess so, sort of," I answered.

"Well, you should. Anyway, we went to get horehound plants up there near the old ranch. Rolling Thunder knew right where they were. He agreed to show me because he knew I needed horehounds. As soon as we got there Rolling Thunder made his prayer and his offering. Then I saw that the plants were absolutely covered with bees. I'm deathly afraid of bees; it frightens me just to look at them and they always sting me. So I just didn't know what to do. I was just ready to leave. Well, Rolling Thunder talked to me; he was so kind and gentle. He sensed what I was feeling, without my saying anything. He told me I was really not afraid of animals or any living thing. I only thought I was. And he reminded me how I had always loved animals and had taken care of them on a farm in my childhood.

"He told me that the fear of any living thing is based on misunderstanding. He said, 'Now, Alice, I want you to talk to those bees. I saw how you talked to the dogs just a little while ago. You talked to the babies and to the mother and you said the right things in the right way. If you can talk to dogs that way, you can talk to bees, and they will understand. They won't understand the English language, but they'll understand your meaning just as you say it.'

"So he told me what to say to the bees. I was supposed to ask the bees to share the plants with me, to tell them I wouldn't harm them, and to explain that I needed the plants for good medicine, but I would leave enough for the bees and for seeds for the coming year. He told me to say it loud and clear. He said he would be sitting behind me, and he wanted to be able to hear my voice. I did as he said, and, do you know, the bees actually understood me, and they moved! I just can't describe how I felt. All the bees on the plant I was looking at moved. They all moved together to the back of the plant. I took only the front half of the plant which they had left me, and then I moved to another plant covered with bees, and the same thing happened again! On one of the plants, when the bees moved back and I started to cut, they all made the strangest buzzing sound. It felt as though they were somehow speaking, telling me to stop, and I was understanding. I looked at Rolling Thunder and he said, 'There now, you see? You and the bees have agreed to share and now you're cutting back too far. They'll expect you, now, to do as you said.' So I cut only the front half very carefully. Then Rolling Thunder came up to me." She paused and she appeared to be filled with emotion. "And he said that this was a gift of the Great Spirit!" Immediately she turned and walked back along the path as quickly as she had come.

I finished folding the tent and then went back to the railroad track to sit alone and look up at the cliffs. The large hawks still soared in endless circles.

Last night Rolling Thunder had talked about communication with plants and about influencing plants with chanting. He told me he could give me something on two-way communication that I could take back to the Menninger Foundation. Now I could take back the story of Alice talking to the bees and the bees talking to Alice. That would no doubt be met with some disbelief on the part of researchers there. After all, the question of communication with the bees (or any other aspect of nature) could hardly have anything to do with science. The incident could easily be dismissed, since I would have to admit that I had not been present when it occurred. Of course this thing did not happen just so it could be reported. It happened so it could happen. When Rolling Thunder talked to Alice about my writing things down, I knew he was not thinking of bringing reports and verifications to researchers; he was thinking of planting ideas among people who might respond to them. There was no question of proving anything; it was simply a matter of talking to the bees. This was easy to do, something anyone could try. It was also a good example of the predicament of scientists who would dismiss the story as being insufficiently verified. But how long will it be before such communication becomes a widespread practice in spite of the fact that it is not "scientific"?

When I had returned from Korea, after nearly ten years there, I had been surprised to see that a process had begun which made it seem that the Orient and the Occident were changing roles. The Easternization of the West had begun. This change was the more vivid to me since I had been involved in the opposite trend, in teaching the ways of the West to Easterners, I was contributing to the Westernization of the Orient. Working with Swami Rama, I reversed roles and became directly involved in bringing the ideas of the East to Western scientists. I wondered if the day would come when some of the events the Swami described, like speaking to ferocious tigers on the snowy paths of the Himalayas, would become possible here. Talking to dogs and bees and flowers seemed to me a good beginning.

I felt that I could now begin to verbalize a comparison between Rolling Thunder and Swami Rama; I could see the primary difference in the expressions of their knowledge. Swami Rama's method is to work internally, to withdraw the mind's attention from external perceptions: "Withdraw the senses, withdraw the senses!" In this way one identifies with the self within—the Atman, the cosmic mind. Rolling Thunder's way is to work externally, to sharpen the senses, to embrace the world. In every step of his growth, just as in the purification process, man works from the outside in. Man is in and of nature —a microcosm of that universe that he can see around him. Through interaction with his environment man learns about the natural world and then comes to understand his own nature. He becomes one with nature, one with himself, one with the Great

Spirit. I had seen Swami Rama control his pulse and breathing. I had seen Rolling Thunder control the weather. These were perhaps simply different expressions of the same self-knowledge and self-will.

A short while ago I had been thinking about the renaissance of the American Indian tradition and the return of the powers, and about the new-age people—the new "Indians"—who were setting the stage for new things to happen. What I had come to think of as the Easternization of the West was happening through these people. Their development had been helped by the yogis, swamis, lamas and monks who had been coming in recent years from the four corners of the earth, bringing new ideas and insights about a way of life that was more in keeping with reality, with the real nature of things, than anything Western society had to offer. Here in Shoshone country, I discovered that the wisdom these saints and sages had come so far to deliver has been common knowledge among the natives of this land and has preceded not only the wise men of the East, but the pioneers, the automobiles and the scientists.

Looking across the canyon, I could imagine a day when this process would be complete, and there would be a constant dialogue between all the life forms on the planet. I watched the birds that were still circling, and I wondered about the prospect of exchanging thoughts with them.

15

Gathering Herbs

Alice Floto left behind all the foodstuffs she had brought:
honey, jam, canned goods, fresh fruits and vegetables. "I know
you three can certainly use these things up here," she said, "and
you've all been so good to me."

After warm goodbyes, the two cars headed out of the canyon
and down the mountain for Carlin; Rolling Thunder and Alice
were in the red Falcon and Spotted Eagle followed in Rolling
Thunder's red and black Camaro. Anne Habberton, Richard
Clemmer and I were again alone in the canyon. A beautiful
peace settled in with the twilight as we prepared the evening's
campfire.

As we were finishing supper we heard a car coming up the
mountain road. It was dark and we caught glimpses of headlight beams flashing in the sky as the car rounded the bends.

We soon recognized the Camaro, and when it pulled into camp Spotted Eagle got out. He had come to get me.

"Dad and Alice are going to the hot springs tonight and Dad thought you might like to join them. I'm supposed to get you if you want to go."

"You mean Alice didn't leave?"

"No, she's going to start out in the morning. Dad thought she should go to the hot springs once more before she leaves, and tonight's a good night."

"Yeah, I'll go," I said.

We sat in the steaming water staring silently into the night, and time stood still as it had before. Rolling Thunder and Alice and I had walked without words across the dark field, left our clothes on the bank and slid quietly into the water. Then Rolling Thunder had broken the silence only to say, "Alice, get over this way where it's deep and get all the way in the water up to your neck. Find a good warm spot and stay there."

This was another very clear night and I thought I could see every star. Some of them seemed to change colors, from green to blue to red and back to green again. This special medicine stream had captured me. On this second visit, my body and my thoughts stopped almost immediately, and my mind reached out past the stars. I recognized my condition as the fresh, free feeling of transcending motion—transcending the multitude of body feelings and nerve responses and the constant firing of impulses in the brain, all the busy, redundant thoughts of the work and play and worry of the ordinary day. This transcending of motion is not a stoned feeling. It is a feeling of wakefulness. The preliminary steps of meditation could be reached swiftly in this setting. Swami Rama used to say, at the beginning of his sessions, "Withdraw the senses, withdraw the senses." Perhaps the elements which were supposed to be purifying agents helped to withdraw the senses. The clear, calm night, the countless stars, the quiet fields that stretched to the mountains, this stream with its warm muddy bottom that grasped the body, the pulling heat of the mud and water, the chemicals, the strong mineral smells that filled the head—all these combined to produce a powerful change.

I was both still and alert for a long while. I was not aware of time, but then a worldly thought suddenly took part of my attention: Either I would be going to San Francisco in the morning, or Rolling Thunder would go and I would be left behind.

"This is no time for such thoughts," I told myself.

Then I was aware of a strange phenomenon that I knew I had experienced before. In observing myself, I saw not one single person, but several individuals, a number of separate wills. One said urgently, "Oh, that's right, I do have to see about going to San Francisco! I almost forgot." Another, somewhat wiser and more calm, quietly said, "Be still. Pay attention to the purification. This is no time to think such thoughts." After a pause it began again, "There will be opportunity to talk of going to San Francisco after this. Be quiet until then. If you persist I will ignore you until you go away." Still another observed, "You are also going on and on." A fourth looked down, saying and thinking nothing, merely watching as one watches children at play. A fifth was totally aware of fields and mountains and stars.

When Rolling Thunder crawled out of the steaming water, Alice and I followed. We stayed for a long while on the bank, keeping the silence. This night had an Indian summer feeling, and there is no better way to experience such a night than to lie naked on the bank of a medicine spring in a quiet meadow under the stars, still and silent, drying in the gentle wind. I thought I would like to stay there for hours.

Rolling Thunder walked back to where we had left our clothes. Back in everyday consciousness, I followed. I felt invigorated, and I also felt I wanted to go to San Francisco with Rolling Thunder; there seemed little chance left to mention it.

Riding down the mountain I had thought this might be a chance to talk to him about the coming week. Now was the time, but I could hardly destroy the silence. It was a silence that made every sentence I prepared in my mind seem too abrupt to say aloud. How could I speak when no one was talking here this night? We were about to leave.

Then a brief exchange between Rolling Thunder and Alice about an extra towel broke the silence and I was at last able to begin.

"Rolling Thunder, I—"

Immediately he interrupted. "Well, I thought you might just ride along with us. Spotted Eagle can come for you in the morning."

"Okay, fine."

Everything was perfectly arranged in less than ten seconds. I had carried on an internal conversation in the stream and Rolling Thunder apparently had heard.

In the morning I woke before sunrise. I had slept very little. Even so, I felt rested.

I dressed and washed and packed things I would take to San Francisco. I had been using Rolling Thunder's sleeping bag, so I rolled it up to return it. I planned to get another in San Francisco. I waited for Spotted Eagle to come. It was a long wait. Anne and Richard got up, and we ate breakfast together. The sun moved over the length of the canyon, rising high above the cliff walls at the far end, then over our heads and toward the rolling, grassy hills. We ate lunch. I lay on a mattress, looking up through the branches of a tall tree at the passing clouds until my eyes closed. I was sleeping when the Camaro drove into camp. It was midafternoon. I put the things in the car, and we went quickly on our way down the mountain.

Spotted Eagle told me he was sorry he had not come for me as arranged. His father had gotten up late and was in great pain with a toothache or something. Spotted Eagle doubted we would get on our way until very late tonight. I wasn't really surprised or upset by the delay. I had learned that with Rolling Thunder there were no delays, only the right time for everything. Richard Clemmer had remarked as we were eating lunch how Rolling Thunder always seemed to "move as the spirit moves him"; I had been around long enough to know that this was true. What did surprise me was that Rolling Thunder was in pain. It was somehow difficult to conceive of Rolling Thunder suffering from an ordinary toothache. For the past several days I had been bothered by sneezing, or worse, by not sneezing and needing to, and by itchy, watery eyes. While I was waiting this morning I had decided to speak to Rolling Thunder about my discomfort. Now I changed my mind. I couldn't mention my own condition if he was in pain.

We reached Carlin in less than a half-hour and Brandy, the Saint Bernard, gave his usual greeting of flopping his tail in the dust of Rolling Thunder's yard. The easiest way to get through the front door was to step right over this sad-eyed and drooling dog who spent most of his time on the doorstep.

Rolling Thunder and Spotted Fawn were there, sitting in their chairs. Spotted Fawn got up to bring me a cup of coffee as soon as we were inside. She always had a large pot of hot coffee in the kitchen, and more likely than not, a large pot of chicken or beef stew keeping warm on the stove. Spotted Fawn was always feeding people as though it were a part of her life. There was something about her way that made it a pleasure to receive from her even a cup of coffee.

Rolling Thunder and I were talking when he mentioned that he was having great pain. I had almost forgotten about the toothache. There was no sign about him at all that indicated pain, other than his saying so.

"This is a subject that interests me a lot," Rolling Thunder said, apparently meaning the subject of pain. "These things are the price we have to pay, sometimes. Nothing comes free. It's my choice and sometimes I have to pay heavy."

He was not being explicit and so I imagined him having accomplished a healing or having had a confrontation, a contest of will, with what he might have called negative forces. I did not ask. I felt this was not an area for questions. What Rolling Thunder wanted me to hear was not the private details of the event, but the essence of the rule.

He watched me for a moment and then repeated, "Nothing comes free; everything has its cost.

"I'm also interested in how to handle these things," he went on. "Every case of sickness and pain has its reason. And it's always a price that's being paid, either for something past or something future. But that doesn't mean we're not supposed to do something about sickness and pain. The important thing is to know how these things work. Modern doctors—most of them—don't seem to understand that. A medicine man's job is to look into these things. We know that everything is the result of something and the cause of something else, and it goes on like a chain. You can't just make the whole chain go away. Sometimes a certain sickness or pain is meant to be because it's the best possible price for something; you make that go away and the price becomes greater. The person himself may not know that, but his spirit knows it. That's why sometimes we take up to three days to look into things before we take a case, and we may not take it at all."

He paused for a moment, looked around, and then he called for Spotted Eagle. There was no answer.

"Physical troubles have all kinds of reasons, good or bad reasons, we might call them, but they all start on the spiritual level. An infection might be called a spiritual impurity. What happens in the body is not the main thing, so healing requires knowing more than the body. If a modern M.D. sees a sick man, he sees the sickness and not the man. So if the doctor doesn't understand what's going on, what the problem really is, if he then gives someone chemicals so the man won't feel anything or if he finds some troubled part of the body and cuts it off and throws it in the trash, it's probably all unnecessary, and it certainly isn't healing.

"Anyway, I'm very interested in pain, and in relieving pain when it can be done by natural means. There are different spiritual conditions. Every physical thing in nature is a spiritual thing in spiritual nature. So these things can be spiritual helpers. There are ways to find these things and to understand what they are—and not just by the chemical composition. I can take a certain plant, for example, even one I have never seen before, and I can hold it in my hand and understand it."

Again he looked around and called even louder: "Mala!"

Spotted Eagle came.

"Get some empty cartons from my herb cellar, and some knives, and put them in the car." Then he turned to me. "Thought we might go into the hills just a few miles east of here and bring back some good medicine."

"Good," I said.

We headed east on the main highway and drove for about fifteen minutes before Spotted Eagle pulled over and parked the car as far off the highway as he could. The three of us started up the hill with our boxes and cutting tools. "Now we don't want to hurt any snakes, so be careful not to step on any," Rolling Thunder said. In the Nevada desert country things somehow appear closer than they really are, so it seemed that we walked a long time before Rolling Thunder stopped. We were in the midst of tall, leafy, bristly-looking plants that were growing quite thickly in this spot. Rolling Thunder looked at them. Some he squinted at and touched. Was he inspecting them for quality? Finally he walked up to a group of the plants, looked at them for a moment, then turned his back on them and looked at the sky. He took something from his pocket and held it near his face in a half-closed fist while his lips began to move. I wondered whether it was all right to watch. I turned my head away. Spotted Eagle was not watching; he seemed to be staring

into space. Out of the corner of my eye I saw Rolling Thunder
turn and hold the unknown substance to the sun. Then he
turned again. Now he was facing the group of plants. I watched
him stoop to shake his hand under one of the plants, but I didn't
try to see what he placed there. He turned toward Spotted Eagle
and pointed up the hill, making a sweeping motion with his
hand. Spotted Eagle looked at his father, blinked and nodded
his head. Rolling Thunder faced me and pointed to the plant
behind him. He smiled and spoke in a whisper so that I had to
think for a minute before I heard the words: "This one's the
Chief."

Somehow our work was carried out without words. I acquired the job of carting small armloads of the plant and drop-
ping them over a barbed-wire cattle fence we had crawled under
halfway up the hill. Each time I walked down the hill and up
I passed that special plant. I looked at it knowing that it was
the Chief. Even though I knew this, I did not know what it
meant. Was the plant itself different from the others? Had
something different attached itself to the plant? I wondered
whether the plants, particularly this Chief, were aware of us. I
felt they were, but I did not know what that awareness was.
Someone had once said to me, "All this life is conscious, but
it is not conscious of being conscious." I did not know in what
sense these plants were conscious, what life inside them was
like, or how that life would feel to me if I could observe it. My
wish to know increased each time I passed the Chief. About an
hour or so had elapsed when we crawled back under the barbed-
wire fence, stuffed the plants into the boxes and walked back
to the car. It had been a beautiful hour spent in silence on that
sunny hill. Once again with Rolling Thunder I had gotten the
feeling that I was involved in something more real than usual.

When we were near the car Rolling Thunder saw that it had
a flat tire. He seemed not at all surprised. "Okay, now, this tire's
flat, so we'll take it off. Doug and I'll wait here, Mala, while you
go into Elko with the guy who's coming here." Neither the

words nor the tone of voice fit the situation. The tire was flat. There was no spare. There was not a car on the highway, and it was nearly sunset.

We jacked up the car and removed the wheel. The moment the tire was off, a car came speeding by, a new hardtop convertible driven by a young man. He screeched to a halt, turned around and pulled up beside us. He knew Rolling Thunder and Spotted Eagle.

"Come on, Mala," said the man. "I'll take you in with that." Then he looked at Rolling Thunder. "Mr. Pope, I can get you some real good rebuilts cheap."

"Good, I'll look into that."

"Be back pretty quick with this."

Spotted Eagle got inside with the tire and the car sped off toward Elko.

Rolling Thunder looked at me and smiled. "That was the tire man from the gas station."

While Spotted Eagle was gone, Rolling Thunder and I walked up and down the sides of the road without losing sight of the jacked car. At first I thought we were only strolling. Then he stopped to look at a plant only a few inches high with mintlike leaves. He pinched off a few leaves and put them in his mouth. I watched his face. Now, just briefly, his pain was apparent. Rolling Thunder chewed thoughtfully. Sometimes he looked at the ground, sometimes at the sky, or he tilted his head. "I think I've found something," he said finally.

We continued walking. I realized that Rolling Thunder was looking for herbs for his pain. The sun was about to set, and when that happened, Rolling Thunder would pick no more plants. His face looked pleasant and comfortable again. He was apparently relating to his pain in an unordinary way. I believed there actually was pain in his tooth or gum and that he was aware of it, but apparently he did not consciously attend to his pain except when he wished to, as now, when he wanted to find the right herb and feel its effect.

I was having my own feelings; I was being driven crazy by

mosquitoes. The same river that ran through the canyon in the hills to the southwest flowed along this highway not far away. The mosquitoes were thick and sunset was their feeding time. I could hardly wait for the sun to pass. Then we would go back to the car. I thought of speaking to the mosquitoes as Alice had spoken to the bees. I even tried it mentally, but I could not check my irritated waving and brushing long enough to be sincere. I hoped Rolling Thunder was not seeing this, but I felt he was really only pretending not to notice. He chewed on several things as we walked along, and just as the sun was about to set, he found a group of those small minty plants. He paused over the group and then reached into his pocket. He opened his little black coin purse, took out some coins and held them to the setting sun. I looked away. When he began to pick the plants I turned and saw the money lying on the ground. After only a moment or so we were headed back to the car with a handful of the little plants. I thought it was odd for Rolling Thunder to hold money to the sun. Earlier, on the hill, he had used some sort of powder or grain—perhaps tobacco. Evidently there was none of it left, so he had given the little plant family some money. The significance and symbolism of the sacrifice became clearer to me. There was a sense in which the money would be useful to the plants. Plants would not use coins, of course, but perhaps they could sense the regard that Rolling Thunder felt for them. It had been an energy exchange. Money, possessions, and the acts of giving and receiving are all powerful agents and agents can be either good or bad. Here the coins had been a form of love. Rolling Thunder traveled in many states and at great personal expense to be involved in Indian matters. His home in Carlin was often an activist center and he shared what he had with everyone. His phone bills and food bills reflected the great number of people with whom he communicated and for whom he cared, and now he looked into his coin purse for something for the plants. It made me feel good. For a brief moment I even liked the mosquitoes.

*   *   *

It was nearly dark when Spotted Eagle returned with the tire. We were hungry by the time we got back to Carlin and unloaded the herbs. We had supper together and talked until very late. Then Spotted Eagle drove me back up the mountain with my case and Rolling Thunder's sleeping bag. Anne and Richard were surprised to see me. They thought we'd be in San Francisco by this time. "Well, maybe we'll get off tomorrow," I said.

The next day came and went. I waited and no one came for me. It was a long day. I thought of Rolling Thunder's pain and I wished there was a telephone in the tent.

The second night Richard took me down the hill to Rolling Thunder's house. I carried the suitcase and the sleeping bag even though I knew I might be bringing them back again. It was no doubt too late to start for San Francisco now. We thought we would just drop in and see what was happening.

Rolling Thunder came to the door as we pulled up. We stood in the front and talked for a moment. Buffalo Horse walked in and out a few times, stepping over Brandy, who noisily flopped his tail. Rolling Thunder seemed very preoccupied. But he looked all right, I thought to myself, studying his face in the dim light. Then I remembered that his pain would not necessarily be visible. There was something else, I felt, that occupied his attention now. I believed he wanted to be alone. Richard and I were soon on our way back to the mountain, watching the rabbits scamper as we rounded the curves in the road.

The third morning I was getting my gear together for the third time just when the Camaro arrived as Rolling Thunder had promised.

Minutes turned into hours as Spotted Eagle and I sat in the living room waiting for Rolling Thunder to come in from his house across the road. We did not see him until lunchtime. We ate lunch together silently and were still silent later as we sat in the living room. Rolling Thunder puffed thoughtfully on his pipe. Time continued to pass.

The silence did not end until Spotted Fawn called from the kitchen about making up a shopping list for the supermarket. Suddenly Spotted Eagle spoke up impatiently. He complained that it was taking too long to get started. He had promised his visiting friend, Amy, that he would give her a ride back to San Francisco, and there were many things he wanted to do there. He was tired of waiting.

Rolling Thunder looked long at his son before he spoke. Then he spoke quietly. "Now you know what has to be done here, so why don't you wait until you feel those things are done, and then speak? You know I can't think about other things until I get my herbs and business taken care of. If you're feeling impatient, then you're where you think about time, and if you're thinking about time, you should be able to think about the order of things. Things have their order. You know there are certain things I have to do that I can't do until I do other things first."

Spotted Eagle reflected. "That's right," he agreed.

Rolling Thunder had mentioned herbs, so we were soon on our way once again with the tools and empty boxes. We drove back to the place where we had collected herbs two days before. We parked in about the same place, but this time we walked south of the highway, down toward the river. It was late afternoon. I knew the mosquitoes would be thick here and very hungry. I decided I would try not to be bothered. But, again, I was more than one person. Part of me said to the rest, in a rather nagging way, "The mosquitoes will be thick here now." Then I started to notice them. I tried to recall those other parts of myself; I wanted to hear from that level within me that intended to remain undaunted.

Rolling Thunder found some herbs he wanted in a spot right down by the edge of the river. He did not speak about them, and I did not ask. This time he had an offering prepared in a little vinyl bag that he took from his pocket. He performed his ritual. Once again, I did not watch closely. We took only a few plants and cut away only the parts that were needed. They

looked small in the bottom of the box. Along the edge of the
river we came to a place where we couldn't pass. The bushes
were thick right down to the water. We would have to either
walk around the long way or else wade in the river. We started
back around and then pressed through the bushes. Clouds of
mosquitoes began swarming all over me. I nearly panicked. It
would be horrible to make a scene here, yet I could hardly run
away. I walked along behind trying to wave away mosquitoes
and push aside the bushes at the same time. As we passed a
large sagebush I pulled off a fanlike branch to whisk at the
mosquitoes. This might work better than waving my arms. We
came to a stream running down from the hills and Rolling
Thunder found another herb he needed. The little bag of offering was brought out again. The ritual was repeated and Rolling
Thunder and Spotted Eagle began to gather the herb. I just
stood and waved at my face and arms with my sage branch. I
felt ashamed. Here was a medicine man and his apprentice,
solemn and silent, obviously in a peaceful state, doing their
work in a ritual manner while I stood with a piece of the sacred,
purifying sage that I had taken without the slightest thought or
regard, flailing it wildly about in the air. But they did not even
glance at me. I looked at Spotted Eagle; he was covered with
mosquitoes. They walked up and down his arms and across his
face, and some of them were red with blood. He apparently did
not notice them. I looked at Rolling Thunder. He had no mosquitoes on him. I stared hard at him. Swarms of mosquitoes
hovered about him, darting back and forth, but none touched
his skin. Then my attention returned to me and I realized I was
covered with mosquitoes and mosquito bites. I had stopped
fanning with my piece of sage, and now I was ashamed to use
it. I wondered whether to hold it or drop it on the ground.
Indecisively, I held it quietly at my side while the mosquitoes
kept on with their meal.

When at last we started back with our herbs I was too miserable to feel relieved. I had to get rid of the piece of sage even

though I knew it would be wrong to throw it away. I placed it carefully in another sagebush as we reached the road. We put the herbs in the trunk and got in the car. I was itching and miserable, and could hardly control my movements.

Rolling Thunder drove and Spotted Eagle sat in the passenger seat. I rode in back sitting sideways to allow room for my long legs. Rolling Thunder announced he was headed into Elko for Spotted Fawn's groceries. After that there was silence. I closed my eyes and concentrated on not scratching. If I should have to scratch each of my countless bites I would be in a frenzy. Mosquitoes have always bothered me, but this time was the worst ever. I wondered whether I had spoiled the herb-gathering atmosphere. The mosquitoes had certainly ruined it for me. Whether Rolling Thunder and Spotted Eagle had noticed or not I felt guilty about the way I had behaved. Between my gnawing conscience and the irritating itching I was doubly miserable. On top of all this my nose began bothering me. I was sniffing and my eyes burned and watered. I hadn't had a chance to mention this condition to Rolling Thunder and it had grown worse every day. I thought it was caused by the dry grass around our camp, but just now it was coming on especially strong. It became impossible not to rub my eyes. Inside I could feel a trace of good mood, but my body was suffering. It was not a suffering like that of pain; it was an almost intolerable irritation. Then Rolling Thunder said, "There is a way to think about these things so they won't be that way."

Two things happened simultaneously. I had a feeling of shock. His words seemed sudden and forceful in the silence. He had directed them without taking his eyes from the road and I knew they were for me. Even Spotted Eagle knew and politely appeared not to have heard. At the same time I became more vividly aware of that trace of a good mood; it seemed to grow. It had been a beautiful day, I had been gathering herbs with Rolling Thunder, we would soon be having supper, and perhaps tomorrow we would start for San Francisco. My irritation, I realized, was disappearing fast. Soon the itching had stopped and my nose was clear. I looked at myself; there was not a sign of the bites. I blinked my eyes and they felt fine. I was amazed. I couldn't remember ever having gone through such a total transformation. It was as though hours had sped by in a moment.

I didn't know whether to say anything, so I stayed silent. Except for one brief exchange between Rolling Thunder and Spotted Eagle that I could not exactly hear, not another word was spoken until we reached Elko. I felt exhilarated. I was still puzzled, but I was once again elated.

We spent our time in the supermarket filling Spotted Fawn's list and selecting items for the trip. Rolling Thunder constantly questioned me about what I might like. He would point to things on the shelves and ask, "How about this, don't you want some of this?" Somehow this pleased me as it would a young child. I had an urge to buy something for him, and I started once to ask him what I could get that he would like, but he was too busy asking me.

Just as he wheeled the cart to the check stand I walked back, picked up two gallons of pure apple juice and checked them out through the express line. He was genuinely thankful.

When we got to the house there was a wonderful supper. In addition to roast beef and potatoes, Spotted Fawn had prepared homemade banana bread, pickled beets and onions, and a gigantic green salad with herbs and sprouts. She thanked me for the apple juice. She thanked me twice, in fact. Rolling Thunder's was a happy place. It was not so much the cheerful round table by the cooking stove or the comfortable sofas in the sitting room as the good medicine that came from the people.

At supper Rolling Thunder pointed to the lazy Susan spice shelf. "This's the spices here," he said, turning it slightly and squinting at me. "This one here is the vinegar." I thought that strange. I already knew these things. "There's plenty here," he said. "Take all you can." His kindness to me was boundless that night. After supper he sat in his big stuffed chair with its half-circle cushion and puffed his pipe. I sat quietly beside him. At length he took his pipe from his mouth and looked at me. "Did Alice tell you about herself and the bees?"

"She sure did," I said, smiling. "She told me first thing when you got back that day."

"That was something," he said. "Well, she has things to learn and things to offer, but that was something for her." He puffed again on his pipe. "There was a lesson in those bees, too, and we talked about that. I told her if some of those bees were like her they'd be down on the others for being Communist or something. The bees cooperate a lot and don't compete much. The bees don't turn on one another. They don't make factions and investigate each other and trap each other and cut each other's throats; and they don't go out and join the John Birch Society. Bees don't need that kind of nonsense, and we don't need it either." Spotted Fawn brought coffee from the kitchen. I was comfortable and relaxed. I recalled how uncomfortable I had felt a few hours earlier. How suddenly and completely all that had changed.

I'd been in good spirits from the moment I arrived in Sho-shone country, I thought to myself, and the camping situation was beautiful and fun. But there were a few external discomforts. For the first time in my life I had severe hay fever, with the symptoms of burning in my eyes and stinging in my nose, and the mosquitoes seemed an inescapable problem. I recalled Rolling Thunder standing in that cloud of mosquitoes, stooping over the herbs, without a mosquito on him. I glanced at him sitting there. He was watching me through those squinting eyes.

"There is a certain attitude you can have about yourself." Still squinting at me, he puffed awhile on his pipe. "Mosquitoes won't bother you—might not even touch you—if you know how to maintain your good feelings. These attitudes make vi-brations, and they have a smell to 'em. That's what keeps the mosquitoes away. You can make a smell they don't care for. One reason they put that poison in your blood is to make you nervous so the others can smell you. When the chemical works you feel irritated, but if you don't feel irritated the chemical isn't working. So if you do get bit you don't have to let yourself get all swelled up and itchy."

He leaned forward and pointed at me with his pipe stem. "You can control your whole situation by the smell you make —by the vibrations you make. It's not easy, that kind of control. But it's not impossible because you do it yourself. It's all done from the inside."

He smoked his pipe and nodded toward the kitchen. "In the meantime, take vinegar. You can start with that. That'll start on that smell and the mosquitoes won't be so bad. Use it every meal—and in your bath, too; a few tablespoons in the bathtub every time."

Now I understood why Rolling Thunder had pointed out the vinegar. Again I remembered riding in the back seat of the car and feeling miserable. I had made no sign of my misery but Rolling Thunder had sensed it. Could it have been the smell? As soon as Rolling Thunder had spoken my condition changed completely. It was exciting to think about it, yet embarrassing! A series of images passed through my head. I imagined him at the table pointing to the vinegar. He had his hat on and I was looking at the feathers. Then he was standing in a cloud of mosquitoes, holding a glass of water to the sun, saying, "It's all done from the inside." I was still watching his hat. Then I was in the back seat of his car still seeing the feathers. He was driving, pointing as we sped along. In the fields and on the road, on the dashboard in the car and on the seats were herbs, vinegar and spices. Some were growing, some were picked, some were bottled. Leaves floated in the air, and seeds, flower petals, crystals and droplets. We passed by what was outside but in the car things floated right along with us. Rolling Thunder indicated the abundance and variety of these things.

I was only looking at Rolling Thunder's feathers and feeling puzzled. He did not turn to look at me. He was smelling everything. "Can't you see what all this is," he was saying. "Can't you see how all this works?"

The best thing I could think to say was, "I guess you take in and give out whatever you want." I almost spoke aloud.

I was aware then that I was sitting in the room dreaming. Yet the pictures were vivid and real. I had not tried to imagine anything. A thought process had stopped the imagery. It occured to me that Rolling Thunder might actually have "smelled" my vibrations in the car, and after suggesting to me the possibility of change, had somehow produced a vibration to which I had been able to respond, a complete retuning. That could account for his knowing and my sudden change. Or perhaps, in Rolling Thunder's terms, it might have been the overpowering of one smell with another. I wondered if that could be possible. I wanted to find a way to ask. I looked over to where he had been sitting, but Rolling Thunder was gone. His chair was empty. I was startled, even a little frightened. There had been another time in camp when I had noticed Rolling Thunder suddenly standing by a tree. I was sure I had not seen him approach and certain I would have seen him if he had. The event was instantaneous and without detail. I had forgotten it when, some days later, a member of the committee began to tell me of an apparently similar experience with Rolling Thunder and then found that he could not talk about it. Now I sat looking at Rolling Thunder's chair and wondering if he had simply disappeared. This gave me a peculiar feeling. The only other possibility was that I had been in a real trance. But I hadn't closed my eyes, and I thought my mind had wandered only for a few seconds.

I looked around. Spotted Fawn was sitting on the sofa, making a needlework design, looking as though nothing had happened. Spotted Eagle had gone into his room. I could hear music through the door. I considered the fact that Spotted

Eagle had left the room much earlier while we were talking and I had not exactly noticed that. I decided it might be possible for Rolling Thunder to quietly step out of the house without my seeing it at all. But that thought was equally puzzling. That would have meant he had purposely left me alone with my images.

Spotted Fawn got up, put down her work and stepped outside, pausing at the door to let her white cat follow. I sat alone in the living room. In only a moment Spotted Fawn was back.

"Mala?" she called, as she came through the door.

Spotted Eagle came out of his room, smiling.

"Start loading up for San Francisco. Your father is ready."

16
❧

Rolling Thunder's Many Roles

We were on our way west by midnight. We would take Route 80 through Reno, over the Sierra Nevadas, down to the Sacramento Valley, and then to my sister's home in Berkeley. It was over 450 miles from Carlin to the coast and we would be driving from midnight to midday. Spotted Eagle drove first; he felt he could stay awake for at least a few hours. Rolling Thunder held his pipe and his tobacco, but he did not smoke. By the time we got through Carlin and turned onto Highway 80, he was slumped in his seat with his chin upon his chest.

The highway was empty at this time of night, except for an occasional overland truck coming from the west. The sky was without moon or stars; silhouettes of the distant hills blended into the night. We made the long, straight stretch of road to Battle Mountain, then in the dark hills the road began to wind.

Rolling Thunder made a sudden gasp as though he had been surprised in a dream. He lifted his head and looked at the road. As we rounded a tight bend we came upon a large bird sitting in the road. It stretched huge wings to lift itself, but it was too late. There was a loud whack as the car struck the bird. The three of us gasped as Rolling Thunder had done. As far as we could tell, the bird flew on. Rolling Thunder shook his head and then rested it against the back of his seat and closed his eyes again.

In the light of the approaching dawn I could begin to see Spotted Eagle in the rear-view mirror. He looked tired. I asked him if he felt sleepy, but he wanted to go on. The light grew brighter and several times Spotted Eagle began to close his eyes. Each time that happened, Rolling Thunder would lift his head at Spotted Eagle, and Spotted Eagle's eyes would come alive for a time. We stopped for gas and Rolling Thunder took the wheel through Winnemucca, then Lovelock, and into Reno for breakfast. Rolling Thunder drove out of Reno but we had not gone far before he pulled off to the side of the road to sleep. He said ten minutes would be enough. After ten minutes he awoke, cheerful and laughing, his eyes bright. During all the time that Spotted Eagle was driving, he must have been doing something other than sleeping.

We reached my sister's home in Berkeley by midafternoon. Rolling Thunder stopped briefly and then went on. My feeling was that he had some heavy business in the Bay Area, for which he had spent the past few days preparing. I knew vaguely he had come as a healer or a guide in response to people who had asked for his help. He didn't tell me what his plans were, and I didn't ask. After he left me in Berkeley I did not see him for several days.

I had my own business. I felt it was a part of my work to maintain communication with members of the Committee of Concern for the Traditional Indian. My association with Rolling Thunder was based on his idea that we learn the truth by struggling against ignorance in ourselves and in our surroundings. Together, self and surroundings are man's condition. I had observed that the committee people I'd met in Shoshone country—Sara Greensfelder, John Welsh, Ed O'Neill and others—were both working and learning, and they maintained their motivation by the belief that working and learning were the same process. They were in touch with many traditional Indian people. They saw the traditional people's way of life as a spiritual statement, a message for man. It was the content of this message that I had set out to find.

In early August, I joined committee members at the Ecology Center in San Francisco to hear David Monongye, a spokesman for traditional Hopi. The Hopi are thought to be custodians of the spiritual doctrine of traditional American Indians. These teachings and prophecies are written down and kept in secret in Hopi villages. Traditional Indians from many places were known to quote Hopi prophecies. These prophecies are said to have foretold the major wars, the constant oppression of sovereign peoples living upon this land, the recent manipulation of governments in the Far East, and the creation of the UN headquarters on Manhattan Island ("The Land of the Iroquois"). They predicted the moon landings, space stations and the increasing ecological desecration of the continent. The Hopi accurately estimate the timing of these predictions by the order and the relationship of the foretold events. Thus the Hopi and other traditional Indians had been waiting and watching for people like those in the audience at the Ecology Center. The ultimate hope and help for the oppressed native peoples, say the prophecies, is to come from the light-skinned people themselves, from the sons and daughters of the oppressors. The day would come, it was written, when children of the white man would begin to dress like Indians, when they would begin to wear long hair and headbands as the Hopi do, and these people would be the new friends of the Indian.

I had heard about David Monongye in camp some weeks

before and had seen a picture of him. At the Center he looked
older and smaller than I expected. He was eighty years old and
nearly blind. Sara Greensfelder introduced him to the audience.
"Just feel free to ask him any questions," she said. There was
silence. He stood up and took some tiny particles from his
pocket. He held them between his fingers and thumb close to
his face, and moved his lips as I had seen Rolling Thunder do.
Then he gave the offering to Sara, and she took it outside and
laid it on the sidewalk in the sun. He sat down and for a long
while no one spoke.

"Do you have a question?" David asked.

David was asked about conditions at Hopiland and about the
strip mining at Black Mesa. He spoke about the Bureau of
Indian Affairs, the government-formulated tribal councils, the
management of reservation land and people, and the breaking
of treaties. I had thought about these issues as Indian problems,
but now I learned that Indians consider them white man's
problems.

"Up home there are a lot of things going on. In the first place,
these Mormon people have forced themselves in and are building houses up there, right down on the other side of First Mesa,
and the chief there didn't want that. He is trying to get it done
away with, but the Mormons are pretty strong and they are just
about finished. The chief has the authority to give anyone permission, but they forced themselves in and they are building a
Mormon church. In another village they are trying to put up
a low-cost housing project. That is a very sacred place and
should not be desecrated, but they are trying to build a low-cost
housing project where the snake dance society performs their
snake dance.

"We were instructed not to follow any policy of the Indian
Bureau because their intention is to take our land and whatever
really belongs to the Indian people. As you have noticed, most
of the Indian people have no land. Their land has already been
taken away from them. They have no more rights to their land,

no more rights to their water, no more rights to their timber. Their things have been taken from them.

"Therefore we don't want to take part in any tribal council. Before these were formed way back, we were warned not to take part in any kind of clubs or councils that would be newly formed. By doing that, we will only defeat ourselves. These other people around us, our own Indian people, have fallen into the hands of the Indian Bureau, and they have been defeated. They are only depending on the Indian Bureau to borrow a lot of money so they can build houses, build roads. They're not looking ahead. When they borrow money from the Indian Bureau, that's how they get tricked. They run into debt and that's how they get caught, that's how they lose their land.

"Now we are counting on you, as I have said before. You have a right to protest against these things. We don't want to lose our land. We still are kind of a nation. We want to be left alone and to do things in our own way. We want to live, we want to retain our life the way we've been living way back. Way back the life was good. The people respected one another and they were getting along fine—way, way back.

"If you do things right, you're Hopi too. If you have not done something wrong, which might be contrary to the law of the Great Spirit, if you are doing something that is right, you also will be called Hopi. Even if you are not this color or skin, you also will be called Hopi. Hopi means peace. The name Hopi means peace. It's very hard to do things in the right manner, but as long as we do things right, we are in tune with the Great Spirit. No one can do away with our belief, or with the Hopi people, because we have a pretty firm belief in the Great Spirit's life plan and we are still trying to follow that. We were told even if we be going on a stumbled road, not to get discouraged.

"We must put a stop to this strip mining. Most of us do not have good health and we would be the first ones to suffer from the smog and pollution and all the destruction. When the smog will spread all over, it will affect the whole system of the people;

and the little animals, the birds, trees, vegetation and all things will be ruined. Everything will be polluted. That is why we are much concerned. We would like to have that done away with. We would like to have it stopped completely.

"Some of our people are for this strip mining. They are the ones who are fighting against us. They should love the people instead of fighting against them. They should pray for whoever is in need of help. In our religious services we pray for all people —no matter what color skin—and for the animals, and all things around us in Mother Earth.

"I always say we have our own church within our hearts. You have your own church right in here. If you follow that within your heart, you are doing something right with the Great Spirit's instructions. You can follow your own heart even if you do not go to church. That's the way we've been told. You know, sometimes in the morning, sometimes we don't feel good, sometimes we feel angry, depressed about something. Of course, we sometimes have hatred. We all have some arguments with some other people. But if you have trouble with some other man, and you hate that man and think, 'I wish he'd die and go away,' you are just working against yourself. The other man may not be feeling angry towards you, but you are angry at him and thinking thoughts against him. You're just working against yourself. You're bringing pain into your own heart. The other man cannot affect you in any way, but if you hate him, and you're going after yourself, you'll hurt yourself with your own bad feelings. Sometimes we don't feel good and sometimes we have some kind of illness, some fear, some imagination, and we just don't want to mingle with other people. If you come out from your house and if some people are standing over there, maybe half a dozen people talking about something, you think they're talking about you. You think they might be criticizing you. But they're not talking about you. Go up to them and talk with them, and if they talk about some happy things and if they are laughing, join with those people. That's the only way you can do away with your fear or anger or depressed feeling. When you come to people who are happy and who laugh, join with them, that's the only medicine. Happiness is the only thing for people. If we respect one another and not hate one another, we'll all be united and we will be happy people."

Many questions were asked, and most of the answers were long. In all, David Monongye talked for three hours, and while he was speaking my mind went back to some of my conversations long ago with Swami Rama and, more recently, with Rolling Thunder. They were really all talking about the same things: the happiness that could be found within the heart, the disciplines of mind and body, and the techniques for working on the self and for living in harmony with nature.

The committee people hoped that Rolling Thunder would appear at the Ecology Center, but he was busy somewhere in Marin County north of San Francisco. We would see him the following night at a corn feast and round dance in San Rafael.

During the time that Rolling Thunder was in Marin County I stayed in Berkeley with my sister and brother-in-law. We were joined by Antoinette ("Dolly") Gattozzi, a science writer for the National Institute of Mental Health who had been associated with the voluntary controls project at the Menninger Foundation. While I was there I tried to tell them about everything that had happened in the past weeks. There was hardly time. I did mention the Shoshone need for legal help, and we discussed the possibilities of communicating with Berkeley lawyers. During my stay in the city I hoped to make contact with a lawyer, perhaps a young law graduate, who might be interested in working among the Shoshone people in Nevada.

The only time that I had ever recorded Rolling Thunder's voice had been in July 1971. He was sitting under a tree by a stream not far from camp, speaking to members of the Committee of Concern for the Traditional Indian:

"There is no justice under law on the reservations. Off the reservations there is sometimes a pretense of some type of trial, but in most all cases where Indians are involved, Indians are advised to plead guilty with the promise they will get a reduced sentence. That never is the case. The Indian is always, without exception, convicted. In cases where Indians are murdered— sometimes by ex-convicts and criminals, sometimes in cases where it is known who the guilty parties are—nothing is ever done. We would like to have some resort to law to get these cases into proper court, to make appeals to federal courts where we know that there would be a better chance of justice. We would like, if we could, to have some dedicated young lawyers come here and stay. Of course, we realize that they would need not only knowledge of the law, but that they would need also to be very dedicated because the forces of the establishment don't like any opposition. They would try to intimidate any such attorneys and probably try to run them out of this coun- try."

We listened to these words on my cassette recorder in Berke- ley. My sister contacted Jim Woods, a lawyer friend, and talked to him about the lack of legal representation for Shoshone people in Nevada and about the chaining of the pinyon trees to provide grazing land on Indian treaty territory. He was inter- ested in meeting Rolling Thunder. We agreed on a meeting within the week. That evening we would see Rolling Thunder in San Rafael. With luck, the arrangement could be made then.

We drove together to San Rafael. There in a place called the Kundalini Ashram was a large crowd, about half of them American Indians. I had met some of the younger Indians in Nevada, but most of the others I had never seen before. We arrived just after the corn feast was over, but before the dancing had begun. I had wanted to introduce David Monongye to my sister and brother-in-law, but he was pressed in by groups of people and it seemed futile.

We found Rolling Thunder surrounded by people eager to talk or listen to him. I had to tell Rolling Thunder about the

tentative arrangement with Jim Woods in Berkeley. When I
had a chance to talk to him I explained we had contacted
Woods.

"Tell the lawyer I'll be there," he said.

From the other room came the sound of drums. Then a voice,
lively and rhythmic, began a sort of dialogue with the drums.
Everyone listened. It was David Monongye. Standing in the
center of the largest room with a circle forming around him,
this little old man was producing a powerful and moving sound.
Soon everyone in the room had joined that circle, and I wondered whether David knew how large a crowd this was. He
glanced about blankly. He was seeing what was in his head, not
what was in the room. He was beside himself with mirth, cock-
ily hitting his drum and tapping his foot, and occasionally
missing a beat to sweep his arm through the air to insist that
the awkward circle begin to turn.

Finally we made a double ring and people got into the swing
of the dancing. Some began to catch and repeat the Hopi words.
Everyone seemed deeply involved. But as the dance went on
some tired and dropped out. David Monongye did not tire. He
picked up the pace. When the dancers became too few to make
a ring around David the dance stopped—but David did not. He
became a performer and his audience sat around him on the
floor. He introduced ridiculous-sounding songs with funny English words and tried to induce the audience to join in. "David
will go on all night," someone said; "he'll never stop. We'll all
get old and die and David will be singing songs."

Suddenly David stopped. The whole place became silent.

"What's happening?"

"Rolling Thunder's going to do a war dance."

Rolling Thunder was in the center. He wore his usual loose-
fitting clothes, but his pants and shirt were decorated with
Indian designs. He had brightly colored bands around his cuffs
and on those bands were bells.

The drums began to sound again. Now the beat was slow and

steady and the tone was heavy. As Rolling Thunder began to
dance, all the people sitting on the floor craned their necks to
see the stomping feet that were producing the rhythmic mes-
merism of the bells. I had never seen Rolling Thunder dance
before. I could have watched for hours, but it lasted only a
moment. Everyone wanted to see more, but Rolling Thunder
left the room. The drums changed their pattern and David
resumed his singing. Some went out with Rolling Thunder and
urged him to dance again. In a short while he came back and
the war dance was repeated. Again Rolling Thunder left the
room and again David returned to his songs.

The Berkeley meeting between Jim Woods and Rolling
Thunder took place on a Thursday night. Woods had many
questions that I found difficult to answer, so I was glad when
Rolling Thunder finally arrived. He listened to the questions
that had been put to me and then he talked:

"We were told the day would come when the white man
would shake hands with the Indian. But what is needed now
between the white man and the Indian is not merely the shaking
of hands. What is needed now is for the white man to make
some restitution for the wrongs and the crimes that have been
committed. What is needed now is the fulfillment of the treaties
and agreements that have been made. Many people today want
to befriend and understand the Indian and even learn from him.
But the government—the Bureau of Indian Affairs and the
Uncle Tommyhawks, the BIA's puppet tribal councils—are
going in the opposite direction. They continue the cheating and
they continue the taking of Indian lands and the taking away
of the Indians' practical rights and civil rights, and so things
become worse.

"Even today, in this day and time, we are still losing our land
and they are still killing our people, even our young people.
Many of them have been found dead in the town of Elko and
on the reservations. Sometimes they're found dead in the jail.

We can't prove these things, we can't do anything in their courts, we can't convict or even investigate anybody, even when we know full well who does these things. Our people have no legal representation whatsoever. Lawyers in the town of Elko and other small towns in our part of Nevada are bought by the big ranchers and the mining interests and the cattlemen. They do not care for a poor person, especially an Indian, who is the poorest of all. Our people are dragged into your courts, and many times there's no pretense of a trial. The recent Indian Bill of Rights doesn't mean anything out there.

"Only recently a young man was thrown in jail and he was not allowed to have an attorney or witnesses. He was not allowed to see his own mother before the trial, and although he had three witnesses in his behalf, they were not allowed to appear. No one except the agency officials and the puppet council were allowed to attend the trial. And this man's actual crime was that he had had the nerve to run for the tribal council. He was a traditional Indian and he thought that by running for the tribal council he could help his people, and he was thrown in jail.

"The law calls for the hiring of Indians on all government projects on the reservations. Yet even when there is the need for carpenters and builders and Indians are available to do this work—Indians that have been taken out of their homes and sent far away to school to learn these trades—you won't see Indians hired on these projects. They build highways through our reservations where they should be required by law to hire our people and yet they do not hire the available Indian labor —even when they have to import labor from other states far away.

"The kidnapping of Indian children from their own families goes on all over the country. They kidnap Indian children out on the reservations under the guise of some sort of child care or religious programs. Any excuse is all right provided some white family wants a child or someone likes to convert people.

These people will get together with the welfare agents and the sheriffs and the Indian agents and they'll go out on a reservation and take a child. They might say it's because the family is on welfare or has too many children or anything else they can think of as an excuse at the time. Often no papers are served. Religious groups like the Mormons—people who should be our best friends, people who claim that the Indian is of the chosen people—are very much implicated in this kidnapping business.

"We have heard that over in some of those European countries they have what they call the 'iron curtain.' We heard about a bamboo curtain in the last big war over in the East. Well, out here we have the buckskin curtain. The public just absolutely does not know and cannot imagine what goes on out on the reservations."

All these conditions about which Rolling Thunder spoke are not limited to the Shoshone Indians. We had talked about this before. The conditions exist from coast to coast in all the hills, plains and deserts where there are American Indians. It was clear lawyers could be of immense help to Indians. It would be a long and complicated process even when it did begin.

"What is the starting point?" Woods wanted to know. "What are you interested in doing first?"

Rolling Thunder thought the starting point was the forest-chaining issue. He explained about the "Ely Chains," the modern Bureau of Land Management invention to facilitate "vegetative manipulation." These are large ocean anchor chains from naval surplus with short lengths of railroad iron welded across each link. They tear out a forest at the rate of twenty acres an hour. The heavy chain is stretched between caterpillar tractors to drag away pinyon trees, whose nuts are the traditional survival food of the Shoshone. Juniper, Indian tea, sacred plants and herbs are ripped in the path. Wildlife is destroyed to clear grazing land for the private use of Nevada ranchers.

"Whose land is this done on, and who does it?" Woods asked. "Who authorizes it? Who initiates it?"

"Well, it's done by the Bureau of Land Management, or it's contracted out by them. We have a BLM office in Elko and one in Ely. It's all authorized and managed by them. But what they're doing, they're responding to pressure from big power interests in Nevada. These rich ranchers don't care about the future when the land will wash away and the whole area becomes a dust bowl. They are after the instant profits from the use of the so-called public domain. If this land is the public domain, then it belongs to the public and the public might need it someday. Actually, most of this chaining takes place on Indian treaty territory, not the reservations where they've shoved us, but our real Indian land, within our territorial boundaries spelled out in the treaties.

"And the Indians are the custodians of the land."

For Rolling Thunder these were the two reasons why the chaining issue should be the starting point. If the Indians are the custodians of the land, the protection of the land and the will of nature become Indian responsibilities. If the land in question is Indian territory, then the forest-chaining issue is also a treaty issue.

"There has got to be some way for these treaties to be brought to the attention of all people and to force the government to face these treaties, to admit that they are breaking their promises and either live up to their part or mutually negotiate new agreements. We have tried in letters, in protests of treaty violations, and in court cases across the country where the treaties should be involved. We're fighting this pinyon tree chaining for two reasons: to save what's left of the pinyon trees and to save what's left of our treaty lands and rights."

Jim Woods questioned Rolling Thunder about the Shoshone treaty and its contents.

"We have a pretty good treaty with the United States government. The Shoshone treaty is very clearly spelled out and it is quite favorable to the Shoshone people. Of course it is broken in every way possible, but if it were to be observed, things would be quite different today. At least with the Shoshone people, we would not have what you refer to as Indian problems: poverty, alcoholism, the high unemployment rate, the high suicide rate. For the real problem is the broken treaties. The real problem is the cheating of the Indians. This is the problem. People propose a lot of so-called solutions for these problems; they talk about medical solutions, psychiatric solutions, economic solutions, social solutions. The only real solution is honesty. Be honest with the Indian. Begin to observe the treaties as originally agreed; they are still valid. Begin to set right all the wrongs that have been accomplished against the Indian in all the years of cheating."

Woods asked, "What is your position with your people? Do you have a position? Do the Shoshone people consider that you represent them? Are you authorized to speak or act in their behalf?"

"I am a medicine man and I am a legal spokesman for my people. I represent them here in this meeting. Before making this trip here I met with our traditional leaders and with the elders in council in preparation for meeting you and talking to you here tonight."

Jim Woods didn't leave until late in the evening. We all realized that if anything was to develop from this beginning, it would be only after a long difficult process of research and planning.

Curiously I remembered those days of waiting, gathering herbs and waiting again before we left Carlin. Rolling Thunder carried in his brief case a proclamation signed by Chief Frank Temoke naming him legal adviser and spokesman for the Western Shoshone Nation. I had seen that. I wondered, however, about the meeting with the leaders and elders. Where were they? How had Rolling Thunder met with them? I remembered his living room and his empty chair after we had been talking. I wondered about those days when I had thought he was in his little house across the road. I wondered how he had known about this meeting that I thought had been my idea.

* * *

Rolling Thunder left for Carlin the next morning. I decided to stay a few more days to get a sleeping bag and perhaps another tent. I was still hoping to find a lawyer who would be willing to visit Shoshone country.

The following night in San Francisco I met with members of the Committee of Concern for the Traditional Indian. In a second-story flat over a bright red Chinese restaurant in Chinatown, six of us talked for three or four hours about David Monongye, Rolling Thunder and Swami Rama. I learned it was corn that Sara Greensfelder placed outside the door when David Monongye spoke at the Ecology Center. Under theoretically impossible conditions, the Hopi raise corn as their main staple. Corn is the giver of life, and it is a sacred symbol. We talked about David Monongye's lecture. As with other contemporary Indian spokesmen, his message was at once teaching and invocation.

The talk turned to Swami Rama. One of the members had heard Dr. Green lecture about Swami Rama in San Francisco. I had talked about the Swami at camp and now everyone wanted to hear more about "the remarkable things that Swami Rama could do," and about similarities or differences between him and Rolling Thunder. I thought they shared fundamentally the same philosophy, but others there that night thought they saw a difference: while American Indians talk issues such as ecology and human rights, East Indian teachers seem to be indifferent to these problems, advocating complete disinterest in worldly things. I thought that the great difference in the circumstances of both peoples had a lot to do with this. Spiritual leaders in the East have always been treated with reverence far beyond their needs or wishes, while in the West they have suffered scorn and cruelty. The difference, I thought, was more in the circumstances of the teachers than in their philosophies. But this was not really the point. I believed that, as Rolling Thunder had often said, spokesmen of Eastern wisdom have frequently been misunderstood. In fact they have never taught complete separation from earthly responsibilities.

"I don't think any wise or even intelligent person ever advocates such separation." I said. "Orientals have always thought more of responsibilities and duties than of freedoms and rights. They don't share our concept of the self as an isolated, individual identity: Westerners dislike a sense of duty and I think they misinterpret Eastern philosophy and reword it in a way that feels comfortable to them. They are beginning to enjoy using terms like 'karma' and 'spiritual development,' but they want to think of these as personal things.

"When Eastern monks or yogis talk about overcoming attachment to worldly pains and pleasures, it has nothing to do with escaping social responsibility. All they say, again and again, is, 'Do your work in the world. Don't put on robes and go off to some retreat. If you think the city atmosphere is not sufficiently spiritual, then work on the city, don't leave it.' For themselves, they're foreigners here and they're not involved in our racial and political karma.

"I think it's up to us to work out our own collective karma. The spiritual leaders and teachers who are real and meaningful for the people born here and who are supposed to be working with this land, this circumstance and this karma are people like Martin Luther King and Rolling Thunder. No yogi or monk from far away will ever arrive here with a spiritual message that is complete for the people who are living here. In fact, I believe the most complete and appropriate teaching of the way for the people of this land will ultimately come from the native Americans."

John Welch redirected the conversation: "Did I ever tell you about my first meeting with Rolling Thunder?"

I had heard that John Welch knew Rolling Thunder before he moved to California and joined the committee, and that they had traveled together on several occasions. In Nevada, shortly after Rolling Thunder had brought the rainstorm at the abandoned ranch, John Welch had told me about a time when Rolling Thunder had caused rain to stop. On a day when it had been raining for hours Rolling Thunder took him up a high hill, saying that when they reached the top the rain would stop for as long as they were up there. And that, John said, was just how it happened.

"Our first meeting was accidental, before I became involved with Indian people or Indian affairs. I was going through Oklahoma on my way back to Kansas City and I knew that a friend from Ireland was there attending an Indian meeting, so I decided to look him up. The meeting was crowded and the faces unfamiliar, but I ran into a young Indian guy I knew. We looked around and he pointed to an Indian across the hall saying that this man was Rolling Thunder and that I should go over and ask where my Irish friend might be. I went up to this man and asked him if he was Rolling Thunder. He only looked at me. I told him who I was looking for and waited for him to say something. Finally he said some funny-sounding gibberish that I could hardly understand. I thought he didn't speak English or hadn't understood a word. My Indian friend came over and we stood there for a minute. When he realized what was going on he told Rolling Thunder that I was a friend. Rolling Thunder apologized in perfect English and said he was just being careful. When I told him I was on my way to Kansas City, he told me he was going to Leavenworth to see about a Shoshone youth imprisoned for refusing to be a soldier for the U.S. government. He asked me if I would take him there."

Rolling Thunder had talked about this incident at Council Grove. He said he'd gone to a meeting of chiefs and medicine men in Oklahoma. Before he left, his people had asked him to bring back a young Shoshone who had been sentenced to five years in Leavenworth Prison for refusing to go to Vietnam. The Shoshone treaties guarantee that the Indians will not be drafted. Rolling Thunder was determined to bring the boy home where he belonged.

"So I was down there in Oklahoma," Rolling Thunder had said, "and I got transportation from a white man, a teacher over at the University of Missouri, and I made my medicine on the banks of the Missouri River. It was a clear day and the clouds rolled up black. They started coming in fast. The thunder clapped and the lightning flashed, and I knew then that it was going to be all right. We walked to the gates of that penitentiary and the army officers were all out in front. They were watching a black funnel that looked like it might have been two or three miles off, coming toward them. Anyway, I won't go through all the details, but that man is home today in Nevada and he has no discharge papers. He doesn't know whether he should be in prison or in the army or what. They just turned him loose."

In all our conversations at the camp in Carlin, John Welch had not mentioned the event, so I had had no idea that he had been the white man with Rolling Thunder that day. The story had impressed me and I had not forgotten it. Now I was hearing it again from Welch.

"I took Rolling Thunder in my car and we got up to Leavenworth in the late afternoon. Rolling Thunder walked right up to that gate and said that he had come to get this man and take him back to Shoshone country. They wouldn't let us in. In fact, they wanted us to go away, but Rolling Thunder was persistent. Finally some prison officer came out and talked to us. He told us it would be impossible to visit our friend. Rolling Thunder said he had come to get someone, not visit. They took us inside a room and we waited. Finally another officer came in and told us that the man he had come to see had been transferred. Rolling Thunder and I left, but we weren't ready to give up, so we stayed in a nearby motel.

"In the middle of the night, Rolling Thunder began talking loudly. It woke me up. When he saw that I was awake he looked at me and said angrily that he had been lied to, and now he was prepared to do things his way. He said that if they could use lies to accomplish what they knew was wrong, he could use fear to accomplish what he knew was right. When I asked him what he meant, he told me that he had just been inside the prison and so he knew the boy was there. Then he told me to go back to sleep quickly because we would be up before sunrise and then I would see his plan.

"It seemed a few minutes later that Rolling Thunder was moving about in the room and telling me to get up so we could be down at the river before the sun appeared. We went down to the bank of the Missouri River where Rolling Thunder built a fire and starting putting a lot of strange things in it. He lit his pipe and smoked it for a while and then he began weird chanting. He handed me the pipe and told me to smoke. I had no trouble doing that, even though the smoke was very strong, but when he asked me to chant, I thought that would be impossible. He insisted I follow him and somehow, at that time, I was able to do it. We chanted and smoked for a long time while Rolling Thunder kept putting things into the fire. I didn't know how or when he had gotten those things.

"After a while the small fire started producing an intense black smoke which rose straight above the fire and hung high in the air. It grew blacker and blacker above our heads. Then there was thunder—loud and frightening! It seemed to start very far away and come right up against our heads. I could actually feel it. Then black clouds were moving all across the sky and they collected right above us. It got so dark that the flashes of lightning were brilliantly white. The lightning was all around us, and it made sharp, crackling sounds.

"Right in the middle of all these goings on, Rolling Thunder put out the fire and told me to walk with him. We got up over the bank and started walking. I kept turning around and looking back; the sky was clear all around us except for one big black cloud which came down to a point right above where we had been. It looked just like a funnel.

"When we reached the prison gates Rolling Thunder shouted at the guards in a really powerful voice. One of them rushed inside and returned with some officers. They kept telling us to go away, and Rolling Thunder kept saying he wanted the Indian youth. He told them he had seen him in there, so he knew right where he was. They all looked surprised, but they still tried to force us to leave.

"Rolling Thunder pointed back to where we had come from and you could see that black funnel in the sky. He told them to watch it and they did, because it was coming right for us. This was his tornado, he told them, and it was about to rip the whole prison wide open. The funnel moved slowly, but it kept getting closer and closer. Everyone just watched until it was nearly on us, and then some of the people went rushing inside. Sand and rocks started flying through the air, but none of them hit us. Nothing hit me, anyway. I could hardly stand up and I had difficulty seeing. Rolling Thunder appeared calm and steady, and he had his eyes on the prison gate. Pretty soon the gate came flying off, you could hear it rip loose. It went flying through the air, spinning around and around. The prison officials brought out the young man. There was no formality— nothing. They just let him go. He went back west to Shoshone country. As far as I know, he's back home still."

17

American Indians: Custodians of the Land

After the meeting I shipped my new camping equipment by Greyhound freight to Carlin and bought myself a ticket on the Southern Pacific. The train from Oakland to Carlin provided everything anyone could want in a train ride: a winding climb across the Sierra Nevadas with tunnels, bridges, snow-filled forests trailing off into the steep mountains high above the tracks and the tracks themselves plunging into the valleys miles below.

The ride lasted twelve hours, and it was dark long before Carlin. I knew this train would pass through our canyon campsite in Palisade and I hoped to see the campfire from the window. I watched for a long time, but just when I expected to spot the campsite I was interrupted by a crewman with a lantern. He had a uniform like the conductor's, but the gold letters on his hat spelled BRAKEMAN.

"You the one for Carlin?"

"Yes. Are we about there?"

"Few minutes. Had a guy get off in Carlin just last week. How come you're gettin' off in Carlin?"

"Well, that's my stop."

"Need any help with your stuff?"

"No, I just have a couple of small cases."

"Reason I ask, this ain't no passenger stop, just a service stop. There's no baggage service here. You'll see how we let you out right here in the bushes."

"Yes, I know," I said.

"Well, you don't live here, I know that." People were turning in their seats and looking.

"If you lived here I'd know ya. I lived in Carlin fifteen years. Just moved. Mostly railroad people here. Never seen ya on this run before either."

I had no reply.

"How come you're getting off in Carlin?"

"Well, I'm just visiting here."

"Who?"

"John Pope. He's an S.P. brakeman. You might know him."

"I don't want to open this door back here. Step don't go out too good." He walked up the aisle to the front of the car and turned around. "I'm going to let you out up front here. You can wait'll we stop." Then he walked back, and leaned over me. "Yeah, I know him," he said, "I know him."

I stepped out. The air was fresh and cool. The brakeman began efficiently signaling with his lantern.

"Know where you're going? That's Pope's right over that way."

"They'd said they might drive up here, so I thought I'd wait," I said.

"No, you can't depend on them. You can walk right through the bushes if you ain't scared of getting snake-bit. You been there before?"

"Yes, I've been there. I guess I'll walk."

"You'd best do that; you'd be standing here all night! It's a couple minutes' walk."

I started to walk and the brakeman called after me.

"Has he been feeding you that big-chief bullshit?"

"What?"

"Hasn't he been giving you all that Rolling Thunder crap?"

"He's not a chief and that's his name," I said.

"Assumed name, you mean. Nobody's name is Rolling Thunder!" He laughed.

"Well, that's his name," I said softly.

I walked a distance and looked back. I could see the brakeman waving his lantern. I wanted to shout, "Every name's assumed! Where'd you get yours, anyway? Where would an Indian get a name like John Pope?" But I turned and kept on walking.

The whole family was home and Anne Habberton and Richard Clemmer were waiting to drive me up to the canyon. I had arrived about twenty minutes earlier than they had expected.

Before leaving for camp I had coffee and a chat with Rolling Thunder. He and Richard had been talking about the pinyon trees and the chaining project. If they could determine when and where the next chaining might start, they wanted to be there. At twenty acres an hour the tractors and chain can destroy a several-hundred-acre site in little time, Rolling Thunder pointed out, so we had to move fast to catch them in the act.

I told them that I'd seen Jim Woods, the lawyer, just before leaving Berkeley and he had asked about the Shoshone treaty, whether it was ratified by Congress and when, and whether it was signed by the President. "Woods wants a copy of that treaty with the signatures if possible," I said. "He's been reading in the law library. He said if anyone wants to become literally sick, they can read what he has read about Indians in our lawbooks.

"I talked to another lawyer, Mel Dayley. He'd read the note we put up on the bulletin board at the U.C. Law School, and he would like to meet us. He'd had a practice in Utah and then moved out to the Bay Area, and he wouldn't consider taking another state bar exam to practice in Nevada. He doesn't think there's too much hope for finding a good lawyer for Nevada, unless maybe we could find some radical young lawyer, maybe the son of a rich rancher."

Rolling Thunder said, "I suppose we knew it wouldn't be easy." Our conversation was over and we went back up the mountain.

As days went by, I saw little of Rolling Thunder. At first I spent time making improvements on the campsite. Then I made cassette recordings of notes and reports and worked on my papers. I watched Anne do clay pottery using techniques she had learned in Hopiland. Richard was busy with his thesis, a comparative analysis of the effects of non-Indian jurisdiction over Hopi and Western Shoshone communities.

The campsite was pleasant enough, but during the day the sun was scorching overhead and the nights were too cold to be out of bed or away from the fire. The hay fever I had forgotten about in San Francisco returned, and I began taking hay-fever pills and eye drops. I would have found all these little discomforts acceptable if I could have spent more time with Rolling Thunder. I began to wonder at the wisdom of maintaining the camp in this canyon so far from Carlin. We began considering the possibility of renting a place in town, and I decided to discuss it with Rolling Thunder.

But the days continued to pass and there was no chance to talk to Rolling Thunder. One time Oscar Johnny was visiting, so we went down the mountain for an evening. Another day Alice Floto came over from Salt Lake City. She and Rolling Thunder talked about my hay fever and worked out a recipe that would need twelve herbs. Then more days passed and I waited at camp.

Early one morning, when we knew Rolling Thunder would be home, Richard drove me down the hill to the house. I sat in the living room and talked to Spotted Fawn, waiting for Rolling Thunder to come in from his little house across the street. He got up but he did not come. Spotted Fawn took him coffee on a tray. When she did not come back, I sat alone in the living room.

I had made up my mind to talk to Rolling Thunder. As the hours passed my impatience made waiting difficult. I felt uncomfortable; my eyes were running and I sneezed. I had no medicine and, worse, no handkerchief. There was no sense in staying out in weed country. I should be where I could see Rolling Thunder every day, not out in the hills. And now here I was, waiting for hours. I fed my impatience for some time, and then I had another thought: "This is foolish. Your hay fever's making you think like this. Eagerness to learn is natural, but complaining is unnecessary. You are here for the day, and you have an abundance of time. It's ridiculous to feel impatient waiting for Rolling Thunder."

Besides, I suspected Rolling Thunder would not come as long as I was feeling this way. That was it. I was not impatient because I was waiting; I was waiting because I was impatient. I began to think I might produce a change in my state if I worked at it for a while. I closed my eyes. In a few minutes Rolling Thunder walked through the door. He was cheerful.

"I wouldn't be in too much of a hurry about moving in from out there," he said. "Instead you could be thinking about arranging things nice, really fix up one of those old houses. I know it's going to be getting cold, but if you'd start thinking about that now, you could go quite a while out there yet. Your feeling is you'd like to be in closer to the house here, but that's not necessarily where it's happening." He knew exactly what had been on my mind.

"Now, if you want to see Indian medicine, you just have to watch everything that's going on, and maybe you'll see something. Whatever takes place that might interest you, it's just going to happen as a part of all the work. We can't isolate some particular activity and do it just to be doing it; it all has to be part of the work. And if I'm going to be doctoring, there's no telling when that might be. I might doctor somebody tomorrow and then again I might not. But if I do, or when I do, it's more likely to be out there than here. I don't like to do any doctoring here in the house. For one thing, it's best to be in a natural setting, and for another thing, it's not good for the house. If everyone would start coming in here to be doctored, it would get pretty heavy. I've had trouble here before when I've doctored people with mental and emotional problems and then those problems kept hanging around here in the house. Some of them are pretty persistent and pretty destructive. There are ways to handle those things too, but I shouldn't have to be thinking about that all the time in my own home. This is where I live and rest, and this is where I have my family.

"So my hope is to have a good place to doctor people, even a place where people can stay. Then when you go back to the Menninger Foundation you can tell them that I would be willing to work with some of their patients. I would be willing to take some referrals from the right psychiatrists if I could do it in my own place and if I could accept or reject whomever I wanted.

"Of course there are things these doctors up at the Menninger Foundation know that I don't know, but there are a lot of things they don't know, and these are things that I could help with. Some of these things might sound strange to these doctors, like some of the cases they call 'schizophrenia' and some other cases, where people are influenced by other beings. Sometimes a part of a person's energy is taken by another, sometimes people get spaced out on drugs and things and other beings come in and try to take over, and sometimes two spirits try to occupy one body. Doctors' training is very limited and they have little awareness or curiosity outside their training. Some of them are even trained to be cynical. But they have no need to go by their feelings; they have a chance, now, to see how these things work. It's high time doctors and medicine men started working together."

There was no need to say anything and there was nothing to say. No trace of my former state of mind remained. In fact, I realized suddenly that there was no trace of my hay fever, at least not at the moment. Was it possible that the hay fever was very related to my state of mind? I was sure that, feeling as I did now, any hay-fever discomforts would be utterly impossible.

"We haven't forgotten your hay-fever capsules," Rolling Thunder said. "The reason I haven't given them to you yet is because I don't have any marshmallow root. I have everything else and they sometimes have marshmallow root at a health store in Elko. So maybe pretty soon we can make up those capsules. They should clear up that trouble so it won't come back."

Rolling Thunder's constant awareness of my thoughts and feelings didn't appear to me as any kind of strange psychic phenomenon. His was a kind of caring. I had the feeling that if I were able to be with him at his level, Rolling Thunder would not have to do all this talking. Just a few moments ago I had been preoccupied with my feelings of disappointment and frustration at not being with Rolling Thunder more, but now it was hard to believe such feelings had ever existed or could ever return. The afternoon went by too fast. Anne and Richard came for me and we left immediately. I should like to have stayed a while longer but we wanted to get the fire started and supper on before sundown. After supper we sat with empty plates and looked into the fire and I talked about my afternoon with Rolling Thunder. "It's funny," I said, "but I feel that he's always around." They agreed. A few moments later Rolling Thunder drove into camp in his Camaro. He had come to give us proof that what I had just said was true. The evidence was a fresh apple pie that Spotted Fawn had made and sent up for us on a blue pie plate.

* * *

One morning Rolling Thunder had Spotted Eagle pick me up at camp and drive me down the mountain. Two young women, a German and a Dane, were visiting Rolling Thunder. They had come to the United States to gather material on American Indians and had done some work with the Committee of Concern for the Traditional Indian in San Francisco, where we had met them. Rolling Thunder took us on an outing. We carried empty cartons and collected some plants, but with this group it became more a social affair than the usual serious herbgathering.

We headed southwest from Carlin toward the Eureka highway and drove past the winding road that leads up into our canyon. Rolling Thunder looked more to the side than the front as he drove, and when we came to a place that interested him we stopped. Except for the major highway, U.S. 80, roads in and out of Carlin are lightly traveled. This one was the loneliest of all: not a car passed while we were here. We carried our empty cartons perhaps one hundred yards or so off the road. "Now if you see a snake, don't do anything to hurt it," Rolling Thunder said as we started into the brush. We came to a huge juniper tree that was covered with blue-gray berries. Rolling Thunder needed some. He called them "wild cedar berries." The two young women stared fixedly as the sacrifice was made, so this time I watched also. We were far from silent on this gathering. The two women chattered constantly in German and English as we picked the berries, and Rolling Thunder even answered some of their questions. But then he worked himself around to the downhill side of the enormous tree and became silent.

The berries were tiny and the cardboard cartons large. At first we picked them one by one, but that way it would have taken till sundown to gather a cupful. We tried and discussed various ways of picking and decided the most efficient was to hold the carton under a limb with one hand and run the other hand along the branches, knocking the berries off. This was rough on the hands, and it seemed a crude way to treat a medicine tree. I tried using only my fingertips, and while that was gentle, it was painstakingly slow. When we had just enough berries to barely cover the bottoms of the containers, Rolling Thunder walked around the tree with nearly a full box. I would not have said anything, but one of the Europeans asked, "How did you do that?"

"Do what?" Rolling Thunder said, pouring our few berries into his container. Nothing more was said of the matter.

Next we found wild sunflower plants, and Rolling Thunder wanted to get many leaves. Once again, this turned out to be nearly impossible for everyone except Rolling Thunder. He instructed us not to take any leaves occupied by even a single ant, and ants were everywhere. Rolling Thunder was pinching leaves with considerable speed, but we found ourselves slowly and carefully examining every leaf. I tried pushing ants along with the tip of my finger, but they refused to cooperate. If one ran down the stem, two others took its place, or they simply froze, daring me to flick them off in front of Rolling Thunder, custodian of the land—and perhaps of the ants as well.

I watched Rolling Thunder and saw that he was simply wiggling his fingers above the leaves with a sort of herding motion while the ants scurried away. He did it again and again. Each time he waved at a leaf the ants would depart en masse. I saw him point his finger down a stem and move a column of ants as though his finger were a magnet and the ants little particles of iron.

I wanted to try this myself, but not where Rolling Thunder could see. I had just started toward another sunflower when I saw a rattlesnake! My mouth and eyes sprung open. The snake began to slide and the rattle almost brushed against my boot. I was about to become either paralyzed or jet-propelled, but instead I became oddly elated. Every time I had been with Rolling Thunder up a hill, down a river, into the bushes or along a road, he had spoken a few protective words in behalf

of his respected snakes. Now, here was one at last. I believe I
might have smiled at the snake and then at Rolling Thunder.
"Look at this!" I said.

Everyone turned. Even the women were calm. Rolling Thunder knelt down close to the head of the snake and held out his
hand. The snake coiled and raised its head to meet the hand.
His hand and the snake's eyes were only inches apart. They
both began to move. When the hand moved forward, the head
went back. When the hand withdrew, the head followed. Rolling Thunder bobbed his head and the rattles buzzed. Now he
extended both his hands and the snake swayed slowly between
them, first to one side, then to the other. Rolling Thunder and
the snake were eye to eye, and I watched, suspended. It was a
dance. Rolling Thunder stopped and the snake became still,
absolutely motionless. "Now," he said, "watch him go on about
his business." He wheeled around on one foot and stood up with
his back to the snake. The snake went limp, uncoiled, slid
through a drain pipe under the highway, and was gone. No one
said a word.

Many times Rolling Thunder had "seen" animals before they
became visible. Even the little black stink bug had been where
it was needed. I had watched Rolling Thunder in dialogue with
mosquitoes, ants and now a snake. I believed that when he
needed any animal it would be waiting. Rolling Thunder had
his own understanding of these things, but I would have to
account for the facts myself. Chief Joseph of the Nez Percé once
said, "The Earth and myself are of one mind." Rolling Thunder
had said that the Earth is an organism, one body of one being.
I sensed that Rolling Thunder and the deer, snakes, bees, mosquitoes, ants and pinyon trees were one being. And if that were
so, then all of us were of this one being, including my colleagues
at the Menninger Foundation who could never accept such
questionable "rubbish." This kind of knowledge might be ad-
missible in church, depending on the church, but it is not yet
a noticeable part of mental health research or therapy.

Rolling Thunder often wondered out loud why psychiatrists failed to see the causal relationship between mental illness, air and water pollution, and the destruction of forests. Every traditional Indian could see this relationship—this man-mind-nature interaction. Perhaps that is why American Indians are still performing "impossible" agricultural and medical feats; why American Indians are still custodians of the land.

The four of us drove to the campsite and shared a meal in the sunset. I brought up the pinyon tree chaining: "Oscar Johnny says they did some chaining south of here just a few days ago." Rolling Thunder responded. "I had a feeling that was going to happen. Richard Clemmer was in the Bureau of Land Management office several times. They promised to let him know as soon as the next chaining was scheduled."

"I know," I said. "Richard got a card in the mail from the Bureau of Land Management yesterday telling him that nothing was happening but that they would keep in touch. I saw the card myself."

"They probably wrote that just as the chaining was finished," Rolling Thunder said. "They're pretty sneaky people. They know what they're doing is wrong, that's why they have to lie. They can't afford to let anybody see their destruction, not an anthropology student, a land-management student or anybody else. Of course they put out their own propaganda on it, and they probably don't want anyone to pick up any conflicting facts. Well, next time they do it, we'll be right there with 'em —and with cameras."

The following day Anne and Richard returned from a Shoshone festival in Ruby Valley and I told them what Rolling Thunder had said about the chaining. They knew the chaining had occurred because they had talked with Oscar Johnny in Ruby Valley. Richard wondered how we were to record the next episode. He doubted that the Bureau of Land Management would ever give advance warning. Another several hundred acres were sure to be attacked within the next week or two. It

was time for the first frost, the time when, for centuries, the
cones have opened on the trees and yielded their life-sustaining
food. It was the time the Bureau of Land Management usually
chose for the heaviest destruction of the forests.

On the first day of September I got my twelve-herb hay-fever
capsules from Spotted Fawn. I took two capsules three times
a day. When the capsules were gone so was my hay fever. There
has been no trace of it since. The herbs worked differently from
the drugstore chemicals I had been taking. There was none of
that fuzzy, drugged relief I experienced about ten or fifteen
minutes after taking every pill. The effect of the herbs was
gradual. On the first day I felt no effect at all. By the end of the
third day, however, all the symptoms were gone. To be safe, I
continued the dosage until my supply ran out. Spotted Fawn
asked if I wanted more capsules, but there was no need for
them.

The herb capsules were never tested under the most strenuous conditions, I'll admit. On September 3 a policeman arrived
in our camp at the crack of dawn, getting us out of bed and
claiming that he had been instructed to have us leave. He said
that with the freezing weather coming on, our site would become a pretty great fire risk. First we moved into Rolling
Thunder's house trailer, and two days later we moved into a
rooming house on Hamilton Street. I had few regrets about
breaking camp for the winter but I would have liked demon-
strating that my hay fever could never have returned, even in
the canyon. In any case, the twelve herbs, the policeman, the
climate and the dry grass around our campsite were all real
enough, but the effects of all these things upon me had to be of
my own making.

Weeks passed and we heard nothing about any chaining
projects. One day in early November, in Goshute country south
of Ely, in the scenic Weaver Creek area near Sacramento Pass,

the destruction began again and we were there with our cameras.

In mid-September I had gone with Anne and Richard to spend a few weeks back in Topeka, Kansas. While I worked at the Menninger Foundation, Anne and Richard made a trip to Hopiland and back. In October we drove back to Carlin. There were no reports of chaining while we were gone, but we knew that if more land was to be cleared this year it would have to be done soon. This was the season when, years ago, whole Shoshone clans would be out in the forests in temporary villages for the pinyon-nut harvest. We waited until the end of October, wondering whether the bulldozers and chains were at work without our knowing it. On the first of November Richard took off in his dirty white Ford to scout the state if necessary. If any chaining was being done he wanted to find it.

He was gone for several days. Anne and I began to worry. We were safe in our rooms, but the thought of Richard lost, out of gas or marooned in the hills on these freezing nights was an uncomfortable one.

"He's okay," Rolling Thunder told us. "I have a feeling he's about on to something."

Richard returned with urgent news. They were at work! Hundreds of acres, down south. The trees were going fast. We would have to hurry. Richard himself had been fine, sleeping in his car at night and spending the daylight hours searching. "I was about two hundred miles from Carlin and about to give up when I thought I heard the caterpillar tractors far away up in the hills. I drove in as close as I could and listened again. It was a chaining crew on the other side of the hill. I walked an hour through the trees and I found them. Three tractors pulling a gigantic anchor chain. Those trees are being ripped up at an incredible speed!" Richard pinpointed the area on Rolling Thunder's maps and urged that we leave as soon as possible.

Early the next morning we packed sandwiches and picked up

Rolling Thunder. The Danish woman, who had extended her visit in Carlin, joined us with her camera. There were five of us, and five cameras. Rolling Thunder had an 8mm movie camera, and he examined it several times hoping, I suppose, that he would be able to make it perform.

By the time we reached Ely, about halfway, we were hungry. Anne mentioned the food we'd packed.

"I think I'll just stop in a little place down here I know." Rolling Thunder said. "I haven't really had breakfast yet. Got up too late and left too early. I like to kind of start off with a good breakfast. Then too, you know, I have a special stomach and I have to pretty much watch what I eat, although I do know you make fine sandwiches."

We went inside with Rolling Thunder while he ordered fried eggs over easy, hash-browned potatoes, country sausage, toast, jelly and a stack of hot cakes, and asked the waitress if she could please bring him a couple of slices of raw onion and leave the coffeepot right on the table beside his cup. This was Rolling Thunder's special diet. We glanced at each other and smiled. Rolling Thunder knew what he was doing. The first thing any of us would agree on about Rolling Thunder is that he understands himself.

It was afternoon by the time Richard drove up into the hills to the point he had reached the day before. We loaded our cameras and started for the sound of the tractors. Richard thought they sounded much farther away now. We walked a long way but the sound stayed in the distance ahead. They were working away from us. We tried to increase our speed, but the going was difficult because we had to walk through felled and shattered trees. The pungent pine odors and the snapping sound of the trees being ripped from the ground reached us from the valley below. We broke into a run and soon found ourselves behind the chain, stumbling over the ripped trees, struggling to keep up and pointing our cameras like weapons.

It was an incredible scene. Pinyon trees were falling by the hundreds. Dust and debris flew into our faces, and our camera lenses had to be dusted off before every shot. The roar of the engines and the snapping and cracking of the trees made so much noise that we could not talk to each other. All we could do was to keep as close as possible to the chain and try to capture the tragedy all around us.

Suddenly the tractors stopped, and the silence was startling. We were all covered with dust, chunks of dirt and splinters of wood. When we looked back there were dead, sprawling, twisted trees as far as we could see. The huge chain had come to rest against the trunks of those trees next to go. I wondered whether in the consciousness of these trees there was a sense of bewilderment or terror. The pinyon trees were not as majestic as the redwoods, but they had grace and beauty. To the Shoshone Indians they offered more nutrition per acre than anything else, plant or animal, that could be raised in this area.

"Look at these trees," Rolling Thunder said. "Some of the elders here are over five hundred years old."

One of the tractor operators stepped down from his bulldozer and crawled over the chain. The chaining was over for the day. We talked with him for a moment and then left. Our conversation had been friendly, and the operators' curiosity about us had given us a chance to ask about their schedule. We wanted to know how many days more they would be chaining and where they would be going next.

"They were a lot nicer than I expected," someone said.

"Well, they try to be friendly," Rolling Thunder replied. "They're just working people, trying to make a living. You can't blame them too much because they don't know what they're doing. They got a contract and they're doing their job. They have no idea about the long-range implications of this destruction, no idea whatsoever. The guilt is with the Bureau of Land Management and the government. The blame belongs up there with the power and the greed."

The contractors needed two more days to clear this area, so

we planned to come back. This would mean staying overnight and buying meals. Funds were a problem. Rolling Thunder's brakeman's salary supported his family as well as his work. I had my salary from the Menninger Foundation, but I was providing my travel expenses. Anne and Richard were coming to the end of the savings set aside for Richard's thesis. Rolling Thunder remarked how absurd it was that people should have to scrape for nickels and dimes to sustain them through the effort to save trees from millionaire ranchers.

"Some of our medicine people could work on another level and probably block this chaining of the trees. But the problem would still be there, all the ignorance and all the greed, or we would fall into a great spiritual contest. It is most reasonable for us to work in a very practical way, on a human level."

We found inexpensive rooms in an old hotel in Ely. The rooms were all the same, with sagging mattresses on old iron beds; the bathroom was down the hall. After supper Rolling Thunder picked up nearly a dozen old magazines from a table in the hall and took them to his room. Anne and Richard joined me for a game of cards, sitting cross-legged on the bed. Since Rolling Thunder had retired with all the magazines, we decided we could play for at least an hour. In the middle of one of our games I began to laugh.

"I just flashed on the picture of Rolling Thunder standing up there on that hill, holding his little 8mm camera, telling that cat driver we were a camera club from way over in the city. He must have thought Rolling Thunder was the president, with feathers in his hat!"

In the morning we checked out and had breakfast, and drove back over Sacramento Pass. It was midday by the time we reached the tractors. The men stopped and offered to let someone ride to take pictures. Richard climbed on with Rolling Thunder's movie camera, but the caterpillar tractor bounced and vibrated so that Richard couldn't even hold the camera to his face, much less keep it steady. Richard asked the operator to stop. When the tractors started again we tried to follow, stopping now and again to reload and then racing to keep up. The uprooting was done in series of rows, and the caterpillars turned again and again working back and forth down the side of the hill, across a narrow valley and up the next hill. At times we stood among trees that were about to be uprooted to get shots of the approaching chain. It was dangerous business: it was difficult to keep from tripping over fallen limbs and branches or slipping in patches of snow. There were three tractors about fifty yards apart, and the drivers could not see us when we were between them. There was always the chance of getting crushed or spiked by the chain. Soon the sun started getting low and the tractors kept going around the side of a hill and down into another valley. We ran after them but soon gave up, exhausted.

Rolling Thunder gathered some Indian tea and other herbs, tied them all up into a bundle, and walked down to the foot of the hill to deposit the bundle near the road. Then he walked back up the hill to where we were resting.

"They've taken everything," he said, "killed every bit of life here—trees, Indian tea, sacred herbs, everything."

He began to walk and we followed. We were not going in the direction of the car, we were just walking. He picked up a few plants as we went along and then stopped to let us take pictures of him standing beside a felled tree whose roots reached over his head. He stood motionless by the dying tree for a few moments, then filled his pipe and lit it. The four of us stood quietly. He made a simple sacrifice and talked in a quiet way to the Great Spirit. The late evening air was crisp and chilling; the setting sun colored the clouds. The Great Spirit was in the clouds, we had been told, and also in the trees, the nuts, the Indian tea, the air in our lungs and the dirt on our faces. The meaning of Rolling Thunder's prayer was that the government of the United States was grotesque and overbearing, and that with all its dangerously powerful bureaus it was causing disharmony and destruction all over the planet by manipulation, by meddling in the affairs of the Indians, the affairs of other Americans, the affairs of Vietnamese and Cambodians, and the affairs of the pinyon trees. To him the matter was spiritual and not political. He spoke in a gentle manner. He asked that this pinyon tree chaining be seen by those who needed most to see it as a symbol of the misuse of power. He asked that the chaining be stopped, that the trees be allowed to grow again wherever they had been, and that their safe return symbolize the sovereign right of all species of all kingdoms to live in their own nature.

Then he spoke to the trees, as if he felt a need to say some words to them. I looked at him against the background of the thousands of dying trees that covered the hills behind. He had not come only to engage in a futile struggle against the destruction. He had come to be with the trees, and now his thoughts were with them. His voice became muted and I could perceive a tightness in his throat. He spoke slowly, almost stuttering.

". . . and we ask that the trees be allowed to return, to grow again in this place where they belong, and that until that day there be peace presiding over this land. We ask that the shock of this tragedy . . . that this confusion and fear . . ." His voice trailed off. He began to scan the hills on either side, but then he looked into the sky and was stone still. I could hear him breathing. This was too painful a sight for a custodian of the land.

18

Chief Frank Temoke

It was dark by the time we got back to the car. We were tired, cold and hungry.

"Now, how about stoppin' just around this bend for a minute," Rolling Thunder said. "I've got a bundle of herbs by the side of the road up here." He picked up his bundle and placed it in the back of the car. We drove all the way to Ely in silence. After a good supper and hot coffee we talked about what was to be done.

A formal protest could be made to the U.S. government on behalf of the trees and the people: Rolling Thunder, the Shoshone Nation, the Goshutes, the Paiutes and other tribes. This had been done before, but it could be done again. The petition would ask that the trees be allowed to grow on Indian treaty territory, claiming that forests were more valuable to nature

than fattening the ranchers' cattle and that cleared hills would
wash away in time and the land become useless even for grazing. The Indians could say that the pine nuts were an important
food source of native American people, who were otherwise
joining the welfare lists. Those forests provided more nutrition
per acre than the cattle, which would hardly be available to
most Indians anyway. An additional legal approach would be
for Rolling Thunder's friends, the committee people and other
U.S. citizens to make a formal protest. It could be pointed out
that if this land is "public domain," as the U.S. government
calls it, its defacement for the exclusive commercial benefit of
private ranching interests was a questionable use of taxpayers'
money.

It was obvious that protest alone would not save the trees.
There were other possibilities, such as a court injunction against
the chaining, but that would take time. The first order of business, as Rolling Thunder saw it, was to begin the process of
informing people. Few people, even in Nevada, knew about the
chaining, although nearly everyone was adversely affected by it.
Rolling Thunder felt that a meeting in Ely with local traditional
Indians and the committee people from San Francisco would
be the best beginning. The local paper would show up, and we
could get out a mailing; that would begin the information process.

Rolling Thunder hoped that eventually many white people
would help, and thus be helped themselves. This was Rolling
Thunder's way—wherever possible to enlist the support of non-
Indians in eliminating the unjust treatment of the Indian. In
turn, the white man would be helping himself where he needed
help, in learning about himself and becoming wise about the
earth and its inhabitants and how everything works together.
This kind of learning process would contain quite a few surpris-
ing lessons for white students.

We inquired about a meeting place. We were offered free use
of the Copper Room in Ely's Nevada Hotel for the following

Saturday afternoon. The manager took Rolling Thunder downstairs to have a look.

"That's going to work out fine," Rolling Thunder told us. "And they're nice people too, real fine people. Well, we'd better be starting back, I guess."

A few days later, we were prepared to visit Chief Frank Temoke on the Ruby Valley reservation. Rolling Thunder and Richard Clemmer had drafted a letter to the Secretary of the Interior which we hoped Chief Temoke would sign. The letter protested the destruction of thousands of acres of forests on Indian treaty territory and other treaty violations and injustices committed against the Western Shoshone and other tribes of Indians. It also raised the issue of the forced adoption of Indian children into non-Indian families.

Since the Council Grove lecture, I had heard Rolling Thunder speak many times about what he called "the kidnapping of Indian children." For generations the Bureau of Indian Affairs and other agencies and members of the Mormon Church and other Christian sects have been breaking up American Indian families. Under its "educational" system, the Bureau of Indian Affairs purposely assigned Indian children to boarding schools too far from home to maintain meaningful family communication, and forbade them to use their native languages and customs. Christians have looked upon the Indians as heathens and have used forced adoptions as a means to get Indian children into Christian homes. Mormons consider Indians a chosen people of Israel and take it upon themselves to arrange for their "salvation." For most Indians "salvation" means tragedy. Welfare agencies are commonly used by other groups and individuals as a convenient instrument to carry out such unilateral adoption procedings. Often without warning the county sheriff or deputy appears on the reservation to take frightened children from their shocked and protesting families. Whether the purpose is to reeducate or acculturate the children, to Anglicize, modernize or Christianize them, the forcible separation of American Indian children from their parents is kidnapping or child stealing and would be judged a crime if committed against a less helpless people. Paragraph two of the letter protested the kidnapping of Indian children.

"The chiefs are not liberal with their signatures," Rolling Thunder explained as we sat in his living room going over the paper. "That's why I want to get all this in here to get his signature on it. Temoke's signature does not come often, so when the chief does sign it means a lot."

Spotted Fawn reached the chief on the telephone and spoke to him in Shoshone. Spotted Fawn was Shoshone and related to the chief, but Rolling Thunder, a Cherokee adopted into the Shoshone tribe, had to speak to the chief in English. I wondered how this worked; I had heard the chief used very little English.

Chief Frank Temoke agreed to meet Rolling Thunder, but he was not likely to make the trip to Ely. The only way to get his signature on the petition was to go to Ruby Valley—a ride of well over one hundred miles with nearly half the distance unpaved. We started out at eight o'clock at night.

Ruby Valley looked familiar to me even in the dark. I could see lights burning in some of the houses where Rolling Thunder had found no one home that day last summer. We drove far beyond those houses before we reached the home of the chief. I had never seen this place before. It looked large and relatively modern. We drove under an archway and up a long driveway, parked in back of the house, and waited in the car while Rolling Thunder went to the door. He was inside only a moment and then came back to the car.

"Come on in. We'll have to wait a little while. Temoke's asleep, but they're going to wake him up."

That was strange. The chief knew we were coming, and it didn't seem so late that he should be asleep already. "The chief gets up awful early, you know. This is country livin' out here. Temoke's up well before the sun every day, and he works hard, you know, physical labor."

I knew the Ruby Valley reservation was dotted with land leased by white ranchers from the government with the cooperation of the Bureau of Land Management and the Bureau of Indian Affairs. Frank Temoke was a labor foreman on one of these ranches. That a chief in his own domain should have to labor for a white man seemed ominous. Yet Frank Temoke, Oscar Johnny and Rolling Thunder, who perform their labors for the system and still maintain their traditional and spiritual identities, are perhaps more fortunate than those who are less aware of their own true functions. They are certainly more fortunate than the many Indians who have been displaced from their traditional roles and excluded from all others as well.

We went in and sat down in Frank Temoke's living room. He was not yet in the room, and no one sat in the largest chair; that was obviously for the Chief. The room was large and filled with comfortable furniture. The walls, chairs and rugs were in shades of soft brown and beige. At the far end of the room a sofa and chairs were clustered around a television set. An old man, a woman and a boy were sitting in the chairs with their backs to us, watching the set. Perhaps the woman was Frank Temoke's wife, and the boy one of his sons. I recognized the old man as the chief's brother, because I had seen him on the first trip out to Ruby Valley. A most unusual kitten was playing on the floor, scurrying about under the sofas and chairs with a wadded piece of newspaper. It had a squat, square head, tiny ears, and very wide round eyes. Anne told Richard she would love to have a kitten like that.

Rolling Thunder began to tell us about a time years ago when there had been a chaining not far from this house. When winter came that year, Frank Temoke and many of the traditional Indians in the area were cold and hard-pressed to keep their houses warm enough to live in. A few of the thousands of trees that had been razed in the area and left to rot would have provided enough firewood to solve the heating problem. The chained area was close enough so that hauling a few trees would have been a manageable task. The Indian people did not get a

single tree. Some white person "in authority" warned them that
they were not authorized to take any of these trees which, dead
as they were, were government property. They were advised
they had no business in the area. In reality, Rolling Thunder
pointed out, Temoke and his people were the authorities—if
there could be authority over the forests—because the trees
were on Indian treaty land and no one had any business cutting
them down in the first place.

Frank Temoke entered from the back of the house. He
walked in and sat down in his big chair. He was dressed in
boots, well-worn jeans and a heavy-duty red shirt. His gray hair
was cut short, but his face held the Indian nose and deep-cut
culture lines typical of the wise old Indian. He had a calm and
mild bearing. He said something apologetic about having been
asleep. I realized that he could communicate in English, if he
chose to do so. Rolling Thunder made a few pleasant inquiries
and then quickly came to the point. There was no need to waste
the time of a chief with trivial conversation in a foreign language. Rolling Thunder reached into his brief case and said he
would read the paper that had been prepared for his signature.
"Guess I'm getting old," Rolling Thunder allowed, reaching
into his shirt pocket. "I've got to wear glasses for readin' like
this nowadays."

The chief gazed seriously through his own glasses and simply
said, "Me too."

Rolling Thunder arranged himself in his chair and held the
paper so that it would receive the best possible light from the
table lamp at his side. He read aloud:

Western Shoshone Nation of Indians

A Statement:
SUBJECT: Violation of Treaty and Aboriginal Rights

We, the assembled American Indians representing the Western

Shoshone and Affiliated Tribes, and individual members of those Tribes—do DECLARE—

That the present policies of the United States Government as represented by the Bureau of Indian Affairs and other Government agencies are destructive and constitute cultural and economic and human genocide to the American Indian. And furthermore that these disastrous and harmful practices should be corrected and stopped at once:

1) The legal stealing of land under the guise of buying the land through phony claims action and trickery of the Government together with lawyers and puppet Indians and government-organized so-called tribal councils which do not represent the Traditional American Indian people;

2) The kidnapping of Indian children for brainwashing into Indian schools and adoptions to white families for the same purpose;

3) The denial and the stealing of Indian water and grazing and mineral rights;

4) The denial of hunting and fishing rights even where specified by treaty;

5) The knocking down of the pinyon nut trees, destruction of Indians' Traditional food supply as well as destruction of the ecology of the land even in Treaty territory.

While Rolling Thunder read, I wondered whether the words were beyond the chief's comprehension. In fact, it appeared as though this reading were a formality. Rolling Thunder had first talked loudly, as though Temoke was hard of hearing. Now he was reading softly and too rapidly to be really clear. The chief seemed to not even try to understand, for when Rolling Thunder began to read he attended to the television set far across the room. The picture was not easy to see from where he was sitting; the program was in English and the dialogue mingled with Rolling Thunder's reading. Soon he nodded, apparently asleep. Undisturbed, Rolling Thunder read on. When Rolling Thunder stopped reading he sat looking at the paper, and for a moment no one spoke. The family at the other end of the room still watched television, we watched the cat, and Frank Temoke

appeared to be snoozing. Soon he opened his eyes and looked
at Rolling Thunder.

Rolling Thunder walked over to the other part of the room
and began talking to the chief's brother. He knelt beside his
chair. The old man took his eyes from the television and turned
to him. I could hear little of what Rolling Thunder said, and
if the chief's brother said anything, I could not hear that at all.
I did hear Rolling Thunder say, "If I hadn't been real sure
about all of 'em, well, you know I'd never have brought 'em all
out here." I guessed that he was talking about the summer when
three carloads of us made our Ruby Valley expedition.

Frank Temoke began to speak very softly. It took me a
moment to begin to understand. He was repeating, almost word
for word, some of the lines that Rolling Thunder had read him.
Rolling Thunder returned to his chair and Temoke began to say
something about some Indian woman on a reservation, someone who had had her children taken from her. He looked at
Rolling Thunder and said, "You know? Now they can talk
about too much drinking, you know? Read that again."

Rolling Thunder found the part Chief Temoke referred to
and read it again while the chief once more stared blankly at
the television set:

2) The kidnapping of Indian children for brainwashing into Indian
schools and adoptions to white families for the same purpose.

The chief looked at him again and was silent for a moment.
Then he said simply, "Scratch that." There was no discussion.

The chief listened with obvious attention while Rolling
Thunder went over other parts of the paper. At times he repeated parts of the paper Rolling Thunder had read while I had
thought he was asleep. Once he made some comment like, "Got
to stop chaining," and when Rolling Thunder mentioned a
protest clause, I was sure I heard him say "Yeah, man!" Otherwise, he sat still with an expression of agreement on his face.

I was impressed with the chief and his handling of this situation. He was concerned not only with the issues, but also with the document he was about to sign. He was interested in what it said and how it said it. Chief Temoke had managed the task of becoming as familiar with this document as if it had been his own. While Rolling Thunder had been reading, the chief, seeming to be barely conscious, had evidently listened and understood in his own language.

When Rolling Thunder apparently felt that the chief was satisfied and ready to sign, he reached into his pocket for his pen. When the chief was handed the paper he did not even glance at it. With deliberation he placed his signature where Rolling Thunder pointed and handed it back.

"We'd like you to join us for this meeting if you would like to be there," Rolling Thunder said. "It's going to be in Ely on Saturday afternoon at the Nevada Hotel." Rolling Thunder had to repeat it a few times before the chief could answer.

"No, too busy. Got to fix fence."

We left. The chief stayed in his big brown overstuffed chair as we filed past him out the door. He only nodded his head as we said goodbye and looked half asleep again. When Anne Habberton was just beside his chair he looked at her and smiled and I heard him say, "You can keep the cat." Anne looked at Richard. She wanted the cat but she declined the offer.

During the long ride back home Rolling Thunder told us the story of the recent Ruby Valley raid when he and Frank Temoke and some traditional Shoshone put on their so-called war paint and ran a group of hunters off the reservation:

"I told you about the time, didn't I, that we ran all the drunken deer hunters off the reservation land out here? That event is spoken of as the 'Ruby raid.' It might be mostly forgotten about now, but it was sure talked about when it happened three years ago. The hunters went back and told the story in the bars and it was repeated all around the towns of Elko and Ely. It even came out in the local papers. And those hunters who were run off will never forget it.

"It was the way the whole thing unfolded that made cur

people so angry, and if you can understand the way it happened
and the things that led up to it, you can understand why we did
what we did. It was only a few days before the 'raid' that a
young buck from the McDermitt reservation was convicted in
Winnemucka for shooting a deer out of season. In the first
place, our people have been guaranteed the right to hunt food
on our own land in our own way. We don't need hunting dates
and hunting permits because we don't kill for the fun of it. We
hunt and kill animals only when we need to do so to live, to
survive. But that's just another broken promise. Now they say
our rights apply only within the reservation boundaries which
they can limit or change around as they see fit. Well, our
guaranteed rights apply within the boundaries that are spelled
out on our treaties, and that does not mean the reservations. In
the second place, that young man killed a deer that had been
wounded in the hind quarters and would have died anyway, and
he wanted to use it to feed his wife and nine children. His family
was starving because he had been poisoned working for the
white man in the mines and he had been laid off without any
compensation. But he was brought into your courts and fined
a hundred dollars, which is a fortune to a man like that.

"The very next day the white hunters began coming right up
on the reservations and made their camps. They began drinking
like they always do and shooting at our people in the distance.
Even if they claim we look like deer, there is no excuse for
shooting at our people. They began killing deer and throwing
the carcasses in the dump, because they're only interested in
contests that give prizes for the biggest trophies. After what
happened we couldn't take it any more, so Oscar Johnny began
leading scouting parties to keep an eye on the drunken hunters.
One group of whites made their camp right inside the house of
one of our Indians. Frank Temoke went down there to tell those
people that they were trespassing upon an Indian reservation.
But they laughed at him and began horsing around, insulting
him and trying to make him drink some of their whiskey.

Temoke is a good and quiet man but he got angry inside. I was there when he came back and told what had happened and I could see how he felt.

"I asked him if he wanted them off the reservation and he said, 'I want them off.' So the word went out to all our people, and you might have some idea by now about how these things are done. These people have no telephones and many of them live a long, long ways away, but they came. You might ask how many there were, but we don't say. We know, but we don't say. I can tell you there were a great many and most of them remained unseen in the hills. There were enough people for whatever had to be done. Even Oscar Johnny's little niece was there. I objected to some of these people at first, but I was overruled, so I agreed.

"We didn't take matters into our own hands because we wanted to. We had contacted the sheriff's office, the Bureau of Indian Affairs, and the Department of Fish and Game. They all tried to give us the impression they were looking into the matter and finding that nothing could legally be done. The sheriff's office suggested we might all make a hundred-and-forty-mile trip to an office where we could sign a complaint. If a white man ever called from a reservation to say he was being mistreated by an Indian, the law was always out there in no time, so we knew we were being given the run-around.

"Chief Temoke gave the word for us to move on the white camps at one minute after sunset. We took them by surprise. There was no violence—not that time, anyway—the surprise was enough. Our young men were on horseback and they were painted and wore feathers. We approached a group of whites and they all stood paralyzed like statues. Temoke and I walked right up to them with a guard on each side. Our young warriors were behind us. Their guns were loaded and the safeties were off, but they were pointed into the air.

"We stood watching these men for what seemed like ten or fifteen minutes, and I stared hard into their faces. They could neither move nor speak. Then one of the men started stammering. It was real soft. 'Jesus Christ,' he was saying. 'Jesus Christ, oh, Jesus Christ.' He was either cussin' or prayin', I don't know which. Then I saw something I had never seen before or since. The man right next to me, his mouth started moving. His throat, his lips, his tongue, everything was working just like he was talking, and not a sound came out. It was the strangest thing I ever saw, this guy's mouth moving and no sound coming out, not even a whisper. But then a third man spoke up. He was shaken, but his voice was halfway normal. 'I'm a deputy sheriff,' he said. Then he made a mistake. He made a move for his hip and our men lowered their sights upon him.

" 'Don't you move!' I shouted, and he stopped still. 'Don't you make a move, not even a twitch, or you're done.' He was really scared now and he whimpered something about his deputy sheriff's card. I guess he thought that would save him. 'Okay,' I told him, 'I'll look at it if you want me to, but it doesn't mean a thing.' He said he knew it but he wanted to show it to me. Our braves held aim on the man; I told him to turn sideways and move one hand to his pocket very, very slowly. So he turned sideways and slowly took out his wallet while our men watched him through their sights. Then he showed me the deputy sheriff's card he carried and I reminded him again that it didn't mean a thing, that he was on a reservation.

" 'I know,' he said, 'I know. I was just wondering, where are the boundaries of the reservation?'

"I told him he could just go on wondering about that. 'There's only one thing you need to know,' and I pointed to a little dirt road way off down the hill. 'You see that road in the distance? Well, if you can get across that road, you and all these drunken hunters'—although they somehow seemed to sober up all of a sudden—'if you can get across that road, you'll be off the reservation and you'll be safe. But the only way that's going to happen is if you make it across the road in fifteen minutes.' So they stood there paralyzed, looking at the road way off in the distance. I watched them for a moment and I told them that the fifteen minutes had started when I had spoken about it. Then I shouted *'Move!'*

"You should have seen them. They scurried so fast you wouldn't believe it. Within fifteen minutes every single drunken trophy hunter was off the reservation. And they have never been back."

We drove awhile in silence. Then, as if he sensed that we had more questions to ask about this night's events, Rolling Thunder spoke again.

"I know why Temoke had that kidnapping part taken out. The chief is against drinking—strongly against alcohol of any sort. If an Indian parent drinks even a small percentage of what a common white man drinks, they can use that as an excuse to take his children away. Alcohol has been used as a kind of weapon against our people since way back in the beginning, and it's used today to maintain this concept of Indian incompetence. I know the chief is sensitive to the way this works. This image has been successfully projected onto our people, and the stronger the image becomes the greater the problem becomes, because every problem of an individual or a society always conforms to an image that has been established. The chief thinks the traditionals should never even touch a drink because he thinks that's the only way to beat that image, and maybe now we will, because the new young people—Indians and non-Indians—are able to resist the old images.

"What Temoke thinks is that if we bring up this kidnapping business again now, we'll just be providing the chance for the other side to reinforce this incompetence image. He knows about some pretty sad cases that have happened lately. It's a tough problem. The forced adoption of our people is wrong and we should be able to object to it, but we'll have to wait until we're strong enough to show up their lies and false images."

I had wondered why Rolling Thunder had agreed so readily to strike the kidnapping clause. Now I believed I understood.

I knew from the stories how deer hunters had related to this chief and I thought I could guess how the ranch owners related to him; but I believed Rolling Thunder related to him as a medicine man relates to a chief. I believed they both needed a great deal of strength, sensitivity and steadfastness to be who they were.

19

Rolling Thunder's Medicine from Bolinas to Virginia Beach

Richard Clemmer had three prayer feathers to deliver to Rolling Thunder from an old man down in Hopiland. Richard told me about the three feathers as we were driving from Topeka, Kansas, back out to Carlin in October. I had taken Richard and Anne to visit the Menninger Foundation, and while I took care of business there, they had made a side trip to the Black Mesa area to visit an old Hopi Indian friend they had not seen for two years. The old man, an important elder involved in current Hopi struggles, was dying of cancer and he did not want to die just now. So he prepared these feathers for Richard to carry back to Rolling Thunder, the well-known Cherokee medicine man who lived in Nevada. With these feathers Rolling Thunder could look into the nature and circumstances of the old man's condition, and should he decide to make the trip to Hopiland, he would have a safe journey.

It was early evening when we reached Carlin. The October sun had already fallen behind the distant hills where we had spent the summer. We settled in and put together an evening meal. When we finished we thought about going to Rolling Thunder's house. The three feathers had the first priority, we decided, and Richard went alone to deliver them.

He was gone for a long time. I knew Rolling Thunder was home, but I also knew no one rushed a subject with a medicine man. There is always waiting to be done. We began the process of reestablishing our Carlin headquarters, but there was the question of how much to unpack. If Rolling Thunder should agree to make the trip to Hopiland, we hoped the trip would be soon and that we could go with him.

Richard returned from Rolling Thunder's house with no answers. Rolling Thunder would take the traditional three days to look into the matter. We decided to unpack and make no plans for a trip to Hopiland. Richard felt that all was not well at Rolling Thunder's. Nothing had been specifically mentioned, but Richard thought the energy and good cheer that were usually a part of the place were missing.

The following day Anne and Richard and I went to Rolling Thunder's house and spent most of the morning playing with the dogs. There was no sign of life inside. Richard's dog, Turtle, was tied on a rope because dogs caught running loose in Carlin were impounded by police. Turtle's one surviving son, Garnet, was too small to go far, so he was allowed to run free. One of Rolling Thunder's largest dogs, who had lived with us at camp, was back on his rope and having a hard time readjusting to the confinement. Matuse, the beautiful German shepherd, spent his days on a long chain that reached to the door of Rolling Thunder's private house. At night, when he was not inside, he slept under the house trailer. Rolling Thunder's own philosophy did not provide for keeping animals so confined, but he had been fined several times. Only Brandy, the Saint Bernard, could be trusted not to wander.

Rolling Thunder needed his dogs. He, his family and his property had been subject to various kinds of mischief and hostility. Those who came to snoop or to steal were merely annoying, but those who came to damage the houses or the cars were potentially dangerous. Sometimes lug bolts on the cars were loosened or wiring systems tampered with. On one occasion when Rolling Thunder was about to leave on a trip he found that his steering column had been sawed. Only his consistent intuition had saved him from disaster.

Spotted Fawn came out of the house while we were with the dogs. She told us that Rolling Thunder was awake and that he would probably rest all day. But soon Rolling Thunder came out of his place and walked across the road to the main house. He gave his usual warm greeting as he passed. We all went inside for some talk and Spotted Fawn's good coffee. A strange gray statue, perhaps a yard high, was standing just under the outstretched wings of Rolling Thunder's huge stuffed eagle in the living room. It looked like an Oriental image, a Hindu figure, perhaps a Bodhisattva, but it was capped with an American Indian headdress of painted feathers. None of us asked about it. While we sat in the chairs in the center of the living room, the statue was against the wall behind us. Rolling Thunder began telling a story of an encounter with a black magician that had occurred while we were back in Topeka. Saying something about the tools of magic, he nodded toward the strange gray statue.

Members of the Grateful Dead rock group, past and present, were Rolling Thunder's friends. He called them "the whole Grateful Dead family." The group maintained a sort of headquarters in San Rafael and many of the "family" lived on a ranch in Novato. Just before we left for Topeka Rolling Thunder got a telegram from the Grateful Dead. "I'll get out there as soon as I can get away," he said when the telegram came: "Seems they've got some kind of problem, but I can't take off just like that."

A second telegram came two weeks later and he left immediately. "I had a feeling I was really needed," he said, "so I decided to show up.

"There was no one there when I got there, the place was abandoned. I didn't know what was going on. Even the growing things were beginning to die." He said he had searched the house and grounds trying to find some clue. The more he looked around, the more he sensed some strange presence. "Well, when I'm in need of help, or when I really need an answer, I sit down and light my pipe and have a smoke and my answer eventually comes to me." Alone in the ranch house he sat on the floor in the corner of a room and lit his pipe, prepared to stay for hours until he learned what had befallen his friends. The answer came sooner than expected. A young white man dressed in a black jacket flung open the door and stomped into the room. He appeared angry and confused. Then he saw Rolling Thunder sitting in the corner smoking his pipe. Suddenly, when he saw the Indian with the feather and the pipe, he became enraged! He shouted at Rolling Thunder and called him names for interfering with his work. He sat down on the floor next to Rolling Thunder and shouted on and on. He claimed he was powerful and dangerous, and he tried first to make Rolling Thunder afraid and then to make him angry.

"I just sat there and looked at him," Rolling Thunder told us. "I sat there and puffed my pipe and watched him have a fit. I learned everything I wanted to know. Well, it was true that he was a powerful young guy. By that I mean he had learned how to misuse power and he was willing to do it. He could only use his power to cause trouble. That was the nature of the helpers who associated with him. He had gone to South America and trained with a sorcerer and acquired his powers. He used money for that purpose and he wanted to get money as a result of it; but what he was really after was glamour. He wanted glory and he wanted fame. When he couldn't get them, he caused trouble. Everyone became sick, the whole place became sick. That was the way I found things there. Of course now this guy was against me."

In his anger, the young man revealed himself, and the angrier he became, the more he revealed. He soon understood who Rolling Thunder was and why he was there, and what followed Rolling Thunder called a contest of wills. The man was not without means: his hostility was powerful, his will strong, and he carried with him the implements he had learned to use in South America. While he tried to destroy Rolling Thunder with his wrath, Rolling Thunder directed his will against the man's purpose and the instruments of his power. It was an intense and exhausting struggle that had to last until one was defeated. There was a time, Rolling Thunder told us, when he shunned such confrontations. Challenges like this one that were so direct and so decisive, so full of fear, anger and hostility, seemed best to be avoided. Now he had the competence and confidence of many years of medicine. He had learned the secret of the struggle and could remain above the contest. The man's powers did not touch him. The fear, the anger and the hostility did not affect him. Like a tuning fork that vibrates sympathetically, or an ear that responds to external sounds with vibrations of its own, the mind hears and responds with its own nature. Rolling Thunder did not receive the man's anger and hostility, because he didn't have these things within himself.

"The man is no longer a black magician," Rolling Thunder said. "His powers are gone. He was doing no good with them, not even for himself. And his medicine pouch is at the bottom of the river. That happened while we were sitting in that room. When the man came in I saw he had dark clothes and a dark atmosphere about him and he had a medicine pouch on his belt. But right in the middle of his big contest his medicine pouch disappeared. Then he pretty much knew he'd had it." Rolling Thunder grinned slightly and then feigned bewilderment. "Isn't that funny? I was only sitting there, listening to the man's abuse, and his medicine pouch simply disappeared and somehow ended up over in the river that runs near the ranch house. That medicine pouch lies on the bottom of the river. Well, those things can be done. It's there today—anybody can see it—and that's where it's going to stay. I relieved him of his other instruments, too." He made another quick gesture toward the statue. "His tools of magic—I liberated these things."

Earlier that summer at one of our campfires in the canyon Rolling Thunder had told me an interesting story from the past which reminded me now of the extraordinary encounter with the "black magician's" medicine pouch.

"In the old days," he had said, "things happened all the time that would be pretty strange to see today. Our grandfathers used to tell of big gatherings—council meetings and festivals— when they were kids when chiefs and medicine men would get together and play around a bit. Of course, I've always said the powers are not to be misused—they're not for personal use or for show—but long ago when there wasn't the competition and confusion that there is today, the old chiefs and medicine men used to have a little fun just among themselves.

"Some old chief, for example, might take a stick or something and throw it over into a bush and then he'd bet the others they weren't sharp enough to see which bush it had landed in. Of course someone would go look and it would be gone, or way over in some other bush. He'd keep throwing things into the bushes and no one would find them. He'd be moving them, see? And then some old medicine man would come up and play dumb. He'd say he figured he had pretty sharp eyes, and the chief would throw a stone way off in some bush. It would land somewhere in the distance and then right away he'd move it from that spot. The old man would run out there while all the others laughed; but the old man would be moving the stone as he ran, right back to where it landed. Then he'd come back with the stone and all the sticks and everything that had been thrown into the bushes, exclaiming they'd all landed in the same spot, and everyone would roll with laughter. Of course it was all kind of a game they were putting on, kind of like keeping in shape."

Rolling Thunder had said all he was going to say about the young "sorcerer." Spotted Fawn brought me another cup of coffee.

"Have you ever heard of Bolinas?" Rolling Thunder began again. "A beautiful little place up north of San Francisco. I've often dreamed about that place. On this last trip I found it. Of course, I didn't know the name of the place until I got there, didn't even have any idea where it was." He interrupted himself suddenly and walked out of the room. Three cats jumped up into his chair and made themselves comfortable. When he came back the cats scampered away. "This is the place," he said, handing me some picture postcards: "This is Bolinas. Pretty as a picture, exactly as I had dreamed it. I knew the place at first sight, knew it was the place I'd been waiting to get to. Funny thing too, the people I met there had been waiting for me."

We looked at the postcards while Rolling Thunder told us about what had happened at Bolinas. When he finished with the "black magician," Rolling Thunder figured his work with the Grateful Dead was done, and he decided to leave. As he started out, he was struck with the idea that a certain place he had often dreamed about was not far away.

"I knew the only way to find that place was to go there, and I knew that in order to get there I'd have to find the place. So I sort of followed my antenna and drove along winding roads through the Marin hills. I might not have gone the most direct route, but I got there."

The small town of Bolinas is on a tiny finger of land that juts out into the Pacific and points south down the coast toward San Francisco. From the roads that run through the wooded hills you can look out over the blue water and see the Audubon Canyon Ranch across the Bolinas Lagoon. Multitudes of birds come here to rest and feed, and American egrets and great blue herons make their homes. By night from these hills you can see the distant glow of the city lights. Children with long hair run barefooted in the streets between the beach and the hills, spontaneous and carefree as the many dogs at their heels. Rolling Thunder "recognized" this place. He knew that in the old days medicine men had come here to find herbal medicines with special powers that grew nowhere else. This was one of the "energy centers" of the body of the Earth.

"I asked the first person I saw what the name of this place was, and he told me I was in Bolinas. Well, I walked around and talked to a few people, and then I met some doctors who operate a little medical clinic there. It's no ordinary clinic, and they are no ordinary doctors. Well, they're regular M.D.'s with all the establishment credentials, but they know a lot more." It was because of this, Rolling Thunder explained, that these doctors were able to recognize a case of possession when they saw one.

A young lady they had treated had been behaving in a very unpredictable and puzzling manner for some time, and finally succeeded in hanging herself. One of the doctors found her and tried in vain to revive her with mouth-to-mouth resuscitation. When the doctor who had attempted the resuscitation assumed her strange expression and began at once to display the same puzzling behavior, the doctors were willing to hypothesize that the young lady had been possessed and that the doctor had acquired her entity.

"This was another case of my bein' where I was needed," Rolling Thunder said. "They were doing what I guess you people would call praying for help when I showed up. I watched them at work in the clinic for quite a while and I was pretty impressed with what they were doing and the way they were doing it. So I told them who I was and they knew I was the one they were waiting for. They told me the story about the girl who was possessed and hung herself, and they told me how the man who had tried to revive her had changed completely—his face, his speech, everything. His wife was sure there was another being in her husband's body. This had gone on for a couple weeks." The doctor's wife and children were frightened, the whole town was alarmed, and the other doctors were uncertain what to do—especially if their theory was correct. "They asked me if I would do something for this sick doctor, and I said, 'Well, there might be something I can do all right, but if I'm to doctor one of your doctors you might just want to make me an official member of your staff, or an adviser or something.' Well, they thought that might be a good idea, so I'm on their staff now."

There was an American Indian ceremony for exorcism of the spirit. Rolling Thunder did not describe the details of the ritual except that it included a fire on the beach: "That was a tough job, and it took a long time. The spirit was a very strong spirit with a powerful and dominating will. The doctor's own spirit was there all the time, but the other one completely dominated. I could see both those beings—they were both there. There are many cases of two spirits occupying the same body, and often one will dominate and then the other, because they're struggling for control. Well, this other spirit didn't want to give up; it had to be forced hard, and when it left the man, you could almost hear it. He let out a scream and fell over, and then he went into a state of shock. After that the doctor was his old self."

I tried to visualize the ceremony and I wondered exactly what Rolling Thunder had done. I wondered what force was used and how it was made to work. Even though I usually wanted to hear something more than what was said, I never asked him questions about the procedures of the rituals or the secrets behind them. Often when I made up my notes, I heard questions in my head, coming as though I imagined others asking them: "What is it that Rolling Thunder really does? What makes this 'medicine' work? Is it really some force or power? Or is it perhaps only placebo effect or even hypnosis?" Rolling Thunder never explained completely and he never tried to inject into my mind an understanding of him or of his knowledge. If he did lead me to understanding, he did it by providing the elements, the patterns and the inducement for me to arrive at my own explanations. Rolling Thunder had told me early on that no one can explain truth as one would explain the workings of a machine. I was beginning to feel that I was approaching some explanations of my own, but now more than before I felt the need for something more from Rolling Thunder. He watched in the silence that followed his story, and presently spoke again as if in answer to my questions.

"The human body is divided into two halves, plus and minus. Every whole thing is made of two opposite halves. Every energy body consists of two poles, positive and negative. We can control this energy just like we learn to control our physical bodies; and by controlling this energy we produce forces. We can learn to control these forces—as I chased out that spirit by directing my energy—in the right way, in the right place and at the right time. In that case I did it right through the palms of my hands.

"These two hands are connected to the poles, one side plus and one side minus. All the things that are true about electricity are at work everywhere. Even electricity is a kind of spiritual force. So in a way we could say we're working with a kind of electricity energy. You've seen me spit on the palms of my hands, and hold them up and slap them together. At least that's what it looks like to you, right? That has its own use and its own meaning, but you might say it's a kind of a helper."

He paused and looked at his open hands. His face was intent but also relaxed, almost benign. "At that moment I could lay one hand on a man and give him a dangerous jolt, and I don't mean just on the bottom level. So it's possible to do great harm.

"That young magician at the ranch—that former magician, I should say—he knew some medicine, but he used it in the wrong way. The same principles are always at work—the same techniques—and they can be used for good purposes or for bad. So there's good medicine and there's bad medicine. This idea I've found in some modern people that there's no good or bad, that it's all the same, is pure nonsense. I know what they're trying to say but they don't understand it. Where we're at here in this life, with all our problems, there's good and there's bad, and they'd better know it.

"As long as so many people accept this modern-day competition, willing to profit at the cost of others and believing it's a good thing; as long as we continue this habit of exploitation, using other people and other life, using nature in selfish, unnatural ways; as long as we have hunters in these hills drinking whiskey and killing other life for entertainment, spiritual techniques and powers are potentially dangerous. The medicine men and traditional Indians who know many things know also that many things are not to be revealed at this time.

"The establishment people think they have a pretty advanced civilization here. Well, technically maybe they've done a lot, although we know of civilizations that have gone much further in the same direction. In most respects this is a pretty backward civilization. The establishment people seem completely incapable of learning some of the basic truths.

"The most basic principle of all is that of not harming others, and that includes all people and all life and all things. It means not controlling or manipulating others, not trying to manage their affairs. It means not going off to some other land and killing people over there—not for religion or politics or military exercises or any other excuse. No being has the right to harm or control any other being. No individual or government has the right to force others to join or participate in any group or system or to force others to go to school, to church or to war. Every being has the right to live his own life in his own way.

"Every being has an identity and a purpose. To live up to his purpose, every being has the power of self-control, and that's where spiritual power begins. When some of these fundamental things are learned, the time will be right for more to be revealed and spiritual power will come again to this land."

Rolling Thunder was finished for the day, and we left him

and Spotted Fawn sitting in their chairs. I remembered a Korean expression that is commonly used when taking leave of elders: "I heard a lot of good talk." All we said was goodbye.

We didn't see Rolling Thunder or his family again for three days. Finally, on the fourth day since Richard Clemmer had delivered the message feathers, we went back to the house hoping to have some answer from Rolling Thunder about Richard's sick friend in Hopiland. When Spotted Fawn saw us in the yard she came out to tell us that Rolling Thunder had been in bed since we were last there. He was apparently exhausted. Spotted Fawn, too, had been feeling ill, but she was better now. She went across the street to Rolling Thunder's little house and went in for a few minutes. She came back to tell us that he would soon be getting up and coming to the house if we wished to wait.

"I lost one of my cats yesterday," she told us, "one of the orange ones." Among the many animals in this home were two sturdy male cats with long, shiny orange hair. They were both called Orange Julius since no one but Spotted Fawn could tell them apart. "It sure seems strange that one of them just suddenly died and the other one is perfectly okay."

When Rolling Thunder came in he looked tired, but he displayed his usual cheerful manner and he was quick to say that everyone was feeling much better.

"Did you get your coffee?" he asked me.

"Yes, thanks. I've got some right here."

"Well, I'll have me a cup. It's been a pretty heavy week around here."

Rolling Thunder sat down in his big chair and looked toward where the strange statue had stood against the opposite wall. For the first time I realized that the thing was gone. And I noticed that the house had been smoked with cedar. The house was cedar-smoked with such frequency that we had become accustomed to it. Sometimes I walked through the door and into a dense cloud of the fragrant smoke, and could barely see

Rolling Thunder across the room, heating a large can of cedar chips on the old-fashioned gas stove. Perhaps it had been done every day since we had last been here. And someone had removed that strange statue.

I concluded the statue may have played a part in all the past week's illnesses. No one had said that exactly, but Rolling Thunder had let us know that the statue was a tool of the "sorcerer." Now the thing was gone, and everyone was better. Had it somehow also been responsible for the death of the cat?

"I should never have brought the thing in here," Rolling Thunder said, glancing at me. "Well, it's gone now, and I mean gone.

"We have to watch ourselves all the time. Sometimes we're tempted to make challenges that we don't need. It's a kind of indulging. I had no need for the thing, but it was like the end of the contest for me, part of the results. Well, sometimes objects have to be doctored, and the things attached to them too; it was good that I was able to do that." As Rolling Thunder finished talking Spotted Fawn came in and sat for a while. She looked well now. Once again everything seemed right at Rolling Thunder's.

We were back at our apartment before Richard Clemmer mentioned the feathers from Hopiland. With all the time spent in the yard and waiting inside for Rolling Thunder, we'd talked well into the evening. The sky was turning gray. What Richard had wanted from Rolling Thunder was to hear what he had decided about his Hopi friend. Richard had an urgent feeling about the old man. He was disappointed not to have had some decision from Rolling Thunder.

"Well, why didn't you ask him?" Anne said. "The three days have passed. You certainly could have said something."

Richard was not sure. I could understand his feeling. In dealing with Rolling Thunder we had all learned never to feel impatient or appear pushy, but to trust his sense of "the right time for everything." Rolling Thunder would not likely have forgotten the Hopi medicine man's request.

Richard decided he would ask. He did have a certain responsibility: his friend might be wondering whether the message had been delivered. Richard also needed to know if he had to plan a trip to Hopiland. So he went back alone to talk to Rolling Thunder. A few minutes later he returned to tell us what Rolling Thunder had said. He had told Richard that his Hopi friend was involved in a very vast and complicated struggle that was taking place on many levels. The old man's cancer was only a small part of this whole struggle, and he explained that things like this needed to be seen in a wider context. It is always necessary to be aware of and consider the entire situation. It is always necessary to be cognizant of what the spirit wants. It is a mistake to think that the only way to help a sick man is to take away the illness. After Rolling Thunder said this he was silent so long that Richard quietly got up to leave.

"Anyway," Rolling Thunder said, "it's already too late. The old man is alive now, but he'll be gone before we could get there."

We learned later that the old Hopi died the following day.

At Christmas Anne, Richard and I were again at the Menninger Foundation in Topeka. At that time Charles Thomas Cayce, Edgar Cayce's grandson, who had been at the Council Grove conference in April, had invited Rolling Thunder to the Edgar Cayce Foundation in Virginia Beach, Virginia, to speak to the Association for Research and Enlightenment.

After Christmas I traveled back to Nevada alone and Rolling Thunder told me about the healing ceremony he had performed at Virginia Beach. He had asked that four people be chosen by doctors at the conference, stipulating that the patients should be persons who were under the care of doctors and who had medical problems with medical histories. Three patients were selected before the healing ceremony was scheduled. The fourth had not been decided upon. Before the ceremony Rolling Thunder announced who the fourth person would be. "I will pick the fourth one myself, and he will be first," he said.

Standing on an open hillside with many people gathered around, Rolling Thunder described the man so that he could be found in the audience. He made his own hands look gnarled and twisted and held them up in the air so everyone could see them. "His hands," he told the gathering, "look like this. He keeps them in his pockets all the time. He's not going to do anything to help you find him, so look for a man with his hands in his coat pockets."

The man was brought forward and Rolling Thunder performed his ritual. As always, he told me almost nothing of the procedure, but I had seen and heard enough of his work that I could almost see the entire scene in my mind. What Rolling Thunder did mention was the smell.

"I smelled those crippled hands and the ill forces that were holding them that way. The stench was unbelievable. It was so terrible that for a moment it almost stopped me." Rolling Thunder talked about the man and his condition. He mentioned details that were hard to believe he could know about. "Today the man is all right," he concluded. "His hands are normal. This is something that can be checked out. These were all people who had their regular doctors and medical histories, so this can be documented."

Again Rolling Thunder had ended an account in need of further explanation. How had Rolling Thunder chosen this particular man, and why? How had he known about his condition, even that he would not come forward? It was several weeks before I heard from Rolling Thunder the part of the story that answered my questions. In the context of some other conversation, Rolling Thunder mentioned the man again. He told me the story just as before, but he went on to say that during the night the man had come to the room where he was staying in Virginia Beach and awakened him. Here the story became puzzling. Rolling Thunder said that the man was persistent, almost demanding that he help him. But then he claimed that the nature of this man's personality had made it impossible for him to come forward to ask for help.

Rolling Thunder noticed my bewilderment. Then, instead of saying "the man" or simply "he," he began to say "the spirit." "The spirit was so forward and the personality so retreating, that it caused additional problems for the personality, and these problems, such as the crippled hands, only compounded themselves. The spirit became strong and demanding. Of course the spirit's purpose was to help the man."

"But it was the man's spirit, wasn't it?" I asked. "It wasn't some other being?"

"It was the spirit of the man, and so this was the spirit's problem. And it was so persistent. It came right into the room where I was sleeping. I got up and it went on and on—even followed me right into the bathroom—insisting that I agree to help. I agreed and still it went on, insisting that I promise to help."

"Then did the man himself remember it? At the healing ceremony did he remember that he had asked for help?"

"The man never knew a thing about it. The man was not aware."

Then it occurred to me that this was not merely a problem of logic, but had something basic to do with how Rolling Thunder knows what he's treating; how he knows what's wrong with the patient. Dr. Elmer Green had already thought of that question, and he had asked me: "How does Rolling Thunder diagnose?" Apparently one way was by communication with the spirit. That was not really any explanation, but then Rolling Thunder would not need any explanation. He was merely doing his medicine. Others could explain it however they wished.

During my association with Rolling Thunder I frequently met people who had been present at Council Grove or at another ceremony at which Rolling Thunder had performed a healing ritual. Many of them wondered if these healing rituals could be considered valid tests, whether the effects could be substantiated or whether some kind of placebo effect had taken place to account for the apparent improvement.

But a healing ritual is not a test at all. It is simply the helping of someone who is injured or ill.

20

Seeing More than Meets the Eye

In January 1971, I was about to wind up my work with Rolling Thunder when I went with Elmer and Alyce Green to the University of California Medical Center to hear them give a lecture about Swami Rama and Jack Schwarz. Schwarz is a naturopath who is able to demonstrate self-healing and control of pain and blood flow, and is a consultant to the Greens' research project on voluntary control of internal states at the Menninger Foundation.

After the lecture I met with Pat Shaffer, a friend of Schwarz, who was program director for the upcoming conference on healing to be held by the Association for Humanistic Psychology in San Francisco in May. Schwarz was to speak at this conference as were both Elmer and Alyce Green. Stanley Krippner, who had invited Rolling Thunder to Council Grove, had suggested that Rolling Thunder would be a valuable speaker at the conference. Pat Shaffer had written Rolling Thunder twice but had received no answer, and she thought that since I was working with him I could find out if he would be willing to speak. Rolling Thunder almost never made appointments, and I had doubts about his making a commitment four months in advance. I knew he had never spoken before such a general audience. I feared there was little I could do to help the arrangements, but I agreed to talk to him.

Later that evening I talked with Jack Schwarz over a quiet cup of coffee. Schwarz told me that my association with Rolling Thunder had just begun. He predicted that my work to date was the opening of a door and that more interesting developments were ahead. I was only mildly surprised by his "prediction," but I wondered what would happen to my project with Rolling Thunder in coming months.

A few days later I returned to Carlin, accompanied by a Japanese friend I had met in San Francisco during the summer. Tsutomu Hayashi hoped to see some Indians and get a different view of this country, so many times more vast and varied than his own.

I told Hayashi about the tribes who once lived free on this land, about the chiefs and the medicine men and the quiet villages. I related the coming of the white man, the killing of the buffalo and starvation of the people, the purposeful spreading of smallpox, the broken treaties and the broken promises. I told him about the Bureau of Indian Affairs' claims that Indian people are incapable of self-determination. I told him about forced separation of Indian families and the chaining of the pinyon trees. This information came as a surprise to him, but he believed it and was interested. Unlike many of my American friends, he felt no personal need to defend or deny these facts.

By the time it grew too dark to see even the silhouettes of the giant sage, Hayashi was fatigued from the mountains, the sun and hearing too much English; he closed his eyes. He could sleep until the brakeman came back to let us out in Carlin. Perhaps the same brakeman I had met before would be working this train.

I sat silently for the remaining two or three hours and looked at the shiny black window. I felt stimulated and I didn't need sleep, so I gazed in the window and watched reflections of the old-fashioned ceiling lights. My mind reflected on four questions that I had for Rolling Thunder.

I had settled on one of these questions just a few days before with Elmer and Alyce Green in San Francisco. On the day after the lecture I joined them at Dolly Gattozzi's home in the Berkeley hills for a pleasant afternoon of tea, cheese, cookies and organic vitamin C. Dolly Gattozzi had been keeping a bottle of natural vitamin C tablets in her refrigerator for what she claimed was a very long time. She rarely used them, yet when someone sneezed and mentioned a cold she was quick to remember the vitamin C. The bottle was soon on the table as a teatime conversation piece.

While staying with my sister in Berkeley, I had noticed that she used both ascorbic acid and natural vitamin C. My sister's theory was that the ascorbic acid was probably of some small value. I felt, however, that if ascorbic acid had any value at all, its value approached that of natural C in proportion to its price. At camp, Anne Habberton and Richard Clemmer had taken synthetic vitamins every day, and that had seemed incongruous to me, considering how "back to nature" they were about everything else—and I had told them so.

Now the topic had come up again. It was not a new subject for the Greens. Elmer Green said he was not certain that natural and synthetic vitamins were identical, even if chemically the same, because yogic theory implied certain nonchemical differences could exist, essentially a difference in molecules from organic and inorganic sources. I remembered cases the Greens had mentioned in which Jack Schwarz "looked" at people and apparently saw chemical deficiencies in them. This phenomenon, or talent, had never been tested scientifically. I wondered aloud whether Schwarz might be able to see the difference between a natural vitamin C tablet and a synthetic? And I decided to ask Rolling Thunder about this.

At lunch Elmer Green had reminded me what Jack Schwarz had said about my future and what it would mean if this were true. There had never been any structural plan or program in my relationship with Rolling Thunder. Our association had been an unregulated one, and it was probably for this reason that it had worked. Still, I was an employee of the Menninger Foundation, even though I was now covering my own expenses and voluntarily working on half salary to conserve funds. It was doubtful that this arrangement could last much longer. If I were to continue my association with Rolling Thunder I would have to go on leave. It was obviously time for me to discuss with Rolling Thunder whether we had more to do. If he had a plan I was quite willing to manage it. I would ask.

Later I told the Greens and Dolly Gattozzi about Rolling Thunder's confrontation with the young "sorcerer" and the healing rituals at Bolinas and Virginia Beach. Everyone was impressed with the involvement of doctors in these instances. Elmer Green thought it would be useful for me to talk to those doctors for validation, documentation and a follow-up of Rolling Thunder's stories, suggesting that Rolling Thunder had perhaps described the events in the hope that I would carry through with the documentation. This was something else I would ask Rolling Thunder about.

It looked like this meeting with Rolling Thunder would be more of a business meeting than a visit. I now had three important questions for him. Unfortunately, I seldom found it possible to have a discussion with him if I tried to lead the conversation. My first question was whether Rolling Thunder wanted me to continue to be around, whether he had more for me to

learn or do. Second, I wanted to remind him that he had
mentioned the possibility of documentation when he'd told me
what he had done at Bolinas and at Virginia Beach, and I
wanted to ask him whether he was thinking of this as a project
for me. The third question was whether he thought there was
a significant difference between natural and synthetic vitamins.
I had been meaning to ask him this ever since Anne and Richard and I had discussed it in camp some months ago. Now that
all of us had just been talking about this again I wanted to be
sure to ask. Alyce Green had reminded me of the fourth question for Rolling Thunder: I was to ask whether he would be
willing to speak in May at the Association for Humanistic
Psychology conference on psychic healing and self-healing.

A jog of the train reminded me that Carlin lay ahead, and
that I had to think about the order of business. I was coming
here for an additional purpose: to close out the Carlin apartment. I would wait on that until I had talked with Rolling
Thunder, as our need for the apartment hinged upon possible
future work with him.

A different brakeman walked through our car. I shook Hayashi. This brakeman looked fat and awkward and he passed back
and forth without even looking at us. I went to find him to
remind him we wanted to be let out in Carlin. He told me it was
a fair piece to Carlin. He would let me know when. There was
no big panic, he assured me, since the train would sit in Carlin
for nearly thirty minutes anyway.

When we arrived in Carlin, the air was unbelievably warm
and gentle. I had been warning Hayashi how cold it would be.
I had wanted to prepare him for the miserable walk from the
train to the apartment. I had told him that our hands would be
numbed by the freezing cold. Carlin could get colder than
Topeka—in January temperatures usually dropped below
freezing; yet it was warm here now, warmer than it had been
when we had moved down out of the canyon in the fall. The

clear, warm night, and especially the surprise of it, elated me. Hayashi seemed equally enchanted. His surprise was looking into the sky and seeing more stars than he had ever seen in Osaka.

It was a good time to go to Rolling Thunder's house. I had planned to wait until the morning, but the night was pleasant. Besides, I knew that Rolling Thunder was not expecting me, and I wanted to tell him I was here. He was more likely to be home at night than in the morning. If we left our bags at my apartment and then went directly to Rolling Thunder's house, we could call on him before ten o'clock. If it felt right, I would ask for a private meeting and arrange a time. The arrangement of the time might make it easier for me to keep our conversation businesslike.

When we reached the apartment Mrs. Elder let us in. She was happy to see me and had much to say. She seemed to think that I was coming back to stay, but it was too late to tell her I had really planned to close out the apartment and leave Carlin. That would have to wait. With some gifts for Rolling Thunder and Spotted Fawn, we walked through town to the familiar house. Rolling Thunder did not seem to be surprised to see me and he was at ease meeting Hayashi. He called into the other room and a Japanese woman came out. Her name was Yasumi and she was about Hayashi's age. She, too, was from Osaka and had gone to school with Hayashi. I had met Yasumi three months before when she was staying with some of Rolling Thunder's San Francisco friends. He said she was teaching Spotted Fawn how to prepare Japanese dishes, so Hayashi should feel at home. Yasumi could also interpret, since she spoke English rather well. Rolling Thunder seemed to think there was nothing unreasonable about this coincidence.

Spotted Fawn brought coffee and sat down with us, and I gave out the gifts I had brought. I had a copy of the *Last Whole Earth Catalog* for Rolling Thunder and the family. I gave Spotted Fawn some incense and a little idol incense burner. For

Rolling Thunder I had *kinnikinnick*, a traditional Indian smoking mixture, some other Indian herbal smoking mixtures and pure tobacco. I also gave him a handmade medicine pouch. Rolling Thunder relaxed and chatted hospitably with Hayashi. I drank my coffee and watched Spotted Fawn arranging the incense in the little idol with other items on the table. The room was quiet as I glanced at Rolling Thunder. He was looking at me.

"Now there is more," Rolling Thunder said, clearing his throat, "depending on what you mean by more. There is a lot to be done. But then, there's no way to put a time limit on it or fit a schedule to it." That answered my first question. It would be easier now to bring up my second. I could do that tonight.

"One thing we'll be doing is communicating with people. There are a lot of people who want to do something and don't know what to do, and we have to get it together. There are a lot of people ready to learn something and they don't know where it's at. This is a lot of work. Of course, the pinyon tree chaining is still an issue, and that fits into everything. But that's not all. There are a lot of doctors—medical doctors and psychiatrists, especially the young ones and the new ones—who are thinking in new ways, entirely different from the old establishment. Some of our people will be working with these people and they'll be cooperating with us. As I said before, we have knowledge and capabilities that they are going to need, and they have some abilities and techniques that we could learn about, too. I would like for you to talk to these doctors in Bolinas and Virginia Beach and get the documentation on what I told you."

He paused and squinted. I felt very strange. Perhaps it was coincidence, but it was done as if he knew these were my questions.

"If you meet these doctors you'll find them very easy to talk to. And there'll be more—more like 'em. They're not intimidated or disturbed by our medicine. They don't have a sense of competition about medicine and they don't feel threatened. It's not that they understand about Indian medicine, because these things are new to them. But they're open-minded and they think like we do in many ways. They would agree with some of the things we've always been saying. Years ago, for example, it would not have been our place to go to your people and tell them to stop using chemical preservatives and synthetic foods. We knew the time would come when your people would be concerned about and want to talk about these things." He had come to my third question. He stopped and watched. The corners of his mouth twitched slightly. Rolling Thunder was amused. I put down my coffee cup.

"I believe in natural vitamins," he said quietly. He nodded at me. He put down his pipe, lifted a kitten out of his lap, and went into the kitchen and came back carrying as many bottles as his hands could hold. "These are the vitamins that we take. These are the ones I like to recommend when I'm asked."

I felt a strange sensation along the surface of my skin, especially on my face. It was not surprise or amazement but more like appreciation. This had happened before; when I was able to participate in some communication or understanding far beyond my own capacity, I felt gratitude.

"Vitamins are life, a certain life force that can't be synthetically produced. A lot of different things might look the same under a microscope to most people, but there's more to things than meets the eye. There's going to be some way to show that difference, though, so that people can see it—like the difference between synthetic and natural vitamin C. Some instrument or some system exists, I think, that will show that, and I have a feelin' we'll find out what that is and we can use that too. I have a feelin' that's right around the corner." He sat down again and talked about the new doctors and their thinking, the cooperation and mutual endeavor that was to come about in the future. "Of course, there are many things that some of the old establishment doctors will never learn no matter how much chance

they have to learn. It might be mainly because they don't want
to, but then, that's their business. There are other people who
understand, or think they do, almost too easy. They say they
are anxious to learn and that they want to know about all these
things, but yet they don't want to do the discipline and the
purification. They don't want to do the work to prepare themselves. So there is the danger of too much being revealed too
early.

"On the other hand, I know there are many people who are
ready to learn and looking for a way, as I said before. If these
people come together to really learn, doctors and students and
workers who have a real purpose, if they are really sincere and
not just curious, then I would be willing to speak."

The meeting was over. I had nothing to say. There probably
would never be a right time to ask how he had known my
questions, and all in the order I had prepared them. There
would be more to discuss later, but I knew it would work out.
Maybe there were no questions and there never had been any.
There was only this eternal orderly arrangement, a constant
right time and right place for all things.

Hayashi and I stayed in Carlin for a week and the weather
was magnificent, crisp and fresh the entire time. One morning
Hayashi got up before sunrise and hiked to the top of the distant
hills. He had wanted to walk for hours in the silence and open
space, and to see the sun come up behind absolutely nothing but
the earth itself. He had many questions about Rolling Thunder
and we talked about medicine, Indian customs and the Bureau
of Indian Affairs. Hayashi was intensely interested, but our
speech had to be very slow and careful and each meaningful
discussion took hours. We stayed in Carlin for a week and I
arranged to keep my place with Mrs. Elder and to store my
things while I was gone. Hayashi visited with Yasumi. Rolling
Thunder and Spotted Eagle were planning to drive to San Francisco and offered us a ride back with them, but meanwhile

Rolling Thunder was away on a trip for the railroad for several days. We spent time at the house and Spotted Fawn insisted on feeding us every time we were there.

One evening Hayashi and I sat in the living room savoring the smell of supper through the kitchen door. Rolling Thunder was due back and the train was late, so he would be hungry. I spoke to Spotted Fawn in English, Hayashi talked to Yasumi in Japanese, Spotted Eagle listened to rock records in his room, and we waited. When the train pulled into the station Spotted Eagle left the music and took the Camaro up to the tracks to drive Rolling Thunder home. I wondered how the train could be heard over the sound of the loud rock music but when it came, Spotted Fawn had somehow known and shouted to Spotted Eagle.

Rolling Thunder came through the door wearing his coveralls and his railroad hat. He had his usual friendly grin and hearty greeting. He put his brakeman's lantern on the table in a deliberate manner and slowly drew his wrist across his forehead.

"Looks like maybe we've got something good waiting for us out here," he said, looking toward the kitchen and sniffing the air. Suddenly he sniffed again very loudly! Then he held his face straight up and moved his nostrils. I wondered whether something was burning. I couldn't notice any smell. Perhaps he was trying to identify every item on the menu.

He called to Spotted Fawn in the kitchen. "Who all's here?"

"Just who you see," she answered.

"Then who's been here just now? Any strangers been around?"

"Not that I know of."

He sniffed the air again. "They're outside somewhere!" He shouted at Spotted Eagle. Rolling Thunder took a handgun from a drawer and stepped out into the night with Spotted Eagle behind him. I walked to the open doorway and looked. Hayashi looked over my shoulder. Rolling Thunder sniffed

again. "I think they're out there in the shed," I heard him
whisper. He pointed to the shack behind his house across the
road. He waved his arm and Spotted Eagle moved off to the left.
The night was dark and still. There was no sound. I couldn't
see the shed across the road. Rolling Thunder had moved toward the shed and I saw his silhouette. I walked out to the road
where I could see him more clearly. He moved like a silent
shadow. Suddenly he made a bloodcurdling howl that cracked
the atmosphere. I felt an electric shock in the back of my head.
It flashed across my back and into my chest, causing me to gasp.
A sharp cracking noise came from the shed and then the sound
of boots. A figure came rushing toward me, turned suddenly
and ran across the road. My eyes became accustomed to the
darkness and I could see Spotted Eagle running off in the
distance and Rolling Thunder standing by the shed peering into
the night; I looked back toward the house and saw Hayashi still
in the doorway.

"Did you see anybody?" Rolling Thunder began walking
toward me.

"Someone ran across the road right here!" I pointed.

"I think there were three of 'em," he said. "Two of 'em ran
straight out that way." He looked in the direction where Spotted Eagle had disappeared. "Don't know who they were."

We stayed in the road until Spotted Eagle came walking
back. "I couldn't see them," he said. "I was way down here
when they took off. They were pretty far ahead."

"Well, we'll go in and have supper, and then you go see if you
can find out who they were and what they were doing here."

"I'm going to get another couple of dogs," Rolling Thunder
continued as we walked back to the house. "Big ones. And I'm
going to have to rig up a string of lights back here." He made
a wide arc with his arm. All the dogs were in the house or the
prowlers would have alerted them. The only dog that never
came inside at night was Brandy, but Brandy was dead.

Spotted Fawn had put supper on the table. As we sat down

to eat, Rolling Thunder told Hayashi what had happened to Brandy. I knew the story, at least the first part. Some time ago when he visited Berkeley Rolling Thunder had mentioned that sad news. He said someone had come in the night and dragged Brandy off. The other dogs had barked, but the family had gotten used to the barking in the night and no one looked out. Brandy was just a pup, enormous as he was, and he made friends with anyone. He had not made a sound that anyone could hear, but apparently he had not wanted to leave with his strange visitors, for the following morning Rolling Thunder examined the boardwalk and the road and decided that Brandy had been dragged along on his seat to a car across the road. Now Rolling Thunder told us that the dog's body had been found weeks later. One of Buffalo Horse's friends had seen a dead Saint Bernard out at the landing strip near the old mine. Buffalo Horse had gone out to check and found Brandy's decaying body with nearly a dozen bullet holes in it.

Rolling Thunder had told the whole story to Hayashi, as Yasumi was not here at the table to interpret.

"Do you understand?" I asked Hayashi.

"Yes."

"Do you think you really understand?" asked Rolling Thunder. He added quietly, "I don't think I understand it myself." He said nothing more and our supper was less cheerful than usual.

21

An Unseen Enemy

One day in March 1972, Rolling Thunder left the Grateful Dead's ranch house in Novato carrying a blanket, his pipe and his medicine fan, and walked into the woods. When he found a proper spot, he spread the blanket on the ground under a tree and situated himself with his medicine fan before him. He was thin and weak, and his hair had begun to gray rapidly. In the past several weeks he had been too busy to defend himself against the efforts that were being made to destroy him. He did not want contest. He did not want to engage in a struggle. He had hoped to go on with his work and be able to remain aloof from this destructive force; but he was beginning to feel tired and confused and indifferent even to his work. Now he had come to this spot with his pipe and his medicine fan to work on himself, to get himself together and to deal with his unseen enemy. He knew he had not come a moment too soon.

He planned to find some herbs and a special plant to put in his pipe, so he left his medicine fan on the blanket, and holding his pipe, walked into the bushes in front of him to search for the plants. He became disoriented and confused. In the brush under the hot sun, as far as his eyes could see, there was no sign to show where he was. Something was wrong. He began to wonder how he had reached this place and why he was here. He had forgotten where he had come here from. He vaguely remembered that he had come here to doctor himself, and he remembered that he had spread a blanket under a tree, but he could not think where the blanket was. He fought to keep conscious. He knew he must keep breathing, keep his eyes open and get back to the blanket. He must get to his medicine fan. But his thoughts were drifting and he could not hang on to them. He was too tired and too weak. He let go and then there was darkness.

A group of traditional Indian people met in San Rafael in late January to begin the work of establishing a foundation whose purpose would be to preserve the traditional culture and teachings of native Americans. There had been tribal and intertribal powwows, medicine lodges, and chiefs' and elders' council meetings even before the arrival of white men. But the people gathered in San Rafael were responding in a more modern way. They intended to meet those complicated procedural requirements that would enable them to be recognized by the white man and white law and to enjoy the legal advantage of a foundation which could be of immense value to the native people and to the land itself. The January meeting took place at the office of the Grateful Dead in San Rafael with members of the group and other non-Indian friends observing. The Grateful Dead offered to perform a benefit concert in San Francisco and donate the proceeds to this new foundation.

At this meeting also was Semu Huaute, a medicine man from

southern California who frequently traveled with young Indians from many tribes. An Indian woman whom Rolling Thunder had first met at one of his "press conferences," in Caliente, Nevada, was there with her Berkeley lawyer. In the weeks that followed, a number of meetings were held in San Rafael and San Francisco. Each time Rolling Thunder made the 650-mile trip west from Carlin, and Semu Huaute drove up from Los Angeles to attend. As the charter for the foundation began to take form, trouble arose. The Indian woman's lawyer, who had initially volunteered advice and services, had made himself the foundation's attorney and demanded what Rolling Thunder and Semu Huaute felt was an extremely high fee for his work in drawing up the charter. This lawyer's next move had been to make the woman the permanent chairperson of the foundation, certified by the charter and by-laws he was drawing up. She then set up her own office in Berkeley with funds that were to have been used for transportation and expenses of out-of-town members. Rolling Thunder and Semu both felt bewildered by this unauthorized activity, and the two medicine men began to wonder whether the woman and her lawyer might not be working against them and the aims Rolling Thunder and Semu Huaute had so long shared.

Since the woman was the only member of the original group who lived in the Bay Area, her influence had dominated from the beginning. And she had the lawyer. Rolling Thunder had wondered at the wisdom of involving these people, but he had thought it was Semu's wish, since the woman had claimed to be his friend. At the same time, Semu thought that Rolling Thunder had invited her after the press conference in Caliente. When Rolling Thunder and Semu Huaute held separate private meetings these facts finally came out.

On March 5 the Grateful Dead performed their benefit concert at Winterland in San Francisco. Rolling Thunder came to San Francisco for the concert, bringing Spotted Fawn, his sons Buffalo Horse and Spotted Eagle, and his daughter Morning

Star and her husband. The concert was a success and a considerable amount of money was raised for the foundation, but the
events that followed were difficult and dangerous. The foundation did not yet legally exist, as there had been many obstacles
to the completion of the charter, so the Grateful Dead's lawyers
proposed to hold the money until the necessary legalities had
been completed. The chairperson, however, insisted on having
possession, or at least control, of the funds. After several days
of hostility, and threats of violence and lawsuits, the money, in
the form of a check made out to the would-be foundation,
turned up in her hands in such a way that it appeared to be an
accident.

Rolling Thunder began to learn that the faction represented
by the chairperson and her lawyer were willing to use whatever
methods were at their disposal to retain control of the foundation and its funds. After the check had been deposited, Rolling
Thunder and Spotted Fawn were in the Grateful Dead's office
when someone called claiming to be one of the woman's "warriors" and boasted that the place was about to be burned and that
Rolling Thunder's life was finished. Not knowing where Rolling Thunder was, these warriors hunted him. Once or twice
they forced their way into homes where Rolling Thunder might
be staying. They sent for a young Indian witch doctor to "make
powerful medicine" to do away with Rolling Thunder. This
man came from far away and began his voodoolike activities
while the others made sure Rolling Thunder heard the details
about the medicine that was being made against him. They
wanted him to feel intimidated and afraid.

Rolling Thunder did not wish to respond. He wanted to think
of this mischief as a minor annoyance. The opposition was not
important and, he felt, not particularly intelligent. But the work
of these people and their "sorcerer" was beginning to make its
mark on him. Now he, and others around him, were becoming
weak and disorganized. Rolling Thunder often considered that
good, useful thoughts or deeds coexist with an opposing poten-

tial. He was forced to admit that this destructive will and energy represented opposing forces that had been attracted by the good work that he, Semu and the others had begun. The real object of the destructive faction had to be more than money. They had played central roles in the foundation from the beginning and there were many tactics that they could have employed to gain power without revealing themselves so soon. Now the struggle had become tremendous and the very existence of the foundation was in question.

Rolling Thunder continued to work for some sort of harmonious settlement. He hoped that the Grateful Dead's efforts would come to the good for which they were intended and that somehow the right kind of foundation could be created out of this effort. He persevered when the situation seemed to be hopelessly difficult, even when he became increasingly ill. Soon he saw the gravity of what was happening to him. He saw that this was a challenge that would have to be met on every level on which it had come. It was nearly too late.

The big dog that lived at the ranch came trotting back to the house while Spotted Fawn and others sat inside and talked. When the dog reached the door, it appeared that it had a bird in its mouth. Spotted Fawn looked closely. The "bird" was Rolling Thunder's medicine fan. She perceived the situation immediately.

Spotted Fawn had been with Rolling Thunder since the concert at Winterland, through all his efforts—first to resolve the matter of the unfinished charter, and later to trace the missing money and then through the hostile threats and the messages that medicine was being made to see to his death. She had been confident that Rolling Thunder would not be seriously harmed by the witch doctor's devices. She felt sure that if Rolling Thunder could disengage completely he would be unaffected. But recently even she could not pretend that these forces had been without effect. She had watched him weaken. Now she

knew she must find him at once. The dog led the way to the
blanket under the tree. It took only a moment's search to find
where Rolling Thunder lay unconscious.

He was carried back to the ranch house.

Rolling Thunder reached me on the telephone at Dolly Gattozzi's house in the Berkeley hills. "You know that lawyer
you've talked to me about—what's his name, the one we've
been tryin' to get together with?"

"Mel Dayley?"

"Yeah, Mel Dayley. If you could, I'd like you to arrange a
get-together now. It's urgent and I'd like to meet him right
away."

"I'll try to call him now and see what I can set up, and then
I'll call you back."

"That's all right. I'll come on into Berkeley. I can get in this
evening so you and I could meet over there. Meantime, try to
set it up with Mel Dayley for tomorrow."

By the time I saw Rolling Thunder that evening I had contacted Mel Dayley and arranged for a meeting the following
day. I had talked with Dayley many times. Twice before I had
tried to arrange for him to meet Rolling Thunder. Once when
Rolling Thunder was attending a big Indian meeting in Reno
I gave Dayley misleading instructions. He came to Reno and
waited two days for us in the wrong motel. On another occasion, when Rolling Thunder held his press conference in Caliente, Nevada, and many people were driving up from San
Francisco, I had arranged for Dayley to ride with some people
from the Committee of Concern for the Traditional Indian and
had procured a room for him. But there had been a long delay
in getting started and Daley finally hadn't been able to go along.
Now that Rolling Thunder needed Mel Dayley's help, I wished
they had first met under different circumstances, when Rolling
Thunder was in better form.

Since the benefit concert, Rolling Thunder had looked thinner, more tired than ever before, and he seemed to be gradually losing his hearing. Yet he had retained his high spirits, easy laughter and steady enthusiasm. He had been up in Marin County and we had heard nothing from him for days, and when he called me at Dolly Gattozzi's about making an appointment with Mel Dayley, I knew that things must have taken a bad turn. I expected to see him looking more discouraged than ever; but in fact he looked surprisingly better. He was still thin, but his color had returned and his manner was calm and gentle. He had that benign look that I had seen in him before.

We talked long into the night. I learned the details of how Rolling Thunder had realized the urgency of his condition and had gone into the woods to be alone, how he had been found in the brush, carried back and cared for. He then told me about the young "warriors" who had searched for him, boasting that with their Indian witch doctor they could make him sicken and die. He told how the benefit money had disappeared from the office in San Rafael, and the efforts he had made to trace it. By that time the lawyer was refusing to communicate with anyone or to answer any questions. When Rolling Thunder was well enough he planned to work "on every level." He decided, to begin with, to ask the help of Mel Dayley. Then he would call for Semu. If Semu could get away from his own work in southern California, he might spend a few days with Rolling Thunder.

After the meeting with Mel Dayley, Rolling Thunder and Spotted Fawn went with me to stay at Dolly Gattozzi's. Dolly would be away for two weeks at a seminar in Hawaii and she had offered Rolling Thunder the use of her house. It seemed the perfect place for him to be. High in the Berkeley hills, it was in a quiet setting and difficult to find. We felt it was imperative that no one know where Rolling Thunder was.

Rolling Thunder and Spotted Fawn spent much of the afternoon walking in the hills, and they came back with a variety of plants and herbs for a fresh salad in the evening.

"Maybe we'll see more raccoons tonight," I told Spotted

Fawn. "They usually come around just after midnight, sometimes four or five of them. They come right up to the door and we can feed them."

"Yeah, you oughta see 'em," Rolling Thunder agreed. "They come right up here begging, looking like little masked bandits. Pretty smart little things; they learn fast."

On the upstairs level, tall glass doors opened onto a large sun deck in the trees. The raccoons had developed the habit of coming to peer through those doors at night to wait for crackers and nuts. I had brought Rolling Thunder here before. He had watched the raccoons as they devoured the evening handout and distracted them by his watching. They would stop still and stare back at him.

"Why do animals gaze so knowingly at a person's eyes?" My sister had asked him. "Why don't they stare the same way at one's hair or ears? How do they know what eyes are for?"

"They don't know, they just feel it," Rolling Thunder said. "Some people think seeing is just light coming in, but attention is a force that's emitted through the eyes, and it can attract or repel. That's why there's that sensation, that fixation, when eyes meet eyes." We stood on the deck and looked over Berkeley to the bay, Alcatraz and the Golden Gate Bridge.

"It feels really good to be up here. This is just what I needed —to be up here above everything, in this fresh air, sort of out of reach, yet among all these trees and birds with deer and raccoons walkin' around. This is a really healthy place."

I hoped Rolling Thunder could stay for many days. He was looking rested already. "The big contest isn't over yet—I mean on a psychic level. By the way, I liked that Mel Dayley, had a good feelin' about him. Now he'll contact the other lawyer and we'll see if we can find out what's goin' on. But this money episode is secondary. I'm facing a spiritual problem, an effort to destroy us and the work of our group. So I've been thinkin' about that, and what I'm going to do is I'm going to call for Mad Bear."

22

Making Good Medicine

Mad Bear Anderson is a legendary figure in Indian medicine. I had heard much about him, and the impression I had was of a large, bearlike person, rather slow, but so powerful that his style did not matter. Only a few weeks before, Rolling Thunder had told a story that strengthened that impression. Rolling Thunder had just shown my sister's family how to purify the home with cedar smoke. In order to emphasize that it is important during the smoking to leave open at least one door or window, he told a Mad Bear story:

"Mad Bear was purifying a house for some people one time, and he made that mistake—not opening any door or window. Actually, he just forgot. Mad Bear knows a lot. They say he knows so much from so many places he can't remember it all. I don't know about that. He'll do the ritual all right but he'll always leave out some incidental thing.

"Well, there were some beings living in this house who were giving the people trouble. They weren't inhabiting the people but they were inhabiting their house and the people were having problems. Mad Bear knew what the situation was and what to do about it, so he performed the ritual; not just a simple cedar smoke thing, but a more complicated ritual.

"His medicine worked good all right, but like I said, he forgot to leave any openings anywhere in the house. Maybe it was because he was concentrating on his procedure. Well, what was in there had to get out. It looked like it was the smoke going out, but it was nothing like the way smoke usually behaves. The force went rushing up to the attic, lifting a trap door and it went right on out through the window, pushing the window out with it, frame and all! The window lay on the ground below and all the smoke was gone—and it took everything with it. It was too bad about the window, but one thing about it, it showed pretty clearly that Mad Bear's medicine was effective."

"Do you know where Mad Bear is?" I asked.

Rolling Thunder looked out over the bay for a long time without answering. It was as though he thought if he paused for a moment it might come to him. Mad Bear had a reputation as a world traveler, and as someone who sometimes just disappears.

"I don't know," he answered. "Sometimes we'll know where Mad Bear is, and sometimes we won't." Again he stared thoughtfully into space. "And sometimes he's just not around —not anywhere at all. Yet he can be reached. One medicine man reaches another in a spiritual way, in a way where there's no days or miles."

He walked all around the deck looking over the railing, surveying the ground and the sky in all directions. He looked up at the hills to the east and over the city and the water to the west, then he looked up into a nearby tree and watched the birds. He went back inside so quickly and quietly that I was left standing alone on the deck still watching the birds. I thought about Mad Bear. Perhaps Rolling Thunder had gone downstairs to smoke his pipe. "When I want to reach some-one," Rolling Thunder had often said, "I sit down and light my pipe." I looked out beyond the railing in all directions as Rolling Thunder had done and wondered whether the smoke from his pipe could reach farther than my eyes could see.

Mel Dayley telephoned the following afternoon. He was one of the few people who knew where Rolling Thunder was. He had been in touch with the lawyer and they had agreed to meet for a hearing with all the parties concerned, and the meeting had been set for a week hence in the Alameda County court-house south of Berkeley.

A few hours later there was a telephone call for Rolling Thunder. I had never heard this voice before, and it startled me. I feared it was a ploy to find out if Rolling Thunder was staying at this address. I hesitated. I wanted to think of a polite way to find out about the caller without either lying or revealing anything.

"He's asleep," I slipped. It was not what I had wanted to say.

"Maybe he'll be awake now," the voice said very quietly. "This is Mad Bear."

Semu Huaute called Rolling Thunder from Los Angeles the day before the hearing in Alameda. "They'll all be arriving together," Rolling Thunder reported. "Semu, Mad Bear and some of Semu's people. They're coming up from L.A., so if they leave about now they should get here early this evening. Well, we'll have a little powwow up here tonight. And we might have a medicine ceremony, too. Your sister should be told about it in case they would like to attend, and I think it would be all right for Mel Dayley, too, if he would like to see the ceremony. Yeah, you can tell Mel Dayley that he's welcome to be with us."

Rolling Thunder's son, Buffalo Horse, arrived in the after-noon. He had been in the Bay Area since before the first meeting in San Rafael, and he had done a great deal of the foot and head work involved in the communication and arrangements for the concert.

"Now when they get in here," Rolling Thunder said to Buffalo Horse, "that is, somewhere here in Berkeley, they're going to call to let us know where they're at. Then you'll have to go down the hill and lead 'em up here, because they'd never find it. And I hope they make it up here all right in that VW van."

We shopped that afternoon. Rolling Thunder expected a real crowd for the next few days. "Now Semu will have some of his people who are always with him, and of course Mad Bear will be here. Then there's Mel and some of the committee people and other friends who'll probably be around, and there's six of us here right now." I thought for a moment. There would be a crowd of nearly two dozen people in the small house.

"I don't think we'll have anything to worry about," Rolling Thunder said. "There'll be a lot of people and a lot of confusion and it might get kind of heavy, but it'll be okay. Spotted Fawn will be seeing to the cooking and the care of the house, and it'll all work out fine."

When we returned from shopping we discussed the midnight ceremony. It would have to be in a suitable out-of-doors place where many people could gather. "We'll have to have a fire. It can be just a small one, but we'll have to have a fire, as you know. Where do you think that might be all right?"

I knew of a place on top of the hill where some friends once held an outdoor wedding. It would be possible to get all the way up there by car. There was a large clearing and a wide panoramic view of cities, bridges and bay. I went out to the woodpile and filled a few boxes with the smallest logs and sticks.

Rolling Thunder stood on the deck and leaned on the railing, puffing on his pipe. "This'll be a good place for them up here. It's a natural and healthy place and they'll like it. Mad Bear was in L.A. when he called me; said he'd make sure he got up here, and Semu too. He'd been thinkin' about going to Washington, D.C.—he's from back that way, you know, from the Iroquois Nation. He belongs to the Tuscarora tribe—someone from the White House sent him a request to look over some of those moon rocks, but he hasn't answered yet. The government's shook up about some of those rocks they brought back from the moon because they're increasing in size and they've got no explanation. They've got them on display in a museum and they're growin' just like living things. They're like a lot of sick people who wouldn't think of talking to a medicine man until they're almost dead, and then they'll try anything. The government's worked hard to put down the Indian culture and especially the medicine man, but there's been many a time they've been worried enough to call for help. Mad Bear also talked about the L.A. earthquake coming up in April. That's something I've been thinking about, too. We don't like to put dates on things or make them sound too definite. Things can be worked out in various ways, especially when they're seen in advance. But Mad Bear was pretty accurate about the last earthquake in L.A. and he's been looking around there again; he's pretty much pinpointed the time of the next one. If it's not avoided altogether and if it really happens, it'll be sometime in the first two weeks of April. That's not very long from now. Mad Bear will have something to say about that when he's here. Predictions and prophecies are just like any kind of scientific estimate. They require an understanding of all the principles involved, seeing and interpreting all the signs, and knowing what the indications are. As far as most natural things are concerned, I think the Indians understand a lot of the signs."

I finished the preparations. When the van of Indians arrived in Berkeley they telephoned, and I recognized Semu from the meeting in San Rafael. Buffalo Horse led them up the hairpin road, and soon the house was full.

Semu had brought his entourage. He is a spiritual leader and young Indians from many tribes follow him everywhere and call him grandfather.

Mad Bear did not at all match my image of him. I had never seen anyone quite like him before, yet it seemed very reasonable to me that there should be such a person. His name suited him, or perhaps it was the other way around. Big and round, with short black hair, he was wearing a Hawaiian-print shirt and a wide grin which clamped a tipped cigar between big teeth.

Rolling Thunder did most of the talking. He explained the difficulties with the foundation, the waylaying of the benefit money, and the threats and bad medicine that had been made against him. Semu knew about most of this, for he had been a part of it. I felt he wanted to forget the whole thing, but he was here now and intended to see it through. He just hoped the end would come quickly and simply.

Richard Oakes was here, too. I never learned how or with whom he arrived, but when I heard his name I knew he was the well-known Mohawk leader who had initially helped to inspire the Alcatraz movement. He had suggestions to make about dealing with the opposition people and their tactics. He had dealt with them before.

The upstairs sitting room was crowded. The floor was covered with people sitting cross-legged. It was impossible to move around, but this added to the camaraderie. These people were of many tribes and spoke various languages. Yet in many ways they were all like Rolling Thunder. They all thought and spoke in the same simple, undistorted manner. Apparent in every one was the same tolerant attitude and the unlimited respect for everyone that I found in Rolling Thunder. If I had never known these people before—if these had been the first Indians I had met—I would have learned two important things just by sitting with them for three or four hours that night. One thing is the gigantic difference between people, between races and ethnic groups—whatever we call them. Difference in feeling, their behavior in groups, the atmosphere they create among themselves. They seemed remarkably more group-conscious, more "as one" than any gathering of white people. The other thing is that the image of the Indian—of his nature and ways—that had been so carefully and skillfully pushed at me by my "education" is about as far from the truth about these people as it is possible to get.

There was no medicine ceremony that night. The moon

phase was not right for a ceremony and Mad Bear thought a
ritual at sunrise would be more appropriate. So the talking went
on past midnight and then stopped when everyone seemed to
realize at the same time that if we were to be ready on the hill
with a fire at the proper time, we would have to be up an hour
before sunrise.

I slept on the floor in the kitchen under a big antique wall
clock that ticked loudly and chimed every hour.

With the three medicine men we left the house in four carloads and in the morning dark drove up the rutted, twisted road
to the top of the hill. The fire was made ready; then we stood
around it in a wide half-circle that opened to the east and waited
for the sunrise. At the proper moment Mad Bear gave three
piercing calls and his ritual began. It was an elaborate one;
objects and substances I could not identify were either put into
the fire or placed beside it and moved about on the ground and
taken up again. I could follow neither the words nor the actions.
Mad Bear spoke in his own language, moving with unusual
speed and grace. His manner was unlike anything I imagined.
When the ceremony was finished, I was not sure I had seen
what had been done, but I was certain of the purpose and the
nature of the ritual. The sunrise ceremony was nonacceptance
of bad medicine. There was no need to conjure up a counter-
force, or to destroy the sorcerer or his powers. Mad Bear had
made that clear the night before. This ritual simply rejected
what had been done to destroy the group that had set out to
provide for the survival and growth of Indian ways. The evil
would return whence it came.

When Mad Bear had executed all the steps of his ritual, Semu
Huaute and Rolling Thunder stepped to the center of the circle
and in turn stood over the fire and spoke. Their voices were low.
We could not hear all they said, but they were not speaking for
our benefit. They were praying to the Great Spirit, asking for
the best possible end to all the difficulties, and for the realization

of the original purposes of the foundation.

When the ceremony was complete, Mad Bear spoke: "Now, what we have to do is to get these ashes into the hearing. Maybe someone could even get them under the woman's chair." There was discussion on the best plan for getting the ashes to the hearing and into an effective place. Then we drove back down the hill.

Spotted Fawn and Morning Star began cooking in the kitchen the moment we were back. There were so many people and so many things to eat that breakfast lasted for hours. After breakfast Semu and I watched the birds for a long while. When he began to speak about them I could see that his manner of watching was different from mine. He watched birds as I would watch people in a store or a park, seeing who they were and what they were doing. He had gotten a feeling about what sort of place this was and what sort of day it would be.

In the south the signs were different, he told me. Around Los Angeles, jays were seen where they had never been seen before, far below the boundaries of their usual habitat, and the meaning of this was specific. According to Semu Huaute, one could tell about air pollution, the human condition, levels of anxiety and hostility—even about the condition of the earth or the coming of earthquakes and floods—if one knew what to look for in the birds. He was familiar with these birds and their habits as well as with related natural phenomena. I had come to consider such a skill as Semu's truly scientific, an interpretation of complete and accurate observations in the light of countless years of accumulated data. Establishment whites would call it supernatural. How ironic that we who in a few short years have caused imbalance and turmoil among nearly all natural things should have conjured up a word like "supernatural" to label so much of the basic phenomena that we have chosen to ignore. Indians were the most natural of people, and the most supernatural people in the world might well be found among white establishment technologists who, as far as nature is concerned, know so little and still have manipulated so much.

Suddenly there were a lot of people on the sun deck. I had been looking at the birds and talking to Semu and hadn't noticed them. Semu always has at least two young braves at his side, often so still that their presence is hardly felt, but now Rolling Thunder, Mad Bear and the rest of Semu's men had joined us, too. Rolling Thunder brought out his medicine case with its paraphernalia. He opened it and took out his medicine fan and a white powdery substance. Everyone stood around in silence while Rolling Thunder administered his medicine to Mad Bear, Semu and all who came forward in turn. It happened without any apparent arrangement and without a single word. When that was done we got into the cars and drove to the Alameda County courthouse for the hearing.

The hearing room was small and crowded. The conference tables were wide and people stood squeezed up against the walls. It was difficult to move. Rolling Thunder, Semu Huaute and Mel Dayley sat at the table with the Indian woman, her lawyer and other principals. Mad Bear sat beside the woman and smiled at her so dramatically that it became necessary for her to smile in return; then he held out his hand and introduced himself to her. This seemed strange, because the woman knew Mad Bear and said so. Nevertheless, though the woman was not entirely willing, Mad Bear warmly shook her hand. Then he pushed his chair back against the wall and sat with his arms folded upon his large stomach, smiling widely at everyone who looked his way. He retained that smile through the entire proceeding. Even when many people were arguing at once and the air became tense, Mad Bear's expression remained unchanged.

In the middle of the hearing three young Indians entered. They managed to get inside and to stand among the people crowded near the door. I recognized two of them because I had seen them with the Indian woman many times. The third man was shorter than the other two and stood directly behind them so he could neither see nor be seen. He ducked his head as though he were hiding. I saw Mad Bear lean forward in his chair and peer as though he were trying to get a look at the third man. The man peeked between his companions at Mad Bear. He tried to move out of Mad Bear's line of sight, but this was impossible because he could not take his eyes off Mad Bear. He seemed compelled to keep checking whether Mad Bear could see him. Mad Bear never stopped smiling. Those who were at the table went on talking but many standing around Mad Bear and this third man were watching because the staring and dodging looked like some sort of ridiculous game. Mad Bear suddenly thrust out a hand and pointed. As if mesmerized, the man came right up to Mad Bear's finger. He was short and wore glasses. He had a tense face and nervous movements. Mad Bear grinned and shook hands in his friendly manner. At Mad Bear's touch the man jerked his hand away as though it had been burned! He stared at his palm, then shoved his way back through all the people and stood behind his two companions, rubbing his hand on his Levis and jacket.

The young man was a "sorcerer" who had come to make medicine against Rolling Thunder. But Mad Bear, with his beaming face, had caught him. When we'd discussed what should be done with the ashes from the ceremonial fire, Mad Bear had decided to carry them in his pocket. I had noticed Mad Bear put his hand into his pocket before he shook the woman's hand, and again before he shook hands with the young man. He had tried to avoid Mad Bear's handshake, and failed to do so. Later he tried to make his own contribution to the meeting. He walked up to the table and stood behind Rolling Thunder and spoke so sharply that everyone turned. His voice was hostile. Everyone watched him in awkward embarrassment —except Mad Bear, who was still beaming. It was impossible to follow exactly what the man was trying to say, but it was about how Indians should understand that Indian troubles come from association with whites. After a few bad moments he tried to become anonymous again.

The hearing lasted for hours. The woman's lawyer left before anything was settled, but we stayed on. At one point everyone but Mad Bear and the elders of the organization left the room and waited outside. When we returned to the hearing it seemed the elders had reached an agreement of some sort and were in the midst of planning another meeting to decide the distribution of the benefit money. For a time we were sure that an accord had been reached, so it was decided that the settlement should be concluded with the lawyer who had left. Mad Bear and the others drove to his office in Berkeley. At the lawyer's office, however, all the old complications returned and the situation remained where it had started. It was a strange day.

Rolling Thunder, Semu and Mad Bear met with Mel Dayley at the house that night to assess the situation. The woman and her lawyer had agreed that all hostilities would be discontinued. Then later, after agreements had been reached and plans had been made, they had changed their minds. The three medicine men agreed it had now been proved there was no hope for any conciliation. The funds were still tied up and the charter still unresolved. All the time and energy had been to little use.

If Rolling Thunder was disappointed he did not appear so, but Semu seemed despondent. He had apparently held hopes for a workable solution. He was not given to irresolution and dispute. All he wished for was to be able to forget the whole affair. He said he would like to find a way to make the hung-up money and the aborted organization disappear, to let the whole problem swallow itself as though it had never existed.

Mad Bear felt more hopeful. The good medicine had done its job. The hearing had gone rather pleasantly, he thought, unproductive though it may have been. There had been no violence or injuries and almost everyone had been reasonably polite. An honest effort had been made to work constructively with the others and now that it was clear this would not be possible, another course would have to be taken. It was decided that Mel Dayley would draw up a paper that the three medicine men would sign to clarify their position. I brought in my portable typewriter and took down Mel's dictation. Mad Bear stared at me and made some complimentary remarks about my typing. He signed the document and said he would be willing to put his name on a new charter when Rolling Thunder and Semu Huaute were ready to begin again. The events of the day meant that they were free to make a fresh start of things, he said, and if they needed his name they could use it. "You could consider me a member as long as you need me in the beginning, but I would hope it would be very temporary, you know. You understand how I cannot be tied to anything."

23

Conversation with Mad Bear

Semu and his men left in the middle of the night to return to Los Angeles. Mad Bear stayed at the house and in the morning he talked to me while he was getting his things together and while we were having breakfast. With Semu's band, the committee people, Richard Oakes and the others gone, it was quiet.

"This is a nice place you've got here," he said. "It feels good. It's real pretty up here and there's a nice view all around. Yes, it's a nice place."

"I like it here, too. I'm just staying here right now. I live and work in Topeka, Kansas."

"What kind of work do you do?"

"I work for the Menninger Foundation," I said.

"You sure type nice. Is that your typewriter you were using?"

"Yes."

"This is a healthy area here. You can sit in here and look out through these windows and see that things are well. See how the trees are standing? The color and the posture of the trees and plants, these things are good signs. You can tell a lot by the growing things and the living things, like the trees and the birds."

"That's what Semu was telling me the other day."

"Things are not so good down his way. There the trees bend down in despair, seeking the Mother. The polluted air and the gross vibrations are painful for trees and living things, painful for the earth. These conditions we are seeing are the problems of the earth, and Los Angeles is one of the problem centers now. All the signs there point to another earthquake—like the one that happened there not so long ago. There were signs then, too, and our people saw the signs and talked about the earthquake among themselves long before it happened; many of them left. If it happens again soon it will be sometime in mid-April. Maybe something can be done about it this time; there are ways to work on these things. The floods are something else. The floods will come later, up around my country, around New York and Pennsylvania, and I doubt that they will be averted. That's another problem. Our first big problems came when man began to walk around on the earth as though he owned it. Because of this we have to question whether life can continue on this planet. Now man begins to walk around on the moon as though he owns it and a new set of problems arises."

The story of Richard Oakes's near-fatal injury and his recovery in a San Francisco hospital at the hands of two medicine men was well publicized in the Bay Area when it happened in January 1970. Now Mad Bear told me the whole story.

He had been in Oklahoma with Peter Mitten, a venerable medicine man about whom I had heard many stories from Rolling Thunder, when Oakes was hit on the head with a cue stick in a San Francisco pool hall and taken unconscious to a hospital. In the time in which I had come to know Mad Bear, I had learned that he is a highly sophisticated and articulate medicine man who has traveled widely and lived and studied with Druids, Vikings, Tibetans, Hindu yogis, and aboriginal peoples in Asia and Africa. Yet when he spoke of Peter Mitten, I got the impression that his relationship to Mitten was as to "the teacher."

In Oklahoma Peter Mitten told Mad Bear that he felt someone was calling him from way out west. Someone wanted him but he did not think he would go. "I am not of that land," said Peter Mitten. "There are medicine men who work out there. Why should they call me?"

Rolling Thunder had explained that in the old days there was a medicine man for every area and that unless he were specifically asked, or were granted permission, a medicine man did not practice in another medicine man's domain.

But someone came, physically, all the way from California to Oklahoma. They had found out where Peter Mitten was and they had tried to reach him in an Indian way. When he didn't respond, they had sent a man all the way to Oklahoma to speak to him. The man told Peter Mitten they had been calling him for days.

"I know," Peter Mitten admitted.

The man explained what had happened to Richard Oakes. He was nearly dead. Richard Oakes had been in a coma for days and the doctors believed he would not live. He would have wanted a medicine man attend to him, and that was his wife's wish now. It was the only hope.

"There are others there. Why should they need me?" Peter Mitten was firm.

The situation was not only urgent, but also complicated. Richard Oakes was dying in a white man's hospital. As was the way of white establishment doctors, they would neither let "their" patient out nor let others in to try to save him, even though they themselves had little hope.

Peter Mitten went to California with Mad Bear.

They arrived at the hospital in San Francisco, and it became Mad Bear's task to conduct the negotiations. There was a great deal of talk which used up precious hours, because even though the doctors had given up all hope for Oakes they were highly reluctant to allow two medicine men to practice in their hospital. They talked to one doctor first and finally to several doctors. Many times they waited while the doctors conferred in other rooms.

"It is the request of the dying man that we should see him," Mad Bear explained. "If he were a Catholic and wanted a priest you would allow it."

"But he has been unconscious all the time and he cannot request anything, much less see anybody," was the retort.

"In that case his wife's request is as good as his own, and she has spoken for him. It is not necessary that he see us for us to do what we have to do," Mad Bear contended.

Under the circumstances, since Richard Oakes was an Indian, it was possible for the doctors to regard these two medicine men as religious personages rather than medical. It might have been easy for them to get to spend a religious moment over the bed of the dying man as the doctors watched, but what they needed was time alone and unwatched so they could perform Indian medicine. At first the doctors wanted to know beforehand exactly what the medicine men planned to do so they could object to some step in the procedure if they wished. They then insisted that they at least be allowed to watch: the patient would be in an observation room and they could watch the procedure through the window. When Mad Bear had made it clear that they would allow no observation, the physicians began to insist again that the procedure be discussed and approved beforehand. Each time the doctors left the room for their private conference they came back with a new stipulation. Each time Mad Bear refused to meet it; he insisted that they be allowed privacy with Oakes, and the doctors continually objected. Mad Bear talked and talked, and all the while Peter Mitten remained silent, still and stoic. The doctors at last agreed to allow Mad Bear and Peter Mitten to be with Richard Oakes alone and unobserved for as long as they needed if the medicine men would sign a statement taking the responsibility for whatever happened to Richard Oakes. Mad Bear was angered. He felt this was unjust.

While the doctors had been coming and going Mad Bear had been talking to a reporter from the San Francisco *Chronicle* who had been following the Richard Oakes case. The reporter was waiting because he learned the doctors believed Oakes would not survive for another twelve hours.

"You believe Oakes will die today whether we see him or not," Mad Bear protested. "How can you ask us to sign such a thing?"

Peter Mitten spoke his first words. "Be quiet and sign!" he said. "He is dying as you talk. Now we have our chance and you want to go on arguing. I'll sign the thing. What difference could it make?"

So Peter Mitten and Mad Bear signed the paper saying they would accept full responsibility for whatever happened to Richard Oakes. Immediately they were taken to the room where Oakes lay unconscious. A nurse waited outside the door in case they needed anything. Oakes was indeed dying. There was discoloration around the chest and barely a trace of life. The spirit was leaving the body. They would have to act fast. Peter Mitten told Mad Bear that they should have a pair of birds to fly about his head.

"I got a couple of birds in the room," Mad Bear told me, "and while I was doing that, Peter Mitten brought back the normal color in Oakes's chest. Then he wanted some hot water that had just been boiled, so I opened the door to ask the nurse for the water. She had a real strange look on her face. 'I thought I heard birds in there!' she said. So I just told her, 'Yeah, I opened the window,' and she said, 'Oh.' "

Richard Oakes regained consciousness. He recovered. He was here at our powwow and he looked fine.

My speculation about the strange young Indian who had come late to the hearing at the courthouse had proven correct. According to Mad Bear, he was an aspiring witch doctor with whom Mad Bear had had dealings in the past when he had gone to Alcatraz to look into the death of Richard Oakes's daughter. During the Indian occupation of Alcatraz, Oakes's little daughter died when she fell to the ground from a high stairway. Mad Bear's visit was to reconstruct what was happening there, and the meaning behind the circumstances leading to the little girl's death. Mad Bear prepared a ceremony on the island one night and everyone involved in the event was supposed to be at the fireside. That was a part of the ceremony: the entire episode was to be reenacted that night. As the ceremony proceeded Mad Bear began to see more of the people involved and their various purposes. Among the protesters were some who had come to Alcatraz to represent a different cause, and Richard Oakes was their opponent. His daughter had met a tragic death that had been intended for her father. Mad Bear could see the entire episode unravel as though it were all happening again, but there was one important character missing at the fireside reenactment. Mad Bear knew he would eventually have to appear, and eventually he did. He had been in the building at the time of the ceremony, conducting his own ritual upstairs in order to avoid Mad Bear below. His ritual failed and he was defeated. He staggered to the stairway, choking and gasping, and doubled over the railing in pain, begging to be released as he was pulled down the stairs toward the ceremonial fire. This was the same man I had seen at the hearing. Recalling how he had been drawn to Mad Bear's pointing finger, I could well imagine how he had been dragged to Mad Bear's ceremony by some force that was imperceptible to me but certainly not to him.

"Now all of those people are more or less finished," Mad Bear said. "That young guy and that woman and all her people. They will fight among themselves and they will go their separate ways. That won't be because we did it to them. All we did was to make it so that we would not receive the results of their work, and it naturally went back on them. The principle of cause and effect is at work everywhere, and somebody has to receive the results of everybody's doings. Every sentence or thought or act has an effect on somebody. If someone has a destructive thought or wish, it has to have an effect on someone. If it doesn't work on someone else, it works back on the person who created it. Of course, in the end everyone gets his own earnings and accounts for his own debts; but just like money it can go around and around and involve many people and it can get very complicated. The purpose of good medicine is to make it simple. There's no need to create any opposing destructive force; that only makes more negative energy and more results and more problems.

"If you have a sense of opposition—that is, if you feel contempt for others—you're in a perfect position to receive their contempt. The idea is to not be a receiver. You people have such anger and fear and contempt for your so-called criminals that your crime rate goes up and up. Your society has a high crime rate because it is in a perfect position to receive crime. You should be working *with* these people, not in opposition to them. The idea is to have contempt for crime, not for people. It's a mistake to think of any group or person as an opponent, because when you do, that's what the group or person will become. It's more useful to think of every other person as another *you*—to think of every individual as a representative of the universe.

"Every person is plugged into the whole works. Nobody is outside it or affects it any less than anyone else. Every person is a model of life, so the true nature of a person is the nature of life. I don't care how low you fall or how high you climb, economically or academically or anything else, you still represent the whole thing. Even the worst criminal in life imprisonment sitting in his cell—the center of him is the same seed, the seed of the whole creation."

When Mad Bear had finished breakfast and packed his things my sister and I drove him to the Greyhound bus terminal in Oakland. Along the way he surveyed the trees and grass and gave a running commentary about the state of the San Francisco Bay Area.

"You know, I was watching you when you were typing the other day," Mad Bear said to me. It was about the third time he had mentioned my typing. I wondered whether that was perhaps the first time he had seen an electric typewriter. "Where did you say you work?"

"For the Menninger Foundation in Topeka, Kansas."

"Well, you should be writing. There are things you should be writing."

24

Peyote Tea Ceremony

When I got back to Dolly Gattozzi's house I found Rolling Thunder on the sofa upstairs puffing on his pipe and looking out at the hills and the bay. Now Rolling Thunder looked his best again.

"I thought we might have another peyote tea ceremony up here tonight, right out there on the deck like the other night. That went pretty well, and it wouldn't hurt to do it again with some of the same people."

Rolling Thunder had conducted a peyote tea ceremony on the night before Mad Bear and Semu arrived. It had been done in the late evening, under the limbs of the oak tree that stretched over the deck. Rolling Thunder had decided to do this for several friends who had helped him over the past weeks. We made telephone calls to invite the people to whom Rolling

Thunder wished to make a gift of his ceremony. We had spread blankets on the deck and built a small ceremonial fire. Before the ceremony Rolling Thunder conducted a brief consultation in one of the downstairs rooms. Those who had a particular request had gone down, one at a time, to speak with him. Then we had gathered on the deck around the fire and Rolling Thunder sat across the fire facing east, as always. After the sacrifice had been made he poured from an enamel pot the peyote tea Spotted Fawn had prepared. We did not drink the liquid until Rolling Thunder finished his prayer and said something special for all those who had privately requested it downstairs. That had been a special evening, an evening of meditation with many hours of silence. It seemed a splendid idea to do it again.

We telephoned those who were to be invited to the second peyote tea ceremony and made ready the wood for the fire. This time we arranged a small brick fireplace on the deck so the fire could be larger and last longer.

When evening came, Spotted Fawn began to steep the peyote buttons in the large enamel pot. To Rolling Thunder peyote was not a drug but a sacred agent, and in our ritual it was a sort of healing agent. People were instructed to put a finger in the cup and rub the mildly bitter liquid on any troubled area of the body.

As I watched Spotted Fawn, I thought about the Potawatomi and other tribes that regularly perform peyote rites in which they eat a number of bitter peyote buttons in elaborate all-night rituals. Rolling Thunder had told us at Council Grove that he was a member of the peyote religion, and since then I had learned from him some appreciation of the rituals. He considered these affairs "serious business." "It's a purification ceremony," he had said, "like most of our ceremonies. It's not used to get high or for foolishness. It's used in a way that we want to cleanse our systems and our minds, so we can put ourselves on a higher plane of life."

Rolling Thunder, like the Potawatomi and perhaps all traditional Indians, considered the use of peyote for "spacing out" or "getting stoned" a gross misuse of the agent and a misuse of the mind. Both the agent and the mind are sacred. In Rolling Thunder's view, the meaningful use of drugs requires a state of mind that can be acquired only through practice and purification, and a great deal of careful preparation. The rituals are conducted by a chief "who directs the meeting in certain ways." Rolling Thunder said he knew that there were a couple of groups of white people now who are using peyote right, "but the great majority of them aren't using it right at all, and they might be punished for it. I've seen some of the results of punishment," he continued. "It's terrible when it kicks back on you. But peyote is good. I've seen it used for many good purposes when it is used right."

Spotted Fawn had talked to me once about peyote rituals in which she had participated, and about the drums that were heard incessantly throughout the entire night: "The drums speak. They talk to you and they help you. They keep you there. I remember times I would start to drift away, 'space out,' as they say, and the drums would say, 'Pay attention, pay attention, pay attention.' " This reminded me of the night of the purification ritual at the hot spring in Carlin when Rolling Thunder had conveyed those words to me without speaking. Rolling Thunder, like Swami Rama and perhaps all "medicine people," gives first priority to the capacity to control the attention, to maintain "one-pointedness of mind." There can be no healing, no meditation, no meaningful spiritual experience without that highest of disciplines—particularly if drugs are to be used and not be dangerously distracting or defeating.

I looked out at the little brick fireplace waiting on the deck and pictured all of us sitting around the ceremonial fire. I hoped someday we could have a real peyote ritual with a group under someone like Rolling Thunder; but I wondered how qualified I was for such an event and what further steps of preparation would be necessary. In our earlier ceremony, the weak peyote tea had had no real druglike effect on me. The only effects I felt were produced by the ritual setting, Rolling Thunder's manner and the symbolic value of the tea.

All the people came and it got late as we waited for the ceremony to begin. Rolling Thunder was downstairs and did not come up. Morning Star went down to see if he wanted to begin.

"He looks like he's asleep," she said to her mother. "I never can tell whether he's sleeping or not. If you want to say something to him you do it."

"Well, I guess he doesn't want to be disturbed," said Spotted Fawn. So we continued to wait. Spotted Fawn had to work to keep the tea warm enough without letting it steep too much.

"Rolling Thunder knows we're here," one of the guests assured the group. "I'm positive he didn't fall asleep and forget us."

Rolling Thunder finally did come, moving slowly up the stairs, looking half asleep. He gave us a dreamy half-smile and then made himself comfortable on the sofa and lit his pipe.

"Everyone's waiting," Spotted Fawn quietly suggested. Rolling Thunder seemed not to hear. He puffed on his pipe and stared through the window into the darkness for a long while. Suddenly he blinked his eyes and looked at Spotted Fawn. "Is everything ready?"

"Yes, I told you, we've all been ready and waiting. I've been trying to keep the tea—"

"Oh!" he exclaimed with an apologetic chuckle. "Well, let's get started."

The ceremonial fire was started again. We had burned much of our wood waiting, so we'd let the fire go out until Rolling Thunder was ready. Spotted Fawn and Morning Star brought out the tea and the others settled on the blankets. Rolling Thunder placed himself at the fire, arranged his sacrifice before him and lit his pipe. There was silence. We had been silent for a long time, but now the feeling was different. The ceremony

was beginning and silence was an important part of the ritual.
Rolling Thunder knelt over the fire and made the sacrifice. He
put several small pieces of fresh meat into the flames and his
words were so soft that I could not hear. He poured tea into
the cups, and then taking one, he stood up. He held it in both
hands in front of his chest and looked down into it for a while.
Then he motioned to Morning Star and she got up and stood
beside him.

"Pass these out," he said.

Morning Star reached for the cup that he was holding.

"Not yet." He looked at the cup for another moment and
then began to speak.

In the previous ceremony Rolling Thunder had passed all the
cups around without saying anything. Then he had spoken and
we had drunk together, slowly and silently, finishing at the
same time with a general sense of oneness. But this night Rolling Thunder picked up the cups one at a time, spoke the name
of one of us, and talked about the person as he looked into the
cup in his hands. Then he handed each cup to Morning Star to
be served. It was like a kind of prayer. Rolling Thunder had
much to say about people's plans and motivations and he made
reference to a variety of problems—physical, emotional,
spiritual. He said nothing demeaning or embarrassing for anyone, nothing that could be considered advice or judgment, but
what he said sounded to me like a very specific and relevant
commentary for each of us. Some of his remarks were suggestions or assurances, some were predictions. No one had conferred with him before this ceremony. He had been lying downstairs as though he were asleep. I wondered how he knew all
the things he was saying.

Rolling Thunder picked up my cup and said, "For Doug,
who lives with us in Carlin, Nevada." Briefly, that made me feel
sorry about not having been there in a long time. Rolling Thunder was speaking for me and what he said was clear, concise and
complete. He told me about my purpose and motivations and

his invocation was for the capacities and states of mind that would be most useful. He talked about the Menninger Foundation, the Research Department, about research funds and other existing problems. He mentioned the voluntary controls project, Elmer and Alyce Green, and others who were involved with this research, and he asked that those who felt bewildered or threatened by some aspects of the pursuit of knowledge be helped to be calm and reserved until they could gain a better understanding of what was being done and a more positive anticipation of the reality toward which all open-minded questioning and investigation lead.

This part of the ceremony lasted for about an hour. After the tea was gone we sat motionless and silent. Nearby four or five raccoons waited and watched. Rolling Thunder held his empty cup and stared into the fire. I wondered if Semu or Mad Bear or someone had been here, whether he would have said something for Rolling Thunder.

Later we moved inside, started a fresh fire in the fireplace and listened to Dolly's stereo LP record of uninterrupted wolf howls. Rolling Thunder had once said, "Even the hearing of the wolves can be a kind of meditation."

Around the fire we kept our silence. I began to think again about what Rolling Thunder had said in the ceremony and about how he had stayed in his room, seemingly asleep, for hours before. I had not been puzzled or surprised by what he had said for and about me, even though I later realized that he was aware of things no one could have told him. The problems, plans and purposes he had talked about were things I had never mentioned. He had said things that from a common sort of reasoning he could not possibly have known. But as he spoke, I had not wondered about this. I felt only gratitude.

25

Closing the Circle

In the last week of April 1972, I telephoned the little market in Carlin, Nevada, and left a message asking that Rolling Thunder call me in Berkeley. He had recently returned from his very long stay in the Berkeley hills that had ended with the peyote tea ceremony, and he was undoubtedly just beginning to get his busy life in order again. Nevertheless I had to ask him whether he would be willing to come back to San Francisco right away. The announcements for the Association for Humanistic Psychology conference on psychic healing and self-healing were out, and Rolling Thunder was named among the speakers. If he could get away a week early, and if he was willing to do it, there were five interviews tentatively arranged for him on San Francisco radio and television talk shows.

It would be a strenuous agenda, and though I would not have

been surprised if he had refused to do even one interview, I was hoping he would do them all. He called me after midnight the following night. He agreed. It was arranged that we would meet him at the Oakland airport in two days.

"Now, this is the schedule for the entire week," I told him. "I've typed up the dates and times of all these programs as well as the places that we have to get to, when we should arrive and whom we should meet, and this copy is for you. I have my own copy and I'll go with you to all these places, so you really don't have to give much thought to the schedule."

We were sitting in the living room in the house in the Berkeley hills. He would stay in this house again until after the conference. The Committee of Concern for the Traditional Indian had offered him the use of the committee car, and Buffalo Horse would drive.

"Now this one right here," I said, pointing to the third day on the schedule, "this one is a live radio talk show with call-in questions and it has a wide listening audience. On all the other programs you'll be alone, but you'll be sharing this one with Sister Justa Smith, so you'll be talking and answering questions together, I think. She's a Ph.D. and a Franciscan nun."

"A what?" he smiled.

"She's a doctor of biochemistry and a Catholic nun."

"Oh, okay."

Sister Justa Smith was the only other speaker who had been able to include a schedule for radio and TV interviews. I was not certain whose idea it was to have her and Rolling Thunder interviewed together. I wondered what Rolling Thunder would think of the Catholic nun and what the nun would think of the medicine man. I hoped it would be all right for both of them.

On the day Rolling Thunder was scheduled for the radio show, Buffalo Horse and I got him to San Francisco early, but Justa Smith came to the studio directly from her New York plane. She sat down in front of her microphone just as the program went on. Rolling Thunder and Justa Smith got acquainted on the air. Rolling Thunder talked about the superiority of such natural foods as pinyon nuts over commercially processed foods. Sister Justa Smith warned about dangerous preservatives and food additives. During the commercials they complimented each other: "That was good. That was important. You should say more about that."

Buffalo Horse and I went to another room to get coffee for Rolling Thunder. Sister Justa said she did not care for coffee and made it apparent she never used it.

"I thought you said she was a nun," Buffalo Horse said as soon as we were outside.

"She is."

"Then where's her outfit or her uniform or whatever you call it?"

"I don't know, but she's a nun. That's what the announcements said. Everyone's calling her 'Sister.' "

"Well, nuns drink coffee, don't they?"

"I think so, but evidently she never drinks it."

When the program was over, Sister Justa Smith called for her transportation. Rolling Thunder and Buffalo Horse and I left. On the way, Rolling Thunder said, "I would have liked to have talked to her more. She was an interesting lady."

"Well, since she's one of the speakers at the conference, we'll be meeting her again," I said.

"She's a pretty nice nun," said Buffalo Horse.

"She's a fine lady. But what I mean is, I think I'm interested in what she's doing. I had a feelin' there was something I wanted to ask her, but I didn't know what it was. What does she do, anyway?"

"I don't know completely what she does, but I heard that she is studying the effects that healers can produce on enzymes in test tubes."

"Oh. Well, we'll be meeting her again, and then I'll see what it is I wanted to find out from her."

The last interview before the conference was a live television talk show called *The Bentley Affair*. Rolling Thunder had appeared on another television interview the second night after he arrived. It was taped at a convenient time in the evening. For *The Bentley Affair* we had to be in the Channel 5 studio in San Francisco by eight-thirty in the morning. Buffalo Horse arrived with the committee car at seven-thirty and wanted to leave right away to allow plenty of time to reach San Francisco.

"Let's go," he said, "It's going to take a long time. We'll be right in the morning rush hour."

Rolling Thunder had gotten up at the last minute. We wanted to give him breakfast. It was all too fast for him, and he left the house without his tobacco. He realized that fact as we were driving through Berkeley. I saw him reach into a pocket of his sports coat, which was lying on the seat beside him, take out his pipe, and then reach into the pocket again. He picked up the coat, put his hand into another pocket and then another pocket. He stretched his legs and checked his pants pockets. Then he looked on the seat where his coat had been. Even on the floor. Suddenly he waved his arm through the air and snapped his fingers loudly.

"What's the matter?" asked Buffalo Horse.

"I forgot my pipe tobacco!" He began to go through the pockets again.

Buffalo Horse felt along the seat as he drove, behind him and on the floor under his feet. I began to look around in the back seat and Buffalo Horse even opened the glove compartment.

"It can't be in here," said Rolling Thunder. "We just came out and got in the car a few minutes ago, you know."

"I know," said Buffalo Horse, "but you've got your pipe right in your hand, so your tobacco's got to be here somewhere."

"Well, I had my pipe in my coat pocket. That's where I put it this morning."

Buffalo Horse put his hand in every pocket in his father's coat.

"Look, the tobacco's not here. It's in the bedroom in the house. I had my pipe upstairs and I put it out before I sat down to eat breakfast. I had my coat with me upstairs. I know exactly where the tobacco is, it's on that little table with the bumpy stone top. I filled my pipe and set it down right there."

"Do you want to go back?"

"We can't go back. We'd never make it."

"Maybe we can buy some in San Francisco," I said. I knew the tobacco was important. Rolling Thunder had always used his pipe for rituals and ceremonies or whenever he was in deep thought or planning. Although he did not light his pipe in the studios, he smoked a pipeful of his strong mixture before every interview. He said nothing all the way to San Francisco. It was a long, slow ride across the Bay Bridge. Buffalo Horse and I talked, but Rolling Thunder, who was usually cheery before these events, only stared silently out the window. Buffalo Horse made his way through San Francisco and we reached the station well ahead of time. We used up precious minutes looking for a parking place. Rolling Thunder still did not speak. He didn't turn his head to look for an open parking space, which was unusual for him. I could not believe he was nervous about the television program; he hadn't been nervous before. I knew he was not a habitual tobacco user, but his pipe may have been really necessary now. I wondered if he was upset about having to rush off without his tobacco. Perhaps he was just enjoying the morning? I could not see his face from the back seat, and I hoped he was all right.

I began to speak to him. "We'll get inside plenty early, I think. If we don't find a place to park you and I can go in first and meet Helen Bentley. They told me she would want to talk to you for a while before air time."

"I've got it!" snapped Rolling Thunder. "All right! I've got it right here!" He turned around in his seat and held out his hand to me. The tobacco pouch was in his hand! "I knew right where it was. It's not so hard when you know where it is." He was waving his tobacco pouch and smiling very broadly. Then he looked at me seriously. "These things can be done. When there's a need for it, it can be done."

Buffalo Horse parked in the block behind the station. Rolling Thunder was busily filling his pipe. Buffalo Horse glanced at me as if to check on my reaction to such a thing. He may have thought I would be shocked, embarrassed or laughing—thinking that I had been kidded. It was difficult for my mind to accept that Rolling Thunder had just "brought" his pouch of tobacco into the moving car from the little bedside table across the bay. Still, I did believe it. My knowledge that the tobacco had not been in the car and my knowledge of Rolling Thunder were much more certain than my knowledge that such things are impossible. I knew that Rolling Thunder would not mention this in any interview or lecture, yet I had been there and he had allowed me to see it. This could have been my chance to know how such things are done, if only Rolling Thunder would have explained it, or if only I could have asked.

The three of us went inside the studio and sat down in the waiting room. Rolling Thunder could sit and puff on his pipe until Helen Bentley sent for him. Pat Shaffer came in with her sister and another of the conference speakers. They wanted to meet Rolling Thunder. "I've heard a lot about you," Pat said, "from Doug and then from Sister Justa Smith."

Pat Shaffer mentioned that Sister Justa's luggage had been lost. She had arranged for someone to get the luggage while Sister Smith rushed from the airport to the radio station. When the person went to pick it up it was gone.

"I feel so bad about it," Pat said. "She has only the dress she is wearing. Her dress for the lecture and everything she needs is in her luggage."

Someone came for Rolling Thunder. Helen Bentley was ready now. I walked back to the studio with him, carrying some pictures we had taken of the pinyon forest chaining in case they could be used. "That's really too bad about the lady's luggage,"

Rolling Thunder said. "It will be necessary for her to have that, and it can be located. I can't concentrate on that just now, but I think after this program . . ."

Helen Bentley was standing at the end of the hall with her hand outstretched. I gave her the pictures and listened while she and Rolling Thunder talked. While they were on the air I walked quietly back and forth between the studio and the waiting room so that I could watch Rolling Thunder alternately before the cameras and on the television screen. During a commercial I walked up to his chair to hand him a paper that had names and addresses of some information sources he wanted to read on the air.

"The lady's luggage is not lost," he mumbled to me. "She may not know it yet, but it isn't lost or missing."

After the show Rolling Thunder had a long conversation with Helen Bentley while I went back to the waiting room.

"I'm afraid I missed most of Rolling Thunder just now," Pat apologized to me. "I've been on the phone almost all the while. But I've got good news! Sister Justa Smith's luggage was not lost. It's just been found at the airport. The person we sent to get it misunderstood the time and place to pick it up and only thought it was gone!"

When Rolling Thunder heard about the luggage he said, "So it was all right all the while then? Well, that's good."

As we drove back home over the bridge he filled his pipe again and was happy. The next thing would be the big lecture itself. It would be his first experience on the stage in front of such a huge crowd of strangers, but he was in great form and I knew it would go well. If I were anybody else, I thought as we rode along, I would probably be asking, "Just how did you know about Sister Justa's luggage being found?"

In the Masonic Auditorium on the morning of Saturday, May 6, 1972, Rolling Thunder spoke to a public audience of nearly three thousand people. This was part of a new beginning;

there had not been a communication like this before.

There have been Hollywood Indians, commercial Indians and Indian curio craftsmen. There have been traditional Indian speakers from many tribes who have told schoolchildren and women's groups about peace pipes, wigwams and moccasins. There have been eloquent Indian leaders and spokesmen who have presented and represented the ideologies and the needs of their people. But Rolling Thunder's was a message of brotherhood—the beginning of a oneness, a true spiritual sharing between the Indian and the non-Indian.

He had been asked to speak about his powers, the powers of Indian medicine, but he stood before the audience now to explain that the time for that has not yet arrived.

"Although there are many new people of good heart and good will who would like to shake hands with the Indian and forget all about the past, that can not be allowed to happen— not by the Indians nor by the law of karma. The time for the sharing will be right when non-Indians are prepared to meet their Indian brothers on a spiritual level. It is the task of the new friends who would like to share the wisdom and experience of their Indian brothers to bring about the conditions in which meaningful intercourse can take place.

"Our teachers tell us that it's up to the good white people to correct what the bad ones are doing. We're not supposed to do that for you. There are things that are being done by your government and we feel that there are a lot of good white people who don't know about these things. It will be up to you to do what you must do in your own way. We are told to do things in our own way. We Indians have to work in our own way, and you people, whatever it is that you know to do, you must do in your own way. We will not tell you what to do, because we ourselves do not like being told what to do.

"You do not claim to have all the knowledge—about medicine or whatever. And not all of the knowledge can be put into books. It includes all nature, all of life, and there's too much of it. I will say that we Indians do know some things the same as other people know some things, and that's why we should share. We would be better off if we could share.

"We Indians are the keepers of the land. We don't claim that we own the land, and nobody else does either. Some give themselves a paper that says they own so much land, but it does not mean anything. We do not own the land, and certainly nobody else owns it. The Great Spirit owns the land, but it was delegated to us. We are the keepers of the land. Wherever you go on this land, if there are any Indians left, any survivors at all, there will be those among the original people who know the law of life and land and air. That's our job, just like other people are delegated for other things. We are supposed to work together to make life good for all of us, all who live upon this Mother Earth. We don't make any claims or demands. We don't say that the whites should go back to Europe or anything like that. No Indian has ever said that. We say there is room for everyone, that we are supposed to live as brothers and share. That is the way it should be.

"Your people did not find a bunch of savages here. You got your Constitution from the Iroquois Nation. Some of your best medicines you got from us: turpentine, quinine, camphor, cocaine. Even the penicillin we got out of the mold of the oak log, and we had that long before you came. Much of our knowledge had to be hidden. Much of this is even written in books; but these things are not to be revealed at this time. We do not want to get into any trouble. We do not look for contests and we do not believe in competition. We flow with nature and we are guided by the Spirit—the spirit of brotherhood and sharing in all things. But until we are all in accord with the Spirit, some of these things cannot be revealed.

"Not too long ago there was an old medicine man named Patrick Sundance who was curing cancer and sugar diabetes and other things among the Mormons and other people over in Utah. He was curing a lot of people. Then the American Medical Association had him put on trial and they gave him the choice of leaving the state or going to jail. That old man was eighty-seven years old. The courtroom was full of people who wanted to testify in his behalf and they would not let one of them testify. The old man is dead now, but they managed to obtain some of the medicines that he had been using and they are still experimenting with his medicines in two universities in this country trying to discover his secret so that they can begin to cure people as they know he did.

"The law of this land says that we are all brothers, we are all sisters, and we are all supposed to share. There will come a time, I am sure, when we can all share our knowledge. And that time will be much sooner when you change some of the stupid laws that have repressed my people—like the stupid law that says a man cannot practice his own medicine in his own country—and help to put things back in their proper order. These are your laws, not ours. We did not make such laws. We have a different law: we recognize one sovereign only, and that's the Great Spirit. Some people say, 'I am not like that, I am different, why can't you do something for me?' Well, think about that. Think about where you are at and then begin to do something to make it better for everyone."

Rolling Thunder had often talked to me about karma. The American Indians, like the East Indians, have been talking about karma for centuries. There may well be a word for karma in many of the tribal languages of the American Indians. Now that the new Americans have begun to use the Sanskrit word, Rolling Thunder has also begun to use it. Karma has no relation to the concept of punishment, for the word is used by those who teach that there is no sin. To Rolling Thunder, karma provides opportunity for giving of oneself to all of life. The giving must be active and unselfish. It is non-self-seeking and non-self-indulging. To Rolling Thunder, it is the resolving of karma—aims, purposes, obligations and action—that moves one along the path toward enlightenment. Upon this path, psychic powers and psychic phenomena are incidental and secondary.

"We are born with a purpose in life and we have to fulfill that purpose. Some of our young men go out when they are twelve or thirteen years old and pray and fast at a certain sacred place. They learn their purpose in life. Now we hear of the new young people talking about finding their identity, their place in life, and they are very wise to do that, if they can do it. Some of them have, I think, and they are now trying to make things better for other people, which is our only purpose in this life—to share with others."

To Rolling Thunder, one's function, identity and karma are not only individual but also racial, national and global. Though it might not be said of other people in other places, Rolling Thunder believes it is true of white society in America; that what stands first between this society and the realization of a higher human potential is this society's racial karma. Rolling Thunder did not speak that day only about problems and tasks. He talked about his homeland and his travels, and about his medicine rituals and some of his patients. He explained how a medicine man must be able to leave the physical plane and to make a conscious trip to "the other side."

"We all live many lifetimes," he said, and it felt as though this idea was no longer strange to hear, even in public.

"We live many lives. We go through different lives; and sometimes we are able to put together the different lives. That is the way it is. We go from one life to another and we should have no fear of death. It is just a transition."

Those who are able to work with concepts of psychic healing and other psychic phenomena would no doubt welcome much more workable hypotheses than the story of the devil and the pearly gates or the postulation that the path of life is from death to death, from nothingness to oblivion. But perhaps they did not expect to hear about reincarnation from an American Indian. Yet this has been a major concept or view of life held by virtually all ancient cultures.

" 'Pagan' means pure in ancient Greek," Rolling Thunder went on, "and 'primitive' means first. These are not bad words. They don't mean savage or ignorant. I have done some studying of your history, too, and I know that there are some of your people, your European brothers and sisters, who still believe in the old ways. But some of your ancestors, who came here from that land across the water, conjured up a hell and a devil. That did not exist before, but they conjured it up—because if you believe in something, and believe it long enough, it will come into being. So they created that and they brought it here with them, and we Indians don't want any part of it. These things we call false teachings. They teach us to fear, to be afraid that we are going to be punished. This is why a person grows up with fears and anxieties and later finds himself seeing a psychiatrist.

"The medicine power is not dying out. In fact, it is coming again to many of our young people. Years ago they were saying that one day there would be no medicine people; but we were not fooled at all, we knew that we would not die out. We knew that one day, as though it had begun overnight, the power would be seen to be returning again. Now it is coming back strong. And I see it returning among other people, too, people who had once lost their identity and their trail—their way of life."

Then Rolling Thunder spoke about San Francisco.

"Now, I'll try to tell you about some spiritual things related to this area. Not too long ago people had made some predictions that this part of the country was supposed to sink under water and I was kind of worried about that. Well, in my country we have a way of coming together—some of the medicine people, the old people—and we compare our dreams and prophecies.

"One night an old man who had never been out of his area —in fact, he couldn't speak English—talked about the place called San Francisco. He said, 'I have seen it like an island with water most all the way round it. And I have seen it like a mushroom, with one little stem under it, holding it up.'

"So what would that mean to you? Well, we interpret these things. They are all symbolic. The meaning was, of course, that San Francisco had water around it and that there was a lot of talk about it going under the water at that time; but that there was something good happening that was holding it up. That's what's been going on here. There are a lot of good things that have been happening in San Francisco from way back. So I started looking into this and I started moving among many different people of many different races. I have met some people who are on a very high spiritual plane like some of our medicine people. There are certain signs and indications when one meets the right ones, and sometimes it isn't even necessary to talk. Race and language makes no difference; the barriers are gone when persons can come together on high spiritual levels.

"Every time I come back to San Francisco I see it much better. There seems to be a kind of a spiritual center here in this area. That's the way it looks to me; that's the feeling I get from it. So, I'm going to carry this message back to my people, because, don't forget, while you're interested, and I'm glad you are, in how the Indians live and about our spiritual beliefs and in how things will be, we also, as your brothers, are interested in what you are doing."

Rolling Thunder walked in his austere and deliberate manner across the stage and down the steps to the aisle. There was a long, standing ovation.

The next event of the day was lunch. We were served in a private room that had been provided for the program participants. I had thought Rolling Thunder might want to leave after lunch, but he decided to stay to hear the afternoon and evening sessions. He looked stimulated and intensely interested.

"Tomorrow at the speakers' breakfast in Tiburon," I said to Rolling Thunder, "you'll have a better chance to talk to all of the speakers."

"Well, we should take the chance to talk to the lady—the

sister we met at the radio station," he said. "There's something of interest to me that I'm thinking I'll hear from her."

This was during an afternoon intermission. We were standing in a side hallway and Rolling Thunder was leaning on the wall puffing on his pipe. We had just heard Elmer and Alyce Green speak about the research at the Menninger Foundation. Rolling Thunder had listened with apparent familiarity as they talked about biofeedback and autogenic training, the parallels of these processes to yogic techniques and their implications for psychotherapy and creativity. After the peyote tea ceremony last month (when Rolling Thunder held my cup of tea and talked about our research project), I was willing to believe that, on some level, he now realized what goes on in the psychophysiology laboratory.

Back in the auditorium Sister Justa Smith got up to speak and Rolling Thunder leaned forward in his chair. If she should give some clue as to what she knew that he wanted to learn, he intended not to miss it.

Sister Justa talked about her work with known psychic healers in the biochemistry laboratory at the Human Dimensions Institute at Buffalo, New York. She explained in technical terms and with a great deal of supporting data how her subjects had produced changes in enzyme solutions in vitro. Then she spoke about another research project that she had recently begun. She described a process called chromatography which showed a visible chemical difference between natural vitamin C and synthetic vitamin C (ascorbic acid). On the large screen were projected impressive color slides of the synthetic and the natural vitamin. The natural vitamin C images looked like a cross section of orange, apple or other living, growing things. One could see what looked like "lines of force." The natural vitamin produced images with brilliantly colored rays or fingers in striking contrast to the dull, flat-looking concentric circles produced by the ascorbic acid.

Rolling Thunder leaned back in his chair and put a hand to

his chin. My mind went back to the January day when he had answered my four questions before I asked them, and talked about natural vitamins: "There's going to be some way to show the difference so that people can see it. Some instrument or some system that will show this, and I have a feeling we'll find out what that is and we can use that, too. I have a feeling that's right around the corner."

I looked at him. He gave me a knowing glance. "See?" he said.

"Just around the corner," I repeated to myself. At this conference people were speaking about man-nature relationships, self-regulation, preventive medicine, self-healing, creativity, yogic and Taoist techniques, and the transcendent human potential. I wondered what was around the corner. I believed now that Rolling Thunder could see around the corner. If only he could tell what he saw. Perhaps just around the corner there was a new society, a new world, a new humanism, life style and awareness.

I recalled words I had often heard from Rolling Thunder and heard again in his lecture that morning.

"Back in Oklahoma some years ago, there was a meeting— the first such high-level meeting in over a hundred years— where chiefs and medicine men came together from all over the continent, and some from South America. The Iroquois came from New York and they brought a board with writing on it. On the last day of the ceremonies we formed a huge circle.

"The circle is the Great Spirit's emblem. All life is a circle. The world is a circle and the atoms are circles. The circle is seen on the rock writings, and it goes around all things, it takes in all things. When we met in Oklahoma, we formed a huge circle of all native tribes and we smoked the peace pipe to the sun, and it stayed lit around that huge circle. Then the Iroquois brought out the board with writing on it and interpreted it. They said 'Today our tribes are united again.' The emblem showed a chain of hands—people holding hands in a circle—and they said, 'Today our people have formed the circle of brotherhood and friendship here.'

"Eventually, this circle will go around the world. The brotherhood and peace that the world is seeking will now start on this land here. All the people here will be joined in the circle of friendship and brotherhood and that circle will go around the world.

"It's not like an organization. It's not a regimented or an organized thing. This is the way Indians do things: It's meant to be, it happens, and that's it."

From Council Grove, Kansas, in 1971, to the Association for Humanistic Psychology conference at San Francisco in 1972, I had made a complete circle with Rolling Thunder. Now as I sat beside him in the Masonic Auditorium—now as he gave me that familiar knowing look—I began around again. I could see this was going to be a larger circle.

26

Epilogue

Our first impression of Rolling Thunder at the Conference on Voluntary Control of Internal States in April 1971 was one of internal silence. To us this was an alerting signal. Having experienced a similar kind of silence during psychophysiological research with Swami Rama of Rishikesh, India, it was natural to wonder whether, and in what ways, these two very different people might be alike. Ironically, by a stroke of fate they are both called Indians. In Idries Shah's terminology both would be called Sufis,[1] and certainly both are "medicine men." Swami Rama's personality is more Western than Rolling Thunder's in that he often puts pressure on others according to the dictates of his personal will. At the same time his view of Nature as the

[1] Idries Shah: *The Sufis.* New York: Doubleday, 1971.

Mother, by whose leave we handle energy both inside-the-skin
(INS)—as in controlling the heart—and outside-the-skin
(OUTS)—as in psychokinesis—is similar to Rolling Thunder's
view of nature as the Great Spirit with whom we can align
ourselves and with whose energy we can then act.

Some scientists are coming to think that there might be something wrong with traditional views of matter, energy and probability. Both Swami Rama and Rolling Thunder "handle" psy-
chophysical energies on occasion in ways that would seem
strange, if not impossible, to Victorian scientists. But modern
science is beginning to have more room for not-easy-to-explain
phenomena. The discovery of the multiplicity of high-energy
particles has given theoretical physicists new views of nature;
matter, fields and energy seem to meet in a subnuclear domain
in which the usually accepted rules of probability may not hold.

A well-known statistician with whom we once worked out-
lined the problem quite clearly when he was asked what was
"the major scientific fallacy" in J. B. Rhine's work in parapsychology at Duke University.[2] The statistician had attended a
conference of a statistical society at which Rhine demonstrated
his equipment and explained his techniques for data analysis.

"There was no fallacy," our colleague said. What a surprise!
He was not noted for belief in parapsychological phenomena,
and if he felt no fallacies were involved in Rhine's work it did
not leave many scientific alternatives. "No," he said, "there are
not many alternatives. In fact, the way I see it there are only
two. Either there is something to it, or there is something
basically wrong with our ideas of physics and mathematics."

Asked about his position on the sticky problem, he answered,
"Due to my conservative and perhaps stuffy upbringing, it is
easier for me to believe there is something wrong with mathematics and physics than to believe there is something to it."

[2]J. B. Rhine and J. G. Pratt: *Parapsychology: Frontier Science of the Mind.* Springfield,
Ohio: Charles C. Thomas, 1957.

What a delightful self-defeating answer! There *is* "something wrong with classical mathematics and physics," and it is partly because there *is* "something to it."

When we say that an honest coin has a fifty-fifty chance of coming up heads or tails when flipped, we are really saying that in our ignorance of the actual factors involved—air density, temperature, humidity, flipping force, momentums, elastic coefficient of the "landing area," path length, and so forth—we cannot predict what will happen. If every variable were known, a computer could easily predict each event while the coin was still in the air. At this gross level, prediction is possible, but if we take a continuously closer and more microscopic view of nature we finally arrive at a position in which the observer significantly influences the observed. The electron beam in an electron microscope can significantly modify the material being examined. Eventually physics and mathematics can no longer determine either what is happening or what will happen, at subatomic levels. No undistorted information can be obtained about all aspects of an investigation. There is a realm of "uncertainty."

Although the mechanisms of parapsychological events are not yet determined, or understood, it is an empirical fact that the observer in a parapsychological investigation often influences the event he is observing. Is the situation analogous to the way in which the electron beam modifies the observed specimen? Possibly, but the point is that mathematics cannot describe nature accurately either in physical science or in psychokinesis, and psychokinetic events, however implemented, are part of the problem of science and mathematics.

How often do physicists unconsciously influence events they observe, and discard legitimate but unexpected results because they contain an element of psychokinesis and therefore do not fit classical theory? This is an interesting question. No doubt a set of theorems and multidimensional equations will eventually describe the observer-observed interaction, so that parapsychological data can be mathematically absorbed into science, but in the meantime, to quote Swami Rama, "Every man can have his own hypothesis, but he still has to account for the facts."

The "facts" so outrage some scientists that their verdict is that the verifiers of the paranormal are either simpletons or liars.[3] Dr. R. A. McConnell of the Department of Physics, University of Pittsburgh, brought another viewpoint to our attention in his *ESP Curriculum Guide*.[4] McConnell quoted Eugene Condon, former head of the United States National Bureau of Standards:

Flying saucers and astrology are not the only pseudo-sciences which have a considerable following among us. There used to be spiritualism, there continues to be extrasensory perception, psychokinesis, and a host of others . . . Where corruption of children's minds is at stake, I do not believe in freedom of the press or freedom of speech. In my view, publishers who publish or teachers who teach any of the pseudo-sciences as established truth should, on being found guilty, be publicly horsewhipped, and forever banned from further activity in these usually honorable professions.

In spite of such admonitions, we must continue to gather data and attempt to understand the "unusual" events of nature. If we go about it in the right way, perhaps we will find that the "reality" of present-day science is a special case of a more general reality. Castaneda's experience with Don Juan,[5] Drs. Edgar Mitchell, Russell Targ, and Harold Puthoff's experience with Uri Geller at the Stanford Research Institute,[6] Dr. Charles Tart's experience with Robert Monroe,[7] our experience with Swami Rama and Jack Schwarz,[8] and Doug Boyd's experience

[3]C. E. Hansel: *ESP: A Scientific Evaluation.* New York: Charles Scribner's Sons, 1966.

[4]R. A. McConnell: *ESP Curriculum Guide.* New York: Simon and Schuster, 1971.

[5]Carlos Castaneda: *Journey to Ixtlan.* New York: Simon and Schuster, 1972.

[6]Edgar Mitchell: "Uri Geller and Psychokinesis." Report presented at the Council Grove conference, April 1973.

[7]Charles T. Tart: "A Second Psychophysiological Study of Out-of-the-Body Experiences in a Gifted Subject." *International Journal of Parapsychology,* Vol. 9 (1967), pp. 251–258.

[8]Elmer E. Green and Alyce M. Green: "On the INS and OUTS of Mind Body Energy." *Science Year* (Chicago: Field Enterprises Educational Corporation, 1974, 137–147.

with Rolling Thunder, to name only a few of the more recent observations, all have similar ingredients—namely, open-minded observers and research subjects who have unusual powers of perception and of energy control.

Our inference from these various investigations and from pondering yogic theory[9] is that a unique energy field, a "field of mind," must surround the planet (expressed in some aspects as electrostatic, magnetic and gravitational fields) and each individual mind with its extension, the body, must have the inherent capability of focusing energy for manipulation of both INS and OUTS events.

We also infer that the individual mind and the general "field of mind" meet in the unconscious. If we grant that most persons cannot perceive or control their own unconscious psychological processes, it is then understandable that most persons would be unaware of this field of mind. Perhaps it is an important clue that the persons who are most aware of their own normally unconscious processes are the ones who seem to most easily control their own nervous systems and physiological processes (heart, blood flow, brainwaves, pain) and who also seem to have the greatest extrasensory awareness of others, and the greatest ability to generate OUTS events, that is, to demonstrate psychokinetic powers.

It seems that we are on the threshold of a breakthrough in human awareness and that "new" energies will be studied by scientists and brought to the service of humans in general. This undertaking is not without danger, for delusion, illusion, fantasy and fact are mixed together in this field, somewhat proportionate to the clarity of the observer. Unless a person is very clear, very straight, he may often find what he *wishes* to find, because his "projections" (mental and emotional constructions)

[9]Sri Aurobindo: *The Synthesis of Yoga*. Pondicherry, India: Sri Aurobindo Ashram Press, 1955. (Available from the California Institute of Asian Studies, San Francisco, California.)

will be "thrown against the screen of substance" which makes up the mind field. In the field of parapsychology it is a well-known fact that the observer's attitude has significant effect on results. In other words, the scientific observer is himself in the test tube, along with his chemicals. In physics and parapsychology, the observer is part of the equation.

Rolling Thunder knows this and reveals it in ways that are not always obvious. But Douglas Boyd is an unusual observer. For one thing, he is not a scientist. He is an observer who can himself be silent, can observe without stirring the waters, so to speak, and so the reflection he sees of Rolling Thunder's reality is relatively uncontaminated by prejudgments. It is for this reason, perhaps, that he has found it possible to understand exotic cultures from the inside, and it was for this reason that we asked him to work with Swami Rama and later invited him to the Council Grove Conference to meet Rolling Thunder.

ELMER E. GREEN
ALYCE M. GREEN
October 1, 1973